POLAND'S JOURNALISTS PROFESSIONALISM AND POLITICS

Soviet and East European Studies: 66

Soviet and East European Studies, under the auspices of Cambridge University Press and the British Association for Soviet, Slavonic and East European Studies (BASSEES), promotes the publication of works presenting substantial and original research on the economics, politics, sociology and modern history of the Soviet Union and Eastern Europe.

Soviet and East European Studies

69 CHRIS WARD
Russia's cotton workers and the New Economic Policy
Shop-floor culture and state policy 1921–1929

68 LÁSZLÓ CSABA
Eastern Europe in the world economy

67 MICHAEL E. URBAN
An algebra of Soviet power
Elite circulation in the Belorussian Republic 1966–1986

66 JANE L. CURRY
Poland's journalists: professionalism and politics

65 MARTIN MYANT
The Czechoslovak economy 1948–1988
The battle for economic reform

64 XAVIER RICHET
The Hungarian model: markets and planning in a socialist economy

63 PAUL G. LEWIS
Political authority and party secretaries in Poland 1975–1986

62 BENJAMIN PINKUS
The Jews of the Soviet Union
The history of a national minority

61 FRANCESCO BENVENUTI
The Bolsheviks and the Red Army, 1918–1922

60 HIROAKI KUROMIYA
Stalin's industrial revolution
Politics and workers, 1928–1932

59 LEWIS SIEGELBAUM
Stakhanovism and the politics of productivity in the USSR, 1935–1941

58 JOZEF M. VAN BRABANT
Adjustment, structural change and economic efficiency
Aspects of monetary cooperation in Eastern Europe

57 ILIANA ZLOCH-CHRISTY
Debt problems of Eastern Europe

56 SUSAN BRIDGER
Women in the Soviet countryside
Women's roles in rural development in the Soviet Union

55 ALLEN LYNCH
The Soviet study of international relations

54 DAVID GRANICK
Job rights in the Soviet Union: their consequences

Series list continues on p. 299

POLAND'S JOURNALISTS PROFESSIONALISM AND POLITICS

JANE LEFTWICH CURRY

CAMBRIDGE UNIVERSITY PRESS

Cambridge
New York Port Chester Melbourne Sydney

Published by the Press Syndicate of the University of Cambridge
The Pitt Building, Trumpington Street, Cambridge CB2 1RP
40 West 20th Street, New York, NY 10011, USA
10 Stamford Road, Oakleigh, Melbourne 3166, Australia

First published 1990

Printed in Great Britain by Redwood Burn Limited, Trowbridge, Wiltshire

British Library cataloguing in publication data

Curry, Jane Leftwich, *1948–*
Poland's journalists: Professionalism
and politics. – (Soviet and East European
Studies: 66)
1. Poland. Journalism
I. Title II. Series
073'.8

Library of Congress cataloguing in publication data

Curry, Jane Leftwich, *1948–*
Poland's journalists : professionalism and politics / Jane Curry.
p. cm. – (Soviet and East European studies)
Bibliography.
Includes index.
ISBN 0–521–36201–6
1. Journalists – Poland – Biography. 2. Journalism – Political aspects – 19th century – Poland. 3. Journalism – Social aspects – 19th century – Poland. 4. Journalistic ethics – Poland. 5. Mass media – Political aspects – Poland. I. Title. II. Series.
PN5355.P6C8 1989
070.92'2438—dc20 1418 CIP
[B]

ISBN 0 521 36201 6

RB

To Andrew, Matthew, and Megan
who were born into this book

Contents

Acknowledgments

This book is the product of what was once intended to be boring dissertation research and what became, very rapidly, exciting living history. Its research and writing have been spread over the years as the events of Solidarity and its suppression commanded my attention and that of the journalists about whom I was writing. In the end, the events of the eighties became the final test of the professionalism I had found in the seventies.

It is also a product of the willingness of Polish journalists to be subjects of my research, and their own queries about themselves and their place in Poland. They were interesting for what they had done and written or produced in periods of quiet and of revolution. But, more than that, on an individual basis and as staff members on journals or as the Association leadership and faculty of the School of Journalism in the seventies, they were far ahead of their time – not only in allowing but in facilitating my research into what was still a minefield of taboos for them. I was, thus, able to research them "as people" and not just as words in an archive. What that opened for me was the valuable level of real action in communist societies which, because of the limits imposed by the rulers, must go on behind the scenes. It also meant that my life has been enriched by friendships that continued even after this research ended.

Although the interpretations and errors are very much my own, I am grateful to the journalists I interviewed, the press specialists I asked for information and advice, and the librarians I hounded for more and more access to archives for their time, their willingness to share, and the special sources they shared with me. Some journalists and press specialists not only met with me but continued, as this book evolved, to be willing to answer my continuing queries and search out whatever answers they did not have. Some, who shall go unnamed, even gave of their time to read this manuscript in its various stages and pick up my errors or challenge my interpretations. Although we did not always agree, my understanding is far richer for their help.

This research was made possible by funding, at various times, from the International Research and Exchanges Board, the Fulbright Commission, and the Rolf Kauntenbourne Foundation. I am also very grateful for the tactical and real support that I received over the years from the faculty and students at Manhattanville College, Columbia University, Vassar College, and Santa Clara University.

Some sections reflect, in part, the additional research that I did on the mass media while I was a consultant on the Rand Corporation project on the Media and Intra-Elite Communication in Poland and the Soviet Union. There, not only was I able to test my data and evaluations with interviews we did with *emigré* Polish journalists but I also received the invaluable mentoring of A. Ross Johnson who, with truly unlimited patience, honed my thinking and writing.

My colleagues provided me with seemingly unlimited personal support and remained convinced that Polish journalists were at least almost as interesting as I thought they were. For this, I am particularly grateful to Jarek Piekalkiewicz, Andrzej Korboński, Sharon Wolchik, Sarah Terry, Owen Johnson, Charles Gati, Erik Hoffman, George Liber, Bill Balderston, Steve Dubrow, Robert Scott, and Anne Snodgrass.

Elsa Dixler and Sheila McEnery did much to make my prose as readable as it is. Małgorzata Terentiew, Renata Siemieńska, and Angela Lauer all did the yeoman's task of keeping the details straight in my writing. Any errors, however, remain my responsibility.

Finally, on a personal level, I am grateful to my parents for their presence, to all those who gave me the time to write (especially Elizabeth Closs, Carolyn Lindsey, and Paul Bignall) and to my children, Andrew, Matthew, and Megan, who provided me with joy and companionship as I researched and wrote. I only hope that the difficulties of having a mom who was always "almost finished" have been made up for by the Poles who have come to be uncles and aunts.

1 Journalists as professionals in theory and reality

> Propaganda, a program of creating opinion, should serve the state as well as political, social and union organizations. But, the journalist should not feel he is a worker for the propaganda apparatus. Naturally, in the process of gathering information, the journalist will represent some point of view but this should be his point of view spoken in his name.
>
> Stefan Bratkowski, Chairman,
> Polish Journalists Association, 1980–81

Who speaks here? One of the "mouthpieces" of communist rule, carefully schooled in the rules and rhetoric of communism so that he could lead the population? Yes, but these are also the words of a professional journalist committed to his rights as a professional to work without interference for his own professional goals of service to the society and to professional leadership. Bratkowski's words were spoken, after the victory of Solidarity, as Polish journalists moved to reclaim their professional rights. The words are those of both a consummate professional and a committed political actor.

Although Bratkowski was a leader in the profession, he was hardly unique. He, like his colleagues, is a product of explicitly political indoctrination. Yet, his message was a call to try to improve the system not merely to serve the Party. In his case, like that of many of his colleagues, he had strived for some thirty years to make his work his own rather than merely to shape it to fit Party doctrines and censors' regulations. Like his colleagues, he turned to his professional association not for instruction but liberation, however much it had been concerned primarily with instructing. Like his colleagues, he used his profession to involve himself in policy and politics. And, like his colleagues, he was a product of and actor in Poland's traumas and revolts beginning in 1948 and culminating, for his generation at least, in the hopes and disappointments of Solidarity and its repression in martial law. His professionalism and that of his fellows defies traditional Western theories. It demands explanation.

Journalists and journalism in Poland were important actors and elements in the battles of Solidarity. The media they produced was a major concern for both Solidarity and the government. And, while battles went on between Solidarity and the government over issues related to the mass media, journalists fought with both sides to be allowed to produce what they felt, as professionals, was right. Some of their number used professional positions to take active roles in government and others used them to take roles in Solidarity. Still others used the journalists' association to increase professional power and autonomy and to negotiate policy as their profession's representatives. But, whatever their personal or institutional politics, journalists almost universally agreed on what their professional demands and stances should be, just as they had done in earlier years. Most of those stances made it difficult for them to conform to the ruler's wishes.

When martial law was imposed, journalists were the first of the professional groups in Poland to organize to resist it. In addition, their actions during the Solidarity period appeared so threatening and powerful to the rulers that journalists, as a group, were directly attacked in the initial martial law declarations. More than one-third of Poland's journalists in those first days were either fired from their jobs or refused to work in their old positions in the face of the retreat from media freedom. The journalists' professional association then became the first formal professional group since the communist takeover in 1945 to be permanently disbanded and replaced. The group's undeclared "crime," both before and after martial law, appears ultimately to have been its insistence on acting and being treated as professionals rather than as obedient followers of political leaders.

Their apparent defeat under martial law, when the various legal gains they had made previously were essentially rescinded or reduced and their professional elite was forced to leave the profession, makes their professional life no less significant. Past experiences of this group explain how professional groups develop out of a very politically controlled atmosphere, how professionals work around various kinds of political pressures, and what the countervailing forces are against the politicization of all decision-making. The actions of journalists after martial law was declared and the concern of the regime with controlling the profession (especially those who had earlier supported communist regimes) demonstrate the strength of the professional impulse for independence and the viability of professional links in creating this independent world. Finally, pressure was continued for the same professional rights and privileges by the quisling journalists' organization established in 1982. This is a further measure of the significance of professional values.

Traditional Western theories of socialization, of interest group behavior, or of change in communist societies do little to explain Polish journalists' behavior in this crisis situation and in earlier periods of crisis in Poland (1956, 1968, and 1970). Nor do they explain their behavior, in the public eye and behind the scenes, under more normal conditions. Such behavior is more usefully explained by Western theories of professionalization and professional group behavior. This theory provides a model for groups (like doctors, lawyers, accountants, social workers, and other self-defined or publicly recognized "professions") who control unique bodies of knowledge not shared by the rest of society. The possession and use of this knowledge is regulated by the groups' internal structures as well as regulations reinforced by the broader society.[1] Furthermore, professionals are defined as being part of occupational groups that have gone through a process involving the establishment of professional organizations and schooling, developing full-time work commitments, and pressing for the right to control their own work and membership.[2] In any society these groups, one of which is usually defined as the journalism profession, are able to claim some autonomy and self-control – as journalists in Poland have.[3] They also have a higher level of formal and informal interaction and organization than other social or occupational groups. This they have by virtue of their controlled membership, common interests and values, close connections with each other for large parts of their lives, and their self-claimed special roles in society.[4]

The stress in professionalization theory is on the importance not of formal structures and formally stated positions, actions and demands (the least significant form of professional activity in the West and the one that most depends on the "permission" of the political leadership in the East), but on informal group formation as well as the development of values and action based on the rewards and pressures inherent in professional work anywhere.[5] Even though some of these demands and rewards differ from those of journalists' counterparts in the West, the mechanisms of professional life appear to be comparable.

This approach then gives dimension to the label of "professional" and "professionalized" that so often is used to label any independent contribution by intellectuals in a communist society.[6] It also provides a model for what goes on behind the lines before the political leadership invites professional participation in policy decisions. In fact, this sociological theory helps explain what has been unexplainable in studies of communist systems: apparent independent professional action and reaction in the context of politically controlled professional organizations.

The place of Marxism–Leninism and the mass media

The significance of the mass media in any society, but especially in those where mobilization and modernization are primary goals, sets the journalism profession apart from other professions. Journalists play a broader social and political role than other professionals for whom politics has limited political relevance in their work lives. Journalists and their media are charged with being, at least, the "gatekeepers" for all but interpersonal communications in the society.[7] The nature of their professional life weighs directly on this role. As research on the role of the mass media and its messages done in the West, developing societies, and communist states has shown, the professional life and attitudes of journalists are critical influences on the nature of the news presented.[8]

In the European press tradition, where the press initially developed as, and remained, a partisan force that accepts responsibility for the "good of the society," the role of journalists as professionals is further increased.[9] Polish journalists were not only representatives of various political factions and spokesmen for them throughout Polish history, but they were also representatives of the national interest and national culture during the entire Partition period. Then, the three powers occupying Poland allowed Poles virtually no avenues other than their controlled press to express their nationalism and their political ideas.[10] The Marxist–Leninist tradition grows out of this European tradition. In postwar Poland, Marxism built upon, even as it distorted, the historical responsibilities of the Polish press.

Ironically, the ideological basis for the current "Marxist–Leninist" press is, in fact, a product of the Stalinist period. Neither Marx nor Lenin discussed in detail the organization and role of the press in a post-revolutionary society. Marx merely termed the press "a mirror of the spirit of the nation."[11] Lenin saw the press as the most effective instrument for fomenting revolution.[12] Only with the advent of Stalinism was this revolutionary image transformed into a structure for the press system of a ruling party. The Stalinist structure has remained the basis for press organization in the Soviet Union and Eastern Europe and the ideological touchstone with which journalists and political leaders justify their actions.

Discussion in this section will be limited to the political ideology presented to Polish journalists. It is not intended to be a comprehensive discussion of the Marxist–Leninist theory of the press. The Leninist definition of "freedom of the press" on which communist states' ideology is focused is one in which there is economic control by the "workers" over the means of press production and, thus, workers' interests have precedence over those of the producers of the press.[13] Communist ideologists stress this use of the press as an instrument both to influence and to reflect working-class opinion. Party domination over the press is, thus, inherently justified by its role as the "vanguard" of the proletariat and by the need to solidify popular opinion to further the revolution.[14]

This Stalinist version of the Marxist–Leninist press was imposed on Poland after World War II. When this was done, the press' target audience was shifted from the literate, urbanized intelligentsia to the workers. The goal was mobilization not policy debate. But the focus on advocacy and analysis aimed at structuring the population's thinking to fit historical traditions. This, combined with the respect for the prewar national media which had long upheld national goals while operating under external political controls, helped preserve the legacy of Polish press traditions even in the Stalinist period.

The crucial tract in Polish and Soviet scholars' discussions of the ideological foundations of the communist press systems is *What Is To Be Done?* (written by Lenin in 1902 as a plan for the revolution in Russia). In it, a heavy burden is placed on the press to serve as the political leadership for the underground.

> The organization, which will form around this (all Russian revolutionary paper) will be ready for everything, from upholding the honour, the prestige, and the continuity of the Party in acute revolutionary "depression" to preparing for, appointing the time for, and carrying out the nation-wide, armed uprising.[15]

This activist image of journalism makes the press "not only a collective propagandist and collective agitator but also a collective organizer."[16] On the other hand, the publication of information for its own sake never entered into these discussions. Professional journalism is, thus, inseparable from political action and the development through the press of ties with workers and peasants and between workers and peasants.[17]

The Stalinist contribution to this ideological basis of journalism was a tipping of the balance in favor of journalists as political propagandists rather than as independent agitators. Journalists' popular ties were intended to be made and maintained by worker-peasant correspondents. This made the press and the journalists that produced it a part of the "thread from the Party, through the newspaper, which extends to all worker-peasant districts without exception so that the interaction of the Party and state, on the one hand, and the industrial and peasant districts, on the other, is complete."[18]

This reduced both journalists' control over the media and the significance of the press as an independent institution. At the same time, the Soviet-model press is also a monitor of the bureaucracy and its administrative practices. As such, the press is responsible for collecting citizens' complaints, checking their validity, and forcing action on the valid ones.[19] Finally, there is a clear stress on economic and social modernization.

> The Soviet press over the years has been one means by which a predominantly illiterate Soviet population was taught to read, and by which it acquired much of the information necessary for daily living in a nation being transformed from an agrarian into an industrialized, urban society.[20]

Journalism is, thus, by definition, a political profession in communist societies like Poland. To be politically involved is not necessarily to be less professional or professionally active. In fact, for journalists, being politically active is often a way to forward one's career and do professional work just as, for many lawyers in the United States, political positions and activities are a career enhancement.[21] And, just as political pressure has often increased journalists' professionalization, the use of political channels and ties has been their way to perform one of their key self-declared professional roles, that of monitor and ombudsman.

In describing their work, Polish journalists in the seventies emphasized that they were experts first and then communists and not an amalgam of the two or simply professionals in the service of the Party. At the same time, they made it clear that, although they earned their salaries from having articles published or programs broadcast, much of what they regarded as professional work involved "behind the scenes" work with political and governmental authorities through a variety of channels and on a variety of levels. For them, then, participation in Party and governmental bodies by making use of their personal ties and connections, serving as experts on commissions, working on professional and policy issues as advisors to citizens' groups as well as government groups, revealing information, speaking at public forums, or being censored and then reprinted in the censors' reports for top Party officials were all useful channels in professional work. In the Solidarity period, journalists' self-defined professional work also involved journalists participating in intellectual committees to draft press and censorship legislation, schooling young aspirants to the profession, and organizing or acting in bodies discussing policy. And, particularly after the declaration of martial law, for some, professional work was extended to writing in dissident publications or keeping up to date on events and verbally spreading information.

Clearly then, in comparison to most other professions, Polish journalism is a special case. Journalists, more than any other profession in Poland, are expected to participate in political activities as part of their professional work, as defined by their own professional values and the state ideology, simply because the media plays such a critical political role. They also have the least clearly defined professional qualifications and skills so they are the most easily politically regulated and penetrated profession. However, from their own reports and the limited published data that exists, it is clear that, no matter how long and at what level journalists hold political positions, they maintain strong connections with the profession. So, whatever their ostensible tasks or goals, they act first of all as representatives of the journalism profession.

Regardless of the rhetoric about the media being the handmaiden of the Party and "vanguard of the working class," until the introduction of martial law, the presence of professional journalists on Party and state bodies and on citizen groups (including Solidarity), as informal contributors to policy discussions, was of benefit to the political leadership. If they participated in Party or state bodies publicly, journalists tended to lend an aura of credibility to these bodies. They also gave their usually faceless membership a clear, publicly recognizable face. And, as recognizable participants in decisions or as behind the scenes actors, journalists and editors served, throughout the postwar period, as necessary links between individuals and groups who shared their interests and expertise. Journalists were, after all, normally the links between groups and with the population and its problems for other actors in policy-making.

This balance between professionalism and political involvement is not without tension. On the one hand, since journalists are so closely intertwined with the Party and state elite, they are well aware of the conflicts, problems and policy shifts within that elite. Hence, they can and do exploit conflicts, problems or shifts to protect their ability to do their work and to push issues that are of interest to them. They also can make public disputes that the leadership is trying to cover over. On the other hand, although the number of formal positions journalists hold in Party and state bodies and the intensity of personal contacts between top leaders and journalists is determined by non-journalists, these outsiders cannot create or control journalists' desire to be involved or their persistent pressure to be heard. Nor do their demands do anything but exacerbate the conflicting pressure on journalists to be advocates and monitors of the state and the society around them. After all, journalists' reading of their ideologically mandated role, however they see the system, is that they should be "a loyal opposition party in the British sense," monitoring the carrying out of policy and proposing adjustments to it, while protecting their ability to perform professional work correctly.

Traditional approaches to groups and policy making: a critique

Western scholars have observed journalists and other white-collar groups in Eastern Europe and the Soviet Union as the key interest articulators of these systems. Even in taking into account the extent to which journalists and other professionals are "political," the growing strength and independence of specialists and professionals as well as the resulting divergence between stated policy and its execution in communist countries have been undeniable. How this all happened has remained a puzzle for which the only key has seemed to be the desire of the political leadership to use professionals' expertise on particular issues.

Groups and the aggregation of group interests in socialist states have virtually no ideological justification in Marxism–Leninism. The evolution toward communism is supposed to result in an evolution away from individuals seeing themselves as part of separate and competing groups.[22] The structures of the Party and state, as well as of social organizations, have been designed to insure that autonomous group interests do not develop and are not articulated. Instead, organizational structures for professional and social organizations are intended to be "transmission belts" for guidance from the political elite to be communicated to organization members and for information on membership activities and concerns to be transferred back to the political leadership. So, they are not intended to articulate or aggregate specific interests, much less develop an insular group identity.[23]

How does professional expertise develop independently enough for the leadership to hear more than simply approbation of its policy proposals? Why, in times of relative freedom, do professionals suddenly appear to present a coherent and consistent set of professional demands almost without time for prior discussion or germination? How does the professional community, which must serve as a basis for all this, develop, given the strict controls over organizations in these societies? These are all parts of the puzzle of the role of the intelligentsia in communist societies. They have never been satisfactorily put together. Western blind spots are increased by a research focus on academic and research specialists and what they write rather than on professionals and their work. Those with whom we have been the least concerned are the practitioners who, like journalists, after all, help create policy from their positions in advisory bodies and who take policy and remold it in their day to day work as professionals.[24]

At the same time, research on the policy process that has focused on individual policies and their implementation in the Soviet Union and Eastern Europe has generally concluded that involved professionals, like "the managers, teachers, educators and scientists" Joel Schwartz and William Keech found to have been the most influential in blocking Khrushchev's educational reform proposal,[25] are the most powerful actors. Yet little is known about why this happens since professional opposition to leadership policies is seldom actually sanctioned or publicized. The impetus for action is assumed to be the desire on the part of individuals "to protect interests derived from occupational roles," as is true for any professional in Western society.[26] The power of these professionals and their specialist counterparts is, further, seen in Western professional literature as deriving from "their technical expertise, their indispensability to the ruling circles, and their access to influential media of communication,"[27] as well as from their less well defined ability to drag their feet or reinterpret the policies they are to follow.[28]

The entrance and involvement of these specialists and professionals into the policy process has been seen by Western researchers as being a result of an invitation from or the weakness of the political leadership.[29] Although the totalitarianism of Stalinist control seems to have been far less strict than it appeared in the 1950s, it is clear that both the level of group activity and the visibility of that activity have increased with the technological modernization of the post-Stalin years. The increase in the technological knowledge and sophistication required for decisions to be made has clearly increased political leaders' propensity to seek advice and defer to it or to allow professionals ever increasing autonomy in the performance of their roles.[30] Beyond the simply technological imperatives, political leaders' increasing claims of deference to specialist and professional interests also have been used as a measure of their desire to involve and integrate an increasingly complex and educated population in the policy process. The claim then is that leadership decisions come from experts and are not politically motivated.[31]

Western theorists have differed on the fundamental nature of groups in these societies. Claims of full comparability between groups and group input in communist societies and pluralist Western societies are not made either in group theory (which has never dealt with "the communist case")[32] or by those who have sought to apply that interest group theory, however imperfect the fit, to behavior in communist states.[33] Furthermore, few parallels have been drawn, in theory or in actual research, between the behavior and demands of specific groups in the West and in the Soviet bloc.

The variety of definitions of "group" in communist politics given in 1969 demonstrates the disagreement among theorists on the nature of "groups" and on the key lines of social and political division in communist societies. In the ensuing years, that definition has been made no clearer:

> Brzezinski and Huntington see policy-relevant groups as forming principally upon occupational lines (and at the upper reaches of the Soviet elite), such as the military, the state bureaucracy, the Party apparatchiki, etc. Meyer, cautioning against all attempts at an *a priori* listing, suggests that interest groups may form around issues or individual political leaders or bureaucrats, in addition to occupations. Barghoorn, following Leonard, argues that the major policy groupings do not form along occupational lines but cut across these to coalesce around issue orientations. They are most usefully identified as "modernizers and conservatives, revisionists and dogmatists." Skilling and Griffiths similarly conclude that groupings most frequently form around issues, but unlike Barghoorn, they see a great multiplicity of viewpoints ... Brzezinski, Azrael, and Barghoorn stress the Party's formal monopoly over decision making and the weakness of interest groups. At the same time, they suggest that certain groups, especially those with relatively high institutional cohesion, such as the military, may occasionally act as successful veto groups, successfully resisting Kremlin pressures. Meyer, while pointing out the serious lack of knowledge of Soviet policy making processes, suggests that the interests of a wide variety of groups are considered by Soviet decision-makers. At the same time, he con-

cludes usually such interests do not count heavily. Griffiths, Skilling and Meissner, by contrast, argue that certain kinds of strategic groupings do count very heavily in Soviet decision-making.[34]

Even studies of the roles of specific professional or specialist groups or of the making of individual policies have hedged on the question of the real meaning and composition of groups.[35] Measurement of strength or influence is done not on the basis of group action but by external evaluation both of the perquisites and position of members in each of these externally defined groups[36] and the correlations between the public statements of group members and the changes made in policies from their initial presentations to their enactment.[37]

Studies of interest groups' input into policy have also failed to grapple with the nature of group interaction. In most of the research that has been done, group interests have been treated as those of essentially "non-associational groups" identified not by their own organization but by their common individual reactions to policy moves and their common social or demographic characteristics.[38] This is done without any clear evidence of interaction and self-identification within a group. Such different entities as formal groups, social groups, and "groups" that represent a common opinion held by individuals with no sense that they have anything in common thus get equated. The assumption is that all affiliations are potentially equal and significant group interests are not recognized by the polity.

The loyalty of Party members to any of the other groups they might join is an open and unanswered question, although most researchers take it for granted that Party membership is the dominant force in an individual's life simply because the Party is so selective and requires such a high level of constant organized activity and identification. Furthermore, since membership in the Communist Party is required for many responsible professional positions, the assumption is that it is the primary force for both institutions and individuals.[39]

Focused as most research has been on academic specialists, the wisdom has been that individuals give advice as individuals or, at most, as members of small institute groups. Group identity and interaction are factored in only where occasionally individuals are identified with a profession and the body of knowledge professionals have from scholarly meetings and journals. Western scholars, and their East European counterparts, have only glanced at "hands-on" professionals. The assumption has been that their only work is done by individuals with little or no sense of how their actions fit with the broader professional community and its goals. "Hands on" professionals' only influence on policy then is assumed to be tied with policy-makers' anticipation of what professionals, who filter and implement the policy, will do to it. In this way, the duel between policy-makers and professionals sounds not unlike the "nondecision making" described in Western pluralist models.[40]

In fact, however, sociological research done on the intelligentsia in Eastern Europe, and particularly in Poland, has demonstrated that, however much Marxist theory denies the existence of groups and group interests, there are clear patterns of group identity and interaction in all of these systems.[41] The identification of individuals with their professional or occupational group is stronger than their alternative affiliations with class, regional, or social groupings. This identification with one's profession or occupation is reinforced by the fact that individuals tend to share a common life-style, set of values, and social circle made up primarily of those in their own profession.[42] Furthermore, professionals have a higher status and more material benefits than workers or party and state bureaucrats.[43] This insures their primary identification with their profession as does the fact that, as long as they remain in a profession, they work with and share pressures and problems with both Party and non-Party people in that profession. Groups, then, exist through informal group interaction based on common values and common friendships growing out of professional life even if formal associational channels are far more controlled than those of Western groups. An individual's ties with a profession are further strengthened by the material and status rewards he receives for his position. Such professional communities clearly appear in periods of crisis, when professional groups respond almost immediately with their own demands and new organizational structures. But, these networks and rewards also clearly continually provide for informal communication of individual professionals' concerns, reactions and gains as well as informal but effective pressure on individuals for group cohesion and adherence to professional norms and values.

Western studies, both of group dynamics and of professional groups as interest groups, stress the importance this informal interaction has in insuring that a group can make an impact on policy.[44] For, as Mancur Olson has pointed out, even in pluralist states where there is no pressure against group affiliation, the activities of an organization or the claim of representation by a formal organization are not sufficient incentives for individuals to align themselves with any organization. Benefits attained by formal representatives are, after all, available to everyone in a group regardless of his participation in the organization. Therefore, two other incentives must be used to bring individuals into organizations: direct material incentives that are available only to members and small group interaction and pressure.[45] In addition, given the strength of the informal connections between professionals and their socialization into a unique value system, professionalization theorists see formal organizations as nothing more than the product of the professionalization of a group and the resulting need to bridge the gap between public and professional "governments" so nonprofessionals recognize the profession and its rights.[46] In effect, informal organizations of colleague networks are the vital links in professional life and political activity. They insure consistent policy preferences and reactions to policies.

A shift, in our approach then, is required to fully understand the role and position of any professional group in these societies. We need to move away from measuring the existence of "group" input on the basis either of formal structures, dominated in Poland and elsewhere in the communist world by the political leadership, or of the public statements of specialists within a profession. Instead, we need to focus on charting informal and internal group activity and the manipulation of structure and policies. We also need, of course, to monitor the public and, where we can, the private statements and activities of individuals and formal organizations.

Taking into consideration the existence of interactive groups with clear group goals and pressures for their cohesion, thus, adds to traditional Western perceptions of policy-making in communist states. Ironically, this assumption that some level of interaction holds individuals in professional circles and insures the influence of professional interests on decisions has long been pivotal in Kremlinological studies of communist elites.[47] But, this basic assumption has not been carried down to the level of individuals and their respective professional groups.[48] As a result, policy decisions have been treated essentially as elite decisions for which specialist and professional advice is commissioned or sanctioned by the leadership.[49] Little or no consideration is given to competition or cooperation between groups except when they are pictured as "opinion clusters" composed of individuals from various fields with a common perspective on a specific issue.[50] Nor has there been sufficient consideration of the ability of groups to make their own policies in areas that are not of direct interest to the political leadership. In addition, the natural reactions of professionals, when policies go against their interests, needs to be taken into account.[51]

And, given the stress by Western research on the formal invitation to participation and the formal, visible participation of individuals and group representatives in stating policy options, there has been little accounting, except under the rubric of "bureaucratic inertia," for the limits on change exerted by professionals.[52] As a result, we have been able to paint only a very rough sketch of the deliberate policy advocacy and manipulation that is done "behind the scenes." Yet, the gap between stated policies and their reality, the inability of even the most repressive regimes to transform all behavior and get full support from professionals, and the number of abandoned policies (as well as policies made without any elite policy commitment) make it clear that much goes on both without political leaders soliciting advice and outside formal public channels.

Finally, as Western studies of decision-making in communist states have shown, it is bureaucratic interests that have the most power.[53] In part, Western bureaucratic theory[54] can be applied to explain the strength of institutional interests in communist societies. But, bureaucracies' strength in protecting institutional prerogatives exists in spite of the penetration of the Communist Party into virtually all institutions – something Western theory maintains would naturally destroy institutional identity. The power of bureaucratic interests, in spite of the Party's penetration, exists in small, less complex institutions as well as in large, professionalized and insulated bureaucracies whose powers are critical to national policy, such as the military and the economic ministries. This suggests that more is involved than simply the model of Weberian-style bureaucracies.

Here, too, Western professionalization theory offers a useful paradigm. For, as the bureaucratic state developed in the West, professionals' life increasingly moved in setting to large bureaucracies. In communist states, political penetration has made independent professional work outside of some bureaucratic setting almost impossible even for the members of the "free professions." To deal with the impact of this bureaucratization on professional life, Western theorists have developed two paradigms:

(1) The paradigm of patronage relations in which the consumer or bureaucratic employer dominates professional behavior by determining how professionals should meet their needs. This is done through the employer's control over the recruitment of professionals. Because of this, professional workers' primary loyalty is to their employer.

(2) The paradigm of mediative relations where a public bureauc-

racy, involving nonprofessionals, stands between the professional and his consumers. It decides, in part guided by the expertise of the professional, what the clients' needs are for services and how they should be met. In this case, professional identification is split between the employing bureaucracy and the professional group.[55]

If one were to follow the totalitarian model, on the other hand, patronage relations would determine professional behavior. Experts would willingly limit their activities to serving as sources of information for elite decision-making and establishing careers solely through ties with members of the political elite. Their loyalty would be measured by their support for elite positions. It would then follow that, because of their ties to the political elite, professionals would make no attempt to articulate independent and oppositional interests. Their only concern would be to move up in the political hierarchy.

Interest group research done on the Soviet Union and Eastern Europe, however, shows that this is not normally the case. Professional demands do occur. Professionals, no matter how closely they are connected in their work or personal lives with the political leadership, do make demands and press for autonomy. And, ultimately, professionals are able to mediate between the public and the political leadership.

The professional model

The conflicts between theories of how groups should and can act under the constraints in communist societies and the realities of group action are, at least, partially explained with the professionalization theory that has been used by sociologists and political scientists to deal with groups or "professions" in the West, ranging from the traditional "free professions," like doctors and lawyers, to those enmeshed in twentieth-century bureaucracies. The occupational groups to which it has been applied are defined in Western sociological theory as groups with unique skills and, therefore, the option of becoming "private governments" with at least some authority and autonomy in their own spheres of interest and expertise.[56] They exist as independent communities with informal organizational structures, unique sets of values, and lengthy socialization processes that are longer than any other period of socialization in an individual's life.[57]

As a result, professionals, as portrayed by these theories, have a permanency of involvement and a set of values that supersede most other group ties. Informal organization, characterized as it is by a colleague network, is the vital link in professional life. Formal professional organizations are really structural concessions to represent a profession to nonprofessionals.[58] Given this model of professional life, explanations of professional behavior focus primarily on less articulated and less public activities and on the professional and his informal network rather than on formal "professional" pronouncements. Professionals are not seen as simply being "invited" into the policy process. They also act independently to formulate professional rules and policies and press to protect and enhance their interests. The political leadership in communist societies serves, then, not as the "gatekeeper" but as the target of professional pressure and, ultimately, the arbiter of professional demands.

Professionalizing

The ability of any profession to reach the point where it can build and maintain a significant amount of autonomy within a bureaucracy is a result of both the process of individual professionalization and the process of professionalization for the group itself. The latter occurs as the group moves to take an increasingly autonomous position by establishing its own formal and informal structures. At an individual level, four elements are involved in transforming an individual into a professional: (1) the recruitment and training process; (2) work experiences and the resulting interaction with fellow professionals; (3) the structures and rules for controlling professionals' behavior that are developed within the profession and codified and reinforced by formal and informal professional associations; and (4) the impact of external images of the profession held by the society.[59] Each of these four elements plays a crucial role in transmitting professional values and expertise and in creating and maintaining an insulated subculture. All of them go on in any environment in which the profession develops. Furthermore, the experience of Polish journalists indicates that political pressure and manipulation of the profession do not stop individuals from becoming professionalized. These political pressures may veil the professionalization, but, in reality, they sharpen and make more urgent the move to professionalization.

The same is true of the effect of political pressure on the professionalization of the group. In spite of the repression of the Polish journalism profession during World War II and under the Stalinist system, as well as the pressure of the political elite against the development of group autonomy and ideals, professionalization has occurred. The Polish journalism profession has followed the same course of development as have Western professions functioning without these kinds of political controls.

The historical pattern common to Western professions and to the case of Polish journalists began with individuals performing the work of the profession on a full-time basis and counting on it for their main income. When individuals were committed to the profession as full-time work, the need to perfect a body of expertise and protect work options then became greater. Professionals pressed for the establishment of training programs and, eventually, for their inclusion in university curricula. This resulted in the development of standards for entrance into the profession that involve lengthy and costly training programs and early recruitment. It also has given the profession more exclusivity and more worth in comparison with other occupations. Schools, in turn, have served as an organizational base for the establishment of a professional association, with the university affiliation simultaneously raising the status of the profession.[60]

Those pushing for specialized training and those involved in it subsequently form a professional association. The title of the profession often is changed to further upgrade a profession's public image. The association then discusses such questions as: is this a profession; what are a professionals' tasks; and, how can the quality of recruits be raised? During these discussions, conflicts develop among practitioners from different backgrounds. Campaigns to separate the competent from the incompetent begin as well.[61] The result of these developments has been that the profession goes through a series of major upheavals. A pecking order for the delegation of tasks develops. The "old guard," who learned through apprenticeships and are committed to their patrons and the use of "talent" as justification for entrance into the profession, fights against newcomers who came from the prescribed university course. This generational conflict stimulates pressure to put hiring and firing under professional group control. At the same time, there is competition for "turf" between the profession and neighboring groups. All of this eventually adds to the development of an entire system, both formal and informal, to regulate professional behavior and emphasize the role of the professional in serving society. It frequently involves political agitation to win the support of law to protect the "turf" of professional work and the profession's own code of ethics. To further protect their "turf" and their status, professional groups also develop rules to eliminate those who disgrace the group, to reduce internal competition and to emphasize that only a member of the profession can provide certain services to the society.[62] In the West, these crises and issues of identification are never fully resolved, so they return off and on as the profession develops and the society in which professionals work changes.

These crises are even less fully and permanently resolved in the communist world. Leadership changes and increase or decrease in political pressure bring each one to the surface again and again. The demographic devastation of World War II in Poland further created an age imbalance that exacerbated the generational conflict and the need for issues to be reconsidered and battled through with each generation. And, the prohibitions on visible and independent group activity make any full public resolution and commitment impossible.

Professionals and the policy process

The nature and significance of professional group and individual professionals' involvement in the policy process is dependent on more, though, than the invitation and interest of the political elite in both Soviet bloc and Western states. The nature of an issue and its relevance to different individuals or groups determine who gets involved and how. Which professionals and professional groups get involved in the policy process depends, as well, not simply on who the policy-makers want to hear but also on the nature of a given profession and the profession's own priorities. Finally, the stage at which groups become involved in a decision or policy and the impact they have are outgrowths of the nature of the policy itself as well as the political leadership's interest in that policy.[63]

From the perspective of professional and specialist groups, policies are not all the same. Some have a direct impact on a profession, its work and its compensation. Formal professional groups play significant roles in organizing around these issues and advocating policies that increase the profession's standing and its benefits. They also act to strengthen professionals' power and the power of the professional association. In doing this, professional groups claim authority and responsibility for themselves.

Other kinds of policies are relevant to professionals only when their expertise is relevant to resolving issues on an individual or informal group basis. In these cases, normally, the policy has no direct impact on an individual's life or work. The professional serves as a representative of other groups through the use of his technical expertise and recognized knowledge in a particular area. Finally, in some policies, professionals are involved as policy administrators. The passage of these policies affects the profession's role but not necessarily either its own interests or work patterns. In this final case, professional involvement occurs through advocacy by the professional association or experts from the profession and through policy administration.

Issues that affect professionals' own lives and work are regarded by professionals and their associations as their exclusive domain. The tendency is to keep the public and the state government away from what they see as professional concerns. In doing this, professional associations, both formal and informal, become "private governments" providing services and material benefits to their members. They also set up structures to regulate individual behavior within the professional community. Finally, they move to represent the interests of the profession to the public government.[64] In acting as representatives of the profession, professional associations jealously guard the ability of professionals to be sources of information and personnel for governmental decisions and committees and also to serve as the links between the professionals and their public.

Internally, each professional association has its own governance. This governance is determined by the profession's goals, the nature of its membership, and its members' socio-economic positions and needs as well as the association's past history.[65] Formal structures are intended to aid the organization in being the chief law-making body for public regulation of professional concerns.[66] These structures also are designed so internal controls can be maintained on association members in order to increase the group's leverage on professional issues.[67] Professional organizations, in trying to control the profession, seek to diffuse conflicts among individuals coming from different specializations, regional bases and social backgrounds. To do this, they divide professionals up into sections reflecting the varied interests and foci of the group's members.[68] They also seek to develop close coordination between local and national branches. By establishing and maintaining this control and coordination, professional organizations influence the public regulation of the profession and its work. They also influence the profession's membership and its public image.

This internal structure is not designed to insure democracy and full participation of all professionals within the organization. Dissent within the profession weakens the organization's negotiating position. So dissent and deviation, either in professional work patterns or behavior, are discouraged both formally and informally. As a service organization, the professional association is involved in lobbying and providing guidance to the government on complex issues. Group democracy and action are replaced by power invested in a permanent bureaucracy and a relatively stable and identifiable elite. So, crucial issues are seldom discussed and voted on by the profession as a whole. Instead, they are normally handled informally by the profession's leaders.

Ironically, though, however strong and visible that formal elite is, it is not the only professional elite. In each profession, there is, on the one hand, a parallel elite of individuals whose professional work is seen as excellent. On the other hand, those who make a career out of professional politics and representation are a self-selected few. They tend to be persons of high, but not top, prestige and authority within the profession. Their work is normally not a model for the profession. In fact, because movement up to the top of the professional organization is usually a result of gradual advancement up through lower level professional offices, most of those in the formal organizational elite spend years of their careers working less than full-time in real professional work. Their relationship with the profession as a whole is skewed by their experiences as bureaucrats and lobbyists. As a result, in Western democracies where professional organizations' dynamics have been studied, these individuals, the bureaucrats, are identified with the professional world they represent and not stellar professional work.[69]

Previous studies dealing with the dynamics of professional groups in Eastern Europe found patterns which seem, on the surface, similar to this.[70] Thus, the dynamics of professional organizations in Eastern Europe and the Soviet Union may be as much a result of their professionalism as of the demands by political leaders that they serve as "transmission belts." For this, the case of Polish journalists serves as a test since journalists are the profession whose loyalty is most demanded by the elite.

Structurally, professional associations in communist societies are hybrids of the two most common forms of professional organization: the guild model of equality among lower level professionals in various workplace and speciality groups[71] and the pyramidal hierarchy model of a bureaucratic structure working to protect the profession against external bureaucracies.[72] Clearly, the pyramidal hierarchy takes on greater significance in communist systems where the pressure and interference that most bedevils the profession comes from external

Party and state bureaucracies' control and direction. This external pressure makes the nonbureaucratic guild model less effective because the ruling bureaucracy of the Party and state both mandates and then responds only to corresponding professional bureaucracies. This same pressure, though, also exists in increasingly bureaucratized Western states.[73]

The structure and effectiveness of professions' and professionals' involvement in policy that does not directly impact on professional work is limited more by political pressures than is professionals' influence on policies regulating their profession. For professional groups in Western and communist societies who contribute to policy-making as advisors or administrators, policy-making is a complex process. It has many stages at which individuals and groups can visibly and invisibly enter and impact on policies. Involvement in the early stages allows individuals and groups to define the issues and solutions they want to consider. It also allows them to determine who will be heard in the debate. Involvement in the middle and most public stages is often limited to tinkering with the basic policy set out early on.[74] Finally, although manipulation and redrawing the administration of a policy often has a significant effect on the public's sense of a policy, it seldom leads to a change in policy and most frequently ends with sporadic and undeclared distortions of it. This, ultimately, may force rethinking of policy but is not well enough articulated to serve as a clear model for a policy reform.

Journalists tend to be one of the most privileged professions because they enter into the early stages of policy-making and play "gatekeeper" roles in later stages. Some have ties with top political leaders and know, from friends, when an issue is being discussed by the leadership. They can use highly personalized and private channels to influence top elite discussions: personal and informal connections with leaders and their assistants that have been built up through years of joint work and social contact; non-published communications to the elite; and part-time or full-time work in political offices. In the most public stage of the policy process the press is one of the major forums for debate and the presentation of information. At a minimum, in the press and professional groups, there are veiled discussions that are monitored by the political leaders or are reflections of private presentations made directly to those leaders. It often is to the advantage of the politicians to allow open discussion so long as this discussion does not jeopardize their ideological power. Only in this way can the top elite be assured of obtaining the most accurate information from the broadest range of experts without those experts limiting themselves to what the elite wants to hear. Such discussions also stimulate non-expert opinion from those directly affected by the policy. This is most often voiced through journalists' reports or letters to journals and public agencies.[75]

Once data has been presented, the elite tends to withdraw to prepare a draft or final proposal for approval by the designated government agency. This normally ends the debate on a specific policy but does not always end the policy process. Individuals, even in strictly regulated communist polities, articulate their interests indirectly and try to get special treatment. Frequently, the aggregate behavior of social groups in response to a policy becomes a significant part of the memory of the elite and of society. This is then taken into account when policy-makers redesign policy. Journalists contribute to both the articulation of individual interests and the visibility of specific group responses to policies by acting as ombudsmen for individual problems and constantly reporting on events and attitudes through their public and private channels. This means that, while citizens are made aware of policies through the media, journalists also serve as channels to modify the impact of policies on individual citizens and to alert policy-makers to problems in how their policies work. Finally, explicit and direct criticism of the impact and administration of a law is made. This broader discussion, characterized in its public form as "press criticism," is, in part, an indication of policy-makers' interest in the administration and the success or failure of a policy in real life. From the perspective of the population, this press criticism is aimed at pressuring the elite to legitimize discussion and modify a policy.

Clearly, journalists are more involved in policy discussions than many professions because of their control over media platforms for public dabate and their ties with political elites. Like the professional organizations that protect professional interests, this involvement is not simply a matter of invitation by the policy-makers. It is a product of the relationship between professional role demands and the requirements of political involvement. Frequently, too, elite policy-making is influenced by the experiences they had, when they worked in one or another profession or policy area.[76]

As in the West, movement from professional work to political work is dependent on the nature of the profession: the congruence of the skills of professionals and those needed by politicians; the ability of individuals in a given profession to abandon their work for temporary or permanent political activity; and the particular occupational needs satisfied by the government.[77] For journalists and lawyers in both the

East and West, movement into politics does not go against professional requirements and traditions. For other professions, like the medical profession, movement into politics requires time and skills which practicing in a profession like medicine does not allow. As a result, some professions are more likely to be actively involved in policy debates not directly affecting their professional worlds than are others.

Thus, Western oriented professionalization theory provides a model for explaining both the power of professionals and specialists and the ability of groups to affect policy in communist systems when neither professional dominance nor group interests are recognized as legitimate. Clearly, the gate-keeper role of the political elite is crucial in any situation. But, the apparent congruence of behavior between Western professional associations and those in Eastern Europe suggests that the natural dynamics of professional interaction may be a significant factor in politics. It also suggests that this will be more true for purely professional issues with low political salience and a limited constituency than it is with other issues. But, in less visible ways, professional input, buoyed by professionalization, occurs on all levels.

Polish journalists: the virtues of atypicality

The atypicality of Polish journalists and their national environment makes their professionalism an ideal and accessible model for looking at the relationship between professionalization, professional group imperatives, and professionals' input in policy-making. Polish journalists, first of all, do not have the normal qualities that are assumed by Western theorists to be necessary for a group to feel that it is imperative to act as professionals. To a greater extent than most professions, journalists do not share a common class origin. They are very involved in politics and very divided as a group in their political orientations. They enter the profession without any single training base.

They have, however, all the characteristics of professional groups: high levels of self-definition as professionals, and of loyalty to their profession. In addition, they have had very high, almost exclusionary, patterns of informal group interaction. Like Western journalists, they have developed this sense of an overriding professional identity in spite of the fact that they are in a highly unregulated, competitive, yet bureaucratized field, and do their work through constant formal and social contacts with individual sources of information from outside the profession. They must maintain and impose their professional identity and boundaries on a world where writing well is not considered either a unique skill or a technological necessity.

Finally, the world of Polish politics is the most tumultuous and unstable in Eastern Europe. It is a political situation into which journalists are constantly drawn. The demands on them, though, are never consistent. This makes them periodically rethink their personal and professional ideals and affiliations.

Research opportunities

For Western researchers, Poland is also an environment where discussion and action are more open and visible than in other more stable and controlled communist states. So, even under the conditions of the mid-seventies, interviews, survey research, and access to internal professional transcripts and reports allowed this study to survey far more than merely what had been published. This primary data, reinforced and enlivened by the words and works of journalists, press scholars, and politicians in the heady discussions and experiments of the Solidarity era and the dramatic changes that came with martial law, provided the data for much of this discussion of journalists' life and work. It reflects the research done on the journalism profession in the West and the research of Polish scholars on the profession as well as the writings of journalists about their work, their profession, and their concerns. In fact, much of the discussion of changes is based on Polish scholars' surveys done in 1958 and 1962[78] among Polish journalists and a survey done by this author in 1976 using a similar sample of Polish journalists. More impressionistic evidence as well as information about policy relevant behavior and non-public negotiations largely comes from interviews with 200 journalists in Poland in 1975–76 and smaller samples in 1979 and 1983. This data was further validated by the comparable interview results when interviews were done with former Polish journalists in Western Europe and the United States between 1976 and 1983.[79]

Professional demographics

Polish journalists, as a group, have been one of the most diverse professions in postwar Poland.[80] Their social composition, particularly in terms of class origins and the level of feminization, have changed dramatically since the communist takeover after World War II. Beginning in 1948, workers, peasants, and women entered the

Table 1 *Percentage increase in membership in the union of journalists 1951–80*

Year	Number of members	Percentage increase
1951	643	?
1954	2,399	273.1
1956	2,826	17.8
1958	2,961	4.8
1961	3,691	24.8
1964	4,406	19.3
1968	4,802	8.9
1971	5,346	11.3
1974	6,055	13.3
1980	9,000	

Sources: SDP Archives, 1976 and 1980

profession in large numbers – far larger than before the war.[81] In the initial postwar years of Stalinism, the profession grew rapidly (Table 1). This Stalinist era group continued to be the core of the profession for the next thirty years since they came into the profession, in the late forties and early fifties, when they were in their teens and early twenties. As a result of this stability, there were places for only a few recruits in the sixties and seventies. And, while a large number of the profession's elite, who had entered soon after the war, retired, resigned, or were kept out of the profession after the declaration of martial law, this generation remained a major professional force both numerically and as role models for professional work in the post-1981 era. The next most numerically and professionally significant group has come from the 1970s entrants who rose to prominence as a result of Solidarity and the changes in the profession.

As a profession, journalists and journalism are considered to be part of the intelligentsia. They have life-styles, values, and social status like those of other intelligentsia groups. But, at least in the forties and fifties, when there was massive recruitment of potentially loyal regime followers into the profession, the majority of those able to get work in the profession were working class. From 1950 to 1955, 66 percent of the students in journalism education programs were working class.[82] These "intelligentsia converts" remained in journalism for the next thirty years. For them, the gains in being raised from the working class to the intelligentsia have been invaluable.

In later years, the smaller groups of entrants into the profession were less working class in origin. By 1964, only 34.2 percent of the profession as a whole claimed to be from working-class backgrounds.[83] This balance did not change dramatically in the 1970s. In fact, in television, the number of journalists coming from working-class backgrounds was so low that one journalist commented that being working class was "an element of snobbism among television journalists."[84] This was, in part, a reflection of television journalism's higher visibility and material benefits. But, basically, it was a result of the fact that television emerged as a "serious" media in Poland only in the 1970s. Then, when most television journalists were hired, the issue of "class background" was less significant.

With the advent of the Solidarity period, the class structure of the profession did not change dramatically. Worker journalists were not treated as members of the profession. Those already in the professional association and in established professional circles simply treated "worker–journalists" as newcomers who would have to serve the customary apprenticeship period before they could be treated as full-scale professionals.

Education and professional training, as is clear from the problems and adjustments in the journalism education programs of the postwar period, are not required for professional work in journalism. In the early period of heavy recruitment, there were more journalists with only high school education than there were with university degrees.[85] Even by 1969, only 58 percent of working journalists had completed a university education and an even smaller percentage had formal journalism training. The legacy of the fifties remained: politics took precedence so 72 percent of journalists under thirty-five had completed their university degrees but only 34 percent of those between forty-five and fifty-five, individuals who entered the profession in the initial postwar years when political qualifications were paramount, had finished their university course work.[86] Furthermore, few journalists in Warsaw actually finished professional training and even fewer of those who worked outside Warsaw had training in journalism.[87] This pattern continued throughout the Solidarity period.

Not only has professionalization occurred without autonomous professional education, but, it also occurred even where individuals entered journalism from other fields. To make this shift involved getting new skills and working in new ways as well as shedding old loyalties. More than half of the journalists surveyed in 1962 had worked outside journalism: 49.7 percent had had no other work prior to entering journalism, 16.5 percent had been government bureaucrats, 8.3 percent had worked in other areas of publishing, 1.6 percent had been in the arts, 1.6 percent had been workers, 1.5 percent censors, 1.3 percent engineers, 1.2 percent military or internal security officers, and 0.6 percent lawyers.[88] A similar question in 1976 showed a comparable relationship between individuals with journalism as a first and only profession and those with training and work experience in some other profession. In fact, because this later survey was done primarily among regional and lower level journalists, even more (60 percent) claimed to have had some other profession prior to becoming journalists. This movement into journalism from other work is reported to have gone on in the 1980 period as well, among those who did make a permanent move into the profession.

Professionals' political affiliations

The prime challenges to the autonomy of journalism come from the political authorities in Poland. They define the journalism profession as an "instrument of the Party" and demand that it be a part of the political establishment in a more direct sense than other professions are. Party membership is, therefore, more common for journalists than for other professional groups in Poland. Nearly half (47 percent) of all members of the Association of Polish Journalists (SDP) and 56 percent of all those involved in work related to journalism were Party members as of 1975.[89]

Ironically, though, whether or not having that percentage of journalists as party members was considered ideal, it is clear that the regime has been able to encourage but not force Party membership. The martial law attempt to get control of the profession and limit its autonomy did not result in journalists taking on Party membership as a prerequisite to professional work. The profession was, at least initially, fragmented because of individuals' intense reaction to martial law and its system of repression. Many journalists left established, high visibility positions and Party membership on their own or because they were blacklisted. Membership in the new Association of Polish Journalists of the Polish People's Republic (SDPRL) also ceased to be a simple matter of membership and became a political statement because the new Association appeared as an imposed substitute for the old Association, involved as it was in 1980–81 with Solidarity.[90] So, since membership was taken as a sign of support for the regime, a slightly higher percentage of the Association registered Party membership. As of 3 May, 1983, of the 5,375 members of the SDPRL, 65 percent were members of the Communist Party and 4 percent were members of the two minor parties.[91] The rest had no party affiliations. Still, even under martial law, the authorities could not bring nearly half of the working professionals into Party membership.

As with other professions involved in politics, appointment to important positions in the profession is controlled by the Party through its right to approve all major appointments (*nomenklatura*) at all governmental levels. Therefore, in managerial positions considered important by the Party bureaucracy or leadership, Party membership is higher than in other positions. In 1977, according to a report by the Association of Polish Journalists:

> Membership in political organizations by editors down to the level of managing editor is high. In RSW Prasa [the major publishing house formally sponsored by the Polish United Workers Party], 80% are members of political organizations [including the minor parties]. In Radio and Television, 70% are members.[92]

For purely journalistic positions (beginning with managing editor but not including editorial writers), the percentage of Party members is significantly lower.[93] For those who entered in the Stalinist period of early and massive recruitment, though, Party membership was clearly an advantageous substitute for the previous experience and education new entrants did not have. More of those who entered in this period are Party members than was the case for those who joined in the 1960s and 1970s.[94] Yet, this Party membership did not necessarily guarantee journalists easy advancement into prestigious positions other than the few closely controlled by the Party's *nomenklatura*.

This has been clear not only from the presence of a significant percentage of non-Party members in the upper levels of the professional hierarchy but also by the concentration of journalists who are Party members. Warsaw, the most advantageous and prestigious place to live and work, has a much smaller percentage of Party journalists than other areas where professional work has lower status but staffs are smaller and local officials' surveillance is far higher.[95] While there was a temporary dip in Party membership as a result of Solidarity's power, particularly in smaller cities and towns outside the capital, the prevalence of Party membership in the regions outside of Warsaw returned with the reimposition of media control under martial law. In 1983, then, 70.3 percent of regional journalists were Party members – a clear increase from the late seventies.[96]

Party membership, in the past, has had somewhat greater influence on the field of specialization:

> The highest level of Party membership is found in the Party department (organization department). In that department, 89.1% are P.U.W.P. members. A significant number of Party members are also in the departments of economics (54%), agriculture (51%), information (from news agencies) (52%), international (48.5%) and national (48%).[97]

The high percentage of Party members in the information department (the lowest paid, lowest in status, and most isolated) then is evidence that Party membership has been an aid to entrance but not necessarily any guarantee of mobility within the profession.

Self-identification

Whatever their backgrounds, political affiliations, and past ties, journalists see themselves as journalists. They also see their profession as "the best" of the professions. In fact, measured by the standards of willingness to leave the profession, ranking of occupations, and journalists' rates of interaction with members of other groups as compared to their interaction with fellow journalists, Polish journalists have a higher level of professional identification than has existed in any other professional grouping.[98] Overwhelmingly, in 1976, journalists surveyed said they would not like to leave the profession (86.6 percent of those surveyed said they would not like to leave the profession, 12.6 percent said they would like to leave it). Even in the aftermath of criticism of the media in the Solidarity period and the repression of journalists and media workers involved with the reform movement, ultimately few complete departures from the profession took place. One estimate by a former official of the SDP was that initially some 2,000 left because of expulsions or an unwillingness to work under the military regime; but, within six months of the declaration of martial law, all but a few had returned to the profession in some form – lesser known publications, writing under pseudonyms, underground writing, or publishing jobs – and all but a few who remained outside the profession did so as journalists making symbolic gestures. Even at that, professional circles and information exchanges continued and were strengthened in this period (for a full discussion of the professional response and involvement in Solidarity and during the martial law period, see chapter 6).

Journalists' responses in 1976 to the question "What do you think is the best occupation?" were equally indicative of individuals' commitment to journalism and its basic goals. The largest percentage of respondents listed "journalism" as the best occupation (23.6 percent). Those who did not see their own profession as the "best" tended to focus on other comparable professions. In the case of Warsaw professionals, most saw the non-technical intelligentsia as "the best" but, in the case of regional journalists, technical intelligentsia careers were considered the best. On the other hand, although 9.2 percent of the journalists surveyed held Party positions and 49.4 percent said they performed some official social function, none listed "Party activist" as the "best occupation." Only two respondents listed institutional party and state positions as the "best occupation." Similar results were reported in 1958 when journalists had to rank professional groups. Then, journalists ranked teachers, doctors and engineers highest because of their roles in "educating the society" and "developing Poland" – roles journalists' own professional ideology specifies as primary responsibilities of their profession. Lawyers and artists were ranked lowest because they had "little influence on changes in the society" and "play a minimal role in the society" – again a reflection of journalists' application of their professional values.[99]

The 1976 breakdown of these measures of identification in terms of the other potential pulls on journalists' self-identification indicates that professional identification is overwhelming. In fact, competing pulls for loyalty tend to increase identification with journalism. Members of the PUWP are more positive about the profession than are non-Party journalists: 38.5 percent of PUWP journalists think journalism is the best occupation while 22.7 percent of non-Party journalists ranked it as the "best profession." Working-class background, correlated as it is with Party affiliation and with the profession as the prime mode of upward mobility, yields virtually the same breakdown.

Anecdotal evidence further indicates that, in spite of journalists' own criticisms of their profession's past work and in spite of public attacks in the 1980s on the media, this positive image of the profession has remained. Problems were blamed on outside interference and occasional "weak" professionals not on the professional work itself.[100] Individuals left the profession after martial law because their past work was defamed or not appreciated and they "had fought the battle to be professionals too long." They did not leave because they had found some better calling. Finally, whether or not they remained in their positions, journalists continued to do work related to information gathering and presentation and attacked those who denigrated the profession by violating professional ethics or restricting their professional autonomy to suit political demands.

Informal group interaction

Even more crucial than individual identification in determining a profession's ability to function as a group controlling its own world and acting in the public arena are the patterns of individual social interaction. In communist societies where formal professional organizations are monitored and controlled, independent action occurs primarily through individuals' informal, personal relationships. The more the profession is the prime source for professionals' friendships, the greater its base for group action. To identify patterns of informal group life, three questions were asked of Polish journalists: "With whom do you associate most frequently?"; "How would you characterize staff relations on your journal?"; and "Do you interact with journalists from other journal staffs?"

Journalists in both 1956 and 1976 reported that they spent most of their social time either with other journalists or with their own immediate families.[101] Professional factors (residence, position and years in the profession) and incidental personal factors (such as wartime affiliations) account for variations in journalists' social lives. Those outside of Warsaw spend more time with other journalists than do those living in Warsaw who, on the whole, have much larger intelligentsia circles.[102] Journalists in editorial positions spent slightly less of their nonwork time with other journalists than did those who were simply staff journalists. Party members associate as frequently with other journalists as do those with no Party affiliation, although they do have a slight tendency to see Party activists more frequently (9.1 percent of Party members said they associated frequently with Party activists while 2.6 percent of non-Party members reported contacts with Party activists in their personal lives).[103]

Entry into the profession without the customary educational credentials and class background is also not a deterrent to close primary social contacts with other journalists. In fact, in both 1958 and 1976, journalists' involvement with other journalists was greater for those coming from working-class backgrounds or having less than a full university level education. For them, not only was entry into the profession a significant move for upward mobility but it also was the most comfortable of the intelligentsia professions with which they could associate.[104]

Interaction with journalists from staffs other than their own, a demonstration of professional group as opposed to work place affiliations, is high. Not only are relations between journalists on a single staff close but journalists relate socially and professionally with members of other staffs with high frequency. Given both the high level of primary social interaction among journalists and the extent of journalists' association with members of other staffs (88.5 percent of those surveyed in 1976 said that they associated with journalists outside their immediate work group), there clearly are informal links that draw professionals together outside of their workplace, allowing them to discuss their problems and options as well as to reinforce common goals and behavior patterns. From this data too, there are indications that, even in "normal periods" of external control, there has been an interlocking pattern of contacts holding journalists together as more than colleagues who work together and need to protect their journal or television program.

With the advent of the Solidarity press and the movement of workers and non-journalists into it, these patterns of association by traditional journalists did not decrease. Even those who worked for Solidarity and its press reported in 1983 that, when martial law had closed their journals and offices down, they had little inclination to continue their ties with the workers and new "journalists" with whom they worked during the fifteen months of Solidarity. Instead, they kept their ties with colleagues from earlier years. The only deviation from the pattern that appeared in the 1958 and 1976 surveys was that, after martial law was declared, journalists had a tendency to exclude from their social circles old friends and colleagues who had made different political choices in responding to the declaration of martial law and the closing down of the old postwar association. This split was particularly evident among older journalists who had entered the profession after the war and had their own independent financial cushion. It was less the case for young journalists who were dependent on their work for their livelihood.

The Polish case

The world in which these journalists work has been one of change and upheaval interspersed with longer periods of stability and Party control. It is also one in which even the most control-oriented leadership has been forced to compromise full communist rule and recognize the Catholic Church's right to function and the right of the peasantry to private farming, as well as to show greater tolerance of independent opinion than has existed elsewhere in the Soviet bloc. All of this brought with it a factionalization of the political leadership that gave journalists options in their elite affiliations. With this factionalization among regime politicians and compromise with popular demands on the mass level, Poland has, since the Stalinist period, been a "quasi-pluralistic authoritarian" state rather than a representative of the more authoritarian Soviet model.[105] Leaders have been overthrown by mass action three times, as the Gierek leadership was in August 1980. The media and leadership policies have been subject to scathing criticisms in each of these periods of upheaval. Journalists and other groups, thus, have been pushed and pulled from one set of demands and expectations to another. They also have regularly experienced losses of freedom after the Party leadership quashed popular unrest. With this has come disillusionment and retreat into silent work for individual and group interests.

The instability of political rule in Poland has brought with it a greater freedom for groups to be seen and their demands heard. It has meant, even in the Stalinist period, a decreased level of fear and increased willingness publicly to voice demands and opinions about the political situation.

In these ways, the experience of Polish journalists is an atypical case for Soviet bloc states. But, although the boundaries of tolerance have normally been broader in Poland than in other Soviet bloc states, the state ideology, the Party and state institutions, and the "rules of the game" are the same as those in the other systems in Eastern Europe and the Soviet Union.[106] And, while the shifts in leadership and the periods of free discussion have given journalists a sense of freedom and an acute sense of being controlled when liberalization moves are halted, the direction and pressure of Poland's political leadership has been toward using the media and controlling or coopting the profession.

Journalists' ability to maintain and protect themselves is based not simply on greater freedom in Poland but on their professionalization. This took root not in the uniquely Polish moments of freedom but in the repressive days of the Stalinist imposition of communist rule. Such soil clearly also rooted the journalists of Hungary, who joined the "revolution" in 1956, and Czechoslovakia, many of whom were leaders or observers in 1968.[107] These journalists behaved as Polish journalists did in 1956, 1970, and 1980. And, the realities of professional life, although the restrictions may be looser, are not that distinct from the realities of journalists' lives in the more controlled system of the rest of Eastern Europe and the Soviet Union.[108] The similarities in the system and in journalists' reactions to them suggest that the Polish profession is a more accessible but not necessarily the only professional group, or a more real element, in communist politics than its counterparts in other systems or from other professions.

2 The postwar roots of the profession

The end of World War II and the imposition of communist rule marked the beginnings of what seemed to be a new Polish journalism profession. Few of Poland's cadre of prewar journalists remained at the end of the war. And, most of those who had survived were summarily blacklisted or pushed to the side by the time communist rule was established in late 1947. In their place came a deluge of young men and women for whom journalism and the new communist rule offered a chance "to make it."

The destruction of World War II had left Poland without the basics for a press. Paper, ink, and printing presses were simply not available. And, most skilled and experienced journalists had been killed; had escaped to the West; or had gone into hiding, publishing only under pseudonyms. The prewar Polish press had been outlawed by the Germans and the press that came out during the war, with the exception of a few Polish language papers controlled by the Germans, came from the communist and noncommunist undergrounds. All that remained were memories of the prewar traditions of the press as an independent voice against unwelcome rulers and a forum for intellectual discussion. These traditions fit the realities of a Poland partitioned between three empires and the time of freedom that followed World War I, only to be worn down by a military regime. And, as is clear from the fact that the interwar laws on the press and censorship remained on the books until Solidarity and intellectual groups joined forces to pass a censorship law in 1981, these old traditions and the professionalizing force they exerted fit even after the communist takeover and the Stalinist attempt at control.

Polish journalism history has served as an incentive for the professionalization process to occur even though it has been enmeshed in moves from all sides to control the freedom of the press. It has also led to the creation of "group myths." The role of the profession in the

Partition period was that of a champion of national culture and language. This image of journalists as preservers of the nation has continued to be crucial to journalists' image. Because of its role in contentious interwar political discussions, the journalism profession also has a tradition of keeping political conflicts between journalists out of professional life. So, except in crisis periods like 1956 and 1980, journalists' professional forums since World War II have been comparatively free of political rhetoric. In addition, the focus of the prewar profession on the journals and issues of the educated class has continued into the "socialist workers' press system." This has led to a writing tradition that is primarily analysis, not information, and to one focused on the language and journals of the intelligentsia. Because of the contradictory pressures on the profession during the communist takeover and the Stalinist period, the profession has also never seen itself as truly a part of the political establishment. And, finally, because of the role played by the profession in 1956, the "myth" of the potential "power of the press" has been the dominant one for the postwar journalism profession.[1]

It was, however, Stalinism that taught the most memorable lessons to those who peopled the profession in the years of communist rule in Poland. No analysis of professional beliefs and actions can go far without a look at the first experiences of the profession. It is these experiences, after all, that not only schooled the profession but have also served as its point of reference. It was the pressure of the Stalinist regime for a press that was read and was still an ideological spokesman for the regime that inculcated in journalists the sense that professional and political involvement and obedience could not be integrated. Journalists developed, without articulating their concerns, mechanisms to protect themselves from political interference. They learned to trust those who were most critical and to play politics with those who controlled their work options. And, ultimately, the unmasking of Stalinism and the accumulation of impossible demands and unfilled promises made journalists political cynics and determined professionals.

In fact, the massive political changes and the continual political interference under which the Polish press works forced key professional demands to be resolved at one stage and resolved again when political demands changed. With the reemergence of each issue, be it education, the nature and rights of professional organizations, or external power over the profession, traditions and patterns of earlier periods have matched their challengers. As a result, there has been a real continuity of institutional styles and professional values. Furthermore, political pressures on journalism have served, in the long run, to expedite the professionalization process and strengthen the professionalism of Polish journalism.

First lessons

In 1945, the future of the Polish press was no clearer than the future of Poland itself. Claiming to be a part of a "popular front" aimed at reconstructing Poland, the communist "Lublin government" moved to control news agencies, radio stations, and press distribution ostensibly because of postwar shortages. But, gradually, they used their control to make it exceedingly difficult for papers not supporting the communists to survive.[2] Local Communist Party committees went even further. They recruited and staffed the new press both by using direct instructions and by guiding events through the chief editors they appointed from their own local Party committees. When there were no qualified recruits available, they set up programs of their own to train them even as the Warsaw authorities dragged their feet on promises to reestablish the prewar school of journalism. Party committees also got actively involved in how "their" papers looked and what they said. As this occurred, the Union of Polish Journalists, resurrected from its prewar base, became increasingly powerless. It made rules that limited employment in journalism to its members. The Party committees hired whomever they pleased. Still, the union took complaints about the growing Party control on the press and presented them to political leaders who would listen. But, nothing happened.

By 1947, there was no longer any question about the fate of the press and the journalism profession. The pressures on the press exerted by the Ministry of Information and local communist authorities were hardly veiled: in the battle over the 1947 elections, the communist controlled ministry closed down or restricted most non-communist journals, leaving many prewar journalists finally and firmly out of work and, therefore, disqualified as members of the union.[3] At the same time, resources were poured into the communist press so that it ultimately dwarfed the non-communist journals that had survived all the other attacks.[4]

A new professional elite also took over in 1948. It turned from advocating professional rights to trying to buy political loyalty.[5] Yet, even with the influx of new members, the majority of journalists used professional gatherings to discuss the weaknesses of educational programs, problems in government-press relations, and the fate of older journalists.

Journalists complained most in these meetings about conflicts with officials over access to information. They cited specific places where they were blocked from observing the events they were sent to report[6] and where signs were posted in offices saying, "Entrance by journalists forbidden."[7] The profession's work was, after all, to reflect life in the country and to serve as a critic of institutional failings. What journalists found, instead, was that institutions were unwilling to make information available[8] and "bad humor, strong protests and attacks blaming journalists for their criticism and holding them responsible for the results of bad and dangerously done work abounded."[9] Even the work of local censor's offices was criticized in these meetings.[10]

The new leaders focused on "the reform of the pay code, reorganization of vacation programs, the development of cooperative work with other professionals, the institution of a life insurance program and the building of a joint professional building."[11] At the same time, ideological discussions for journalists were ordered once a month.[12] The national organization worked out a program for regional journalists to come to Warsaw and be apprenticed to more ideologically supervised journals or to take course work that would deepen their ideological training.[13] In the union's journal, the number of ideological articles increased sharply even though direct references to the Soviet model were infrequent. The union sponsored trips for journalists to Czechoslovakia, Hungary, Yugoslavia, and Bulgaria but not to the Western countries where Polish journalists had gone in the past.[14] It even broke with the prewar tradition of political nonalignment when it applauded the union of the Polish Workers Party and the Polish Socialist Party.

In line with the national campaign for "increased production," journalists were judged on "the correctness of their information, the work they did in rapidly informing the public, the ties that they developed with their readers, their punctuality in closing editions, and their exactness in adjusting their material."[15]

The politicization of editorial positions was built into the new salary code. Editors and managing editors were excused from requirements that they publish a set number of articles monthly.[16] The institution of "correspondents," a dominant element in Stalinist journalism, was added as a special class of journalism.[17]

Stalinism: 1949–1953

In the years from 1949 to 1953, the Stalinist press system was imposed to minimize the professional autonomy of journalists. The media policy which would govern this period had two often inconsistent goals: to win support from a hostile population for communist rule in Poland and to sovietize the population. To do this, the media was instructed to:

> be propagandists who day after day convey Marxist–Leninist theories, agitators who day after day speak about the international political situation and about the Party's and people's government policies, and organizers who day after day mobilize our forces for their active part in Socialist construction. This is a powerful instrument of the Party in its endeavor to bring up a new generation of builders of socialism in Poland.[18]

The journalist in this situation was an intermediary. He collected letters and articles from Party propagandists and worker–peasant correspondents. He intervened with low level bureaucrats on behalf of individuals in the name of the Party. His professional talents as a writer of prose were significant only if he produced Party propaganda.[19]

In fact, the intense conflicts between the realities of the work world and the political elite's expectations and demands strengthened the profession's image of itself as a "besieged island." Public opposition and criticism within the union did die out. The union was transformed into a Soviet style "transmission belt" to mold the profession. Its union functions were transferred to the general trade union council. But, members continued to look to the new Association to solve their problems. The intensive journalistic training programs served to isolate the new recruits from all but their professional peers and to develop among them a real sense of community. Peasant–worker correspondents insulated working journalists from the real world. At the same time, whether they came into the profession after an internship as correspondents or not, most recognized how poorly the system worked and how different reality was from the well painted pictures the press was expected to provide. Journalists, too, felt the sting of local pressure for revealing problems. This meant that they had to create for themselves a safe and cherished haven. Also, the pressure on journalists to specialize made them more and more able to see through propaganda and to criticize policies, based on their own knowledge.

Recruitment

Movement into the journalism profession was extremely rapid in the Stalinist era. Between 1949 and 1954, the membership of the journalism organization more than doubled. As the professional journal, *Prasa Polska* stated in February, 1950: "reservoirs of journalism cadres are the Party and social activists, worker and peasant correspondents . . . young ZMP activists [the Communist youth organization] and, most of all, young workers and peasants".[20] Rules for training were eased so new journalists could be registered merely by being recommended by their editor-in-chief and passing a political examination.[21] The parameters of the profession were stretched to include "interveners" and "the government and public institution press apparatus."[22] Since work experience prior to World War II no longer counted towards seniority, journalism rapidly became "the world of the young."[23]

The initial spurt of direct recruitment after 1948 diverted massive numbers of young recruits into professional education programs from which they would emerge only in 1952. This formal education was basically centered at the School of Journalism at the University of Warsaw. The course work was explicitly to reflect "both the Soviet experience and the new methods of teaching journalism used in the West."[24] Faculty consisted, at first, of political activists and not professional journalists. When the school began to produce its own specialists and the need for students who could actually produce a paper was too great, the dominance of political activists and subjects was reduced, professional journalists were brought in as lecturers, and courses on press history and journalistic techniques were added.[25]

Students were recruited into the program on the basis of their political activism and class background as workers and peasants. While they were in the program, they were expected to stretch their time to do an apprenticeship and, more importantly, to be members of the Party youth organization or the Party itself.[26]

By 1950, some 200 students were enrolled in each of the three years of the program.[27] Hence, by 1954, the "early recruits" had finished the program and been working in journalism for two years. The real lessons they had learned in their journalistic education were taking effect as they became secure in their jobs. Their experiences had been none too positive. The experience of being educated to be journalists did not create political loyalists as it was designed to. Instead, it was a professionalizing one even though it was not professionally controlled and did not teach a unique body of professional knowledge. Because of the intensity of the program and the concentration of its students, too poor to live elsewhere, in dormitories, journalism students were together thirty-eight to forty hours a week in classes and then lived together.[28] Their faculty was also so tiny and overworked that students had little contact with their teachers. So, their world was that of their fellow students. From this, they developed a strong sense of membership and identity with "journalists" that has lasted for the last forty years as these once politically trusted recruits molded and led the profession. Their sense of themselves as a group turned against the system as they went out into the real world. Since political slogans and Marxism–Leninism did them little good in the newsroom, these young recruits apprenticed themselves to older, trained journalists who were often far from pro-regime political animals. They found that their education had misled them about the realities of political life in Poland:

> Even on things close to me . . ., I was out of touch with what was really happening. My world was the journalism program. It was like a cloister, things changed when I left. What I saw then was not what I had learned to believe when I was in school. When I got ready to do my first report on all that collectivization had brought the peasants, I was ready to be welcomed by the happy peasants. Instead, my senior colleagues warned me to carry a gun to protect myself from their fury. I knew that my teachers had lied.

To supplement the numbers of journalists produced in this three-year program, there was a shorter program for those who were brought into the profession to fill the many vacancies on various local papers. That program was no less disillusioning. Since editors, however politically committed, did not want to lose their best young staff members, they sent the least skilled to Warsaw. There, the SDP took no interest in the program, established journalists shunned it, and the stipends and housing that had been promised never materialized. In the end, these journalists returned to their towns convinced that the system did not work and that political loyalty was meaningless.[29]

Not surprisingly, then, by late 1954, even without external political change, the young people who were taking over professional positions were far from the ideal loyalists that the system was bent on forming. They were loyal to each other, even to their fellow students who had left the profession and gone into government work ranging from the secret police to the various ministries and Party departments. But, in this, they were professionals, not system loyalists. With all of this, they would have felt the need, under any circumstances, to take full control of their professional lives in the face of political pressures and to force an improvement in their material and professional positions.

Association activities

The association concentrated on managing the journalism produced in the new Poland by raising "the ideological level of its members."[30] *Prasa Polska* no longer reported professional discussions but concentrated on criticizing the way journalism was being done.[31] In editorial offices, the association was an enforcer. It aided correspondents and wall newspapers; organized formal cooperation between journalists and other professions; organized cooperation with administrative workers and printers; worked to increase class consciousness; influenced the material and cultural standards of its members by giving out the "social funds" it controlled; and sent observers to local meetings to get an accurate sample of regional opinion.[32]

On an ideological level, the association itself stressed the Soviet model as the basic model for the Polish press.[33] Journalists were "not only to inform, but also to signal new methods and initiatives and to cooperate in organizing major social campaigns."[34] The aim of the press and the profession was to "educate and train" the population and to "increase the loyalty of the population to the socialist system."[35]

New journals were being opened in regions where there had been no daily press.[36] Journalists, newly trained in the socialist ideology and with little technical training, were expected to produce daily papers efficiently. Their living standards were very low, although they were told they were crucial to the new society. Fulfilling production norms was far from simple. It was hard even to get articles published because journals gave so much space to reports by worker–peasant correspondents. Editors were also unwilling to risk deviating from the standard line so they used agency material.[37] The situation was further worsened by the fact that staff was so rapidly organized and enlarged that there were too many journalists on any given paper.[38] And, finally, no coherent planning was carried out, so journalists had no guarantees that what they wrote would be used.[39] And, in addition to doing their "professional work," journalists were expected to spend extra hours developing a cadre of worker–peasant activists and leading local ideological programs.[40]

Journalists and local managers or directors had conflicting goals. The factory or institution director saw his press bureau[41] as an institution which was "not to inform and enlighten but to advertise for the director of a given institution and to censor the letters addressed to the press."[42] The journalist wanted information, often potentially damaging to the director, to build a story or to solve problems brought up by local correspondents.

Worker–peasant correspondents

The implementation of the Stalinist system of worker–peasant correspondents – who, as citizens, were expected to send their own report to papers'[43] – ultimately led to the increasing isolation and professionalization of journalists. It also had a significant impact on the attitudes of journalists who began their writing career as correspondents.

Throughout the period from 1948 to 1953, it was clear that journalists worked to maintain the distinction between journalists and worker–peasant correspondents. Only a few journals were willing to give worker–peasant correspondents any kind of identification card to give them access to information centers and tie them to the journal.[44] Journalists were also unwilling to have correspondents receive any honorariums for their work: being a correspondent was to be an act of social volunteerism, according to journalists, that was done not to earn additional money but to correct the wrongs in society.[45] What they did, on the other hand, as journalists was professional and should be well rewarded.

Journalists, thus, stressed that the work of correspondents was different in depth and dimension from their work. Correspondents were pictured by journalists as being "like fish in water while journalists are fish in ever changing water."[46] Journalists, in fact, sought to regularize the contributions of worker–peasant correspondents to insure that these contributions served as a conduit of information for them. So, individual journals established a staff of as many as ten workers to handle the letters, decide what should be done with each one, refer them to journalists, and rewrite them. This department was also responsible, in the later years of the Stalinist period, for instructing correspondents as to what to write.[47] Journalists, thus, transformed correspondents into their own controlled body of researchers. This freed them from the difficult trips to rural areas and limited the amount of space used for correspondents. Finally, journalists were able to use this system to select out potential recruits to full-time professional work, based on their proven ability and cooperation with professional journalists. Because correspondents were under so much pressure in their communities if they wrote anything negative, they were both toughened for journalism and made to see it as a safe, separate haven. The profession, thus, established some control over professional socialization at least of those who came in the backdoor by working as worker–peasant correspondents.

Outgrowths of Stalinism

By the end of the Stalinist period, the realities of producing a newspaper or a journal, surviving as writers, and dealing with the conflicts which existed on the local level between the population and any representative of political authority had made journalists cynical and professionalized the interests and perceptions of the more than 1,700 new recruits to journalism. The imperatives of publication further strengthened the position of those who were skilled in producing newspapers and not simply in political maneuvers.

Journalists, even at the height of Stalinism, did modify or circumvent, by individual action or inaction, directions given them for (1) using worker–peasant correspondents; (2) schooling journalists (chief editors refused to have good journalists leave for ideological education); and (3) the hiring and payment of journalists (worker–peasant correspondents work was dropped so that staff journalists' could be published). Journalists and their editors conformed to the topics and "ideological line" required of them by the Party, but, they often did not produce the kind or quality of journalism the Party leadership wanted. Because the political leadership needed the press, on the other hand, it could not prevent journalists from making what they claimed were "necessary modifications" in the Soviet press model. Nor could it insulate journalists from the high levels of citizen disaffection: journalists and their families had to live in the real world and first-hand reports from them on what was really going on were necessary for the Warsaw-based Party leadership.

In the areas of formal education and professional organization and activity, the political elite's goals were less challenged by the growing journalism establishment. Journalists could not control the structure or program of the Association and professional educational program nor did they have the time or money to deal with these issues. They simply used both education programs and "their" organization less and less.

The ferment begins: 1953–1955

Nine months after Stalin's death – even as political terror mounted in Poland[48] – the ironies and conflicts journalists faced had reached the point that the newly come of age journalists began to draw away from their political bosses. The process was not, at least at the start, a clear one. It happened subtly and on different levels. In the Association's journal, *Prasa Polska*, and in journalists' meetings, the "givens" of professional life under Stalinist control were attacked. *Prasa Polska* added two columns: one in which journalists criticized their professional life[49] and one for reprints of journalism-related articles in the press.[50] It also attacked the heavy doses of ideological training student journalists received saying it made them unfit to practice journalism effectively.[51] And, long before the eruption at the Warsaw Party *aktiv* meeting in December 1954,[52] these shifts of emphasis in the association's publication had taken on far sharper dimensions at explosive local and national journalists' meetings.

For journalists, in fact, de-Stalinization began at the Warsaw journalists' meeting, November 1953. This was not only the first meeting of a local chapter of the association but also the first time that, instead of a Party official, a journalist – and not a party member at that – gave a keynote address. As would be the case for Henryk Korotyński's next keynote speech at the National Convention in 1954, this respected editor gave a speech steeped in all the requisite "triumphs of the Soviet system" even though what he said was "revolutionary" in content.[53] What Korotyński voiced were the chief complaints of professionals against their unrepresentative association and the unwelcome controls they had to deal with in doing their work. "We say to ourselves openly that there is a lack both in our editorial offices and in the meetings of the Journalists Association of an atmosphere with an adequate degree of favorable support, frank criticism, and self-criticism."[54] He further pointed out that criticism on a "broader forum than private, one-to-one discussions" had not been possible;[55] journalists were not trusted by readers;[56] journalists were not given the skills or the opportunity to provide enough information to satisfy readers' demands;[57] journalists colored reality rather than reporting on problems or failures;[58] and old forms were much better than current writing styles mandated by the Party.[59] In all of this, Korotyński's underlying call was for professional skills rather than political reliability to rule and determine entrance into the profession. There was a need, he said, "for excellent writing skills to exist among department editors and managing editors [political appointees] as well as those in other positions in the journal."[60]

He also articulated the need for change in the position and work of the Association: "The majority of our colleagues do not value the role of the Association in enlivening the ideological life of the profession of journalism, establishing a climate for developing, discussing and deepening views. This should alarm us about the illness and weakness of our work."[61]

Korotyński's keynote address and the discussion which followed put both the Party and association officials on the defensive. Clearly, neither were prepared for such criticism. Jerzy Kowalewski, Deputy Director of Propaganda and Agitation, made a point by point defense of the editors' and political authorities' right "to see to it that the discussion does not become a false one or go beyond respectable borders."[62] Even as Korotyński had attacked the system for failing to allow real reporting, Kowalewski stressed that journalists should not go into the field without a clear perception of "what they were inspired to find".[63] Nor was he, as spokesman for the Party, able to anticipate the complaints journalists had on their social and material conditions.

The officials of the SDP were no less on the defensive. Some of the Warsaw groups' moves were, after all, less than veiled attacks on the organization and its leadership. Not only did journalists press for improvements in their social and material situation, but they also took matters into their own hands. Committees of journalists were set up to plan activities for Warsaw journalists.[64] Journalists pushed for SDP delegates on each staff to have greater authority in administering SDP activities and in aiding journalists in their work.[65] For the Party and SDP leaders, these moves were a frightening demonstration that journalists would not tolerate the SDP being merely a "transmission belt" and a clear sign that journalists were not totally mobilized behind the Party's political program.

In the first half of 1954, SDP leaders went on the defensive. They belittled the results of the Warsaw meeting, saying the meeting included only representatives of twenty-six of the eighty-two journals in Warsaw,[66] most of whom were "only weakly interested in the activities of the Association"[67] and totally disinterested in its education programs.[68] They further criticized the political reporting of the two journals whose staff members were active participants in the discussion. These included Korotyński's own *Życie Warszawy*.[69] Finally, they pressed for journalists to become more "literary" and suggested that the upcoming journalists' congress focus on the safe issue of bringing journalists and writers closer together.[70]

This ruse did not work. The National Congress of 1954 became a forum for attacking nearly every aspect of professional life and the professional organization. Issues that had been controlled by the political elite were reclaimed as professional issues – schooling, salaries, and the evaluation of professional work. Coupled with this, for the first time, the nominees for the board were questioned and alternative regional candidates proposed. In the end, only two leaders of the previous SDP Executive Committee were renominated and they were reelected with the lowest number of votes of anyone on the list.[71]

The two-day discussion focused on the lack of truthful and effective criticism in the press and on demands for the SDP to become an independent and active agent controlling professional work and recruitment. The material and work conditions of journalists were attacked. In the course of the discussion, also, various speakers indirectly attacked the Soviet Union and its image in the Polish press.[72] Delegates from outside Warsaw complained vociferously throughout the meeting of being excluded from events, ignored by the governing board, disadvantaged in earnings, and given little opportunity and no resources to do creative journalism.[73]

Henryk Korotyński served as keynote speaker as he had six months earlier at the Warsaw meeting. This time he was far bolder.[74] He took up professional issues of how reporting had been done and the links between the press and its readers without the usual requisite reference to the Party and the Soviet model and with clear references to unprofessional work being done by political hacks.[75] In addition, he recognized the split between professional journalists and editors from the party apparatus by saying that journalists should have more independence and individual authority.[76]

The Party position in all of this was a new one. It legitimized the very demands and criticisms that had shocked the same Party representatives at the Warsaw meeting. That there was too little information in the press and only fragmentary analyses based on vague information[77] as well as a real need for readership studies were taken on as calls of Party representatives.[78] Party speakers admitted there were administrative problems that the press could and should criticize.[79] Party leaders reverted to trying to cajole journalists out of their disaffection and apathy: "If journalists work better, the Party will help them with housing and other material benefits."[80] This softened response was, according to Party leaders, a response to the appearance of an unbreakable wall of criticism reinforced by moves to liberalize in the Soviet Union.

Delegates went far beyond previous boundaries in making statements such as: "Class enemies are now in bureaucratic posts,"[81] and "Russian journalists write criticism on studies done over the years without ever going outside the four walls of their offices and know much less about it than those who write the books which they criticize."[82] Some also advocated a return to prewar models of contacts between readers and journalists[83] and in writing styles.[84] Others even suggested enlivening the press by using Western models.[85] Finally, at least one journalist made it clear that "Marxist–Leninist training does not help to explain reality."[86] Journalists criticized the limitations on information, particularly about foreign affairs, available to them.[87] They made it clear that they knew the press was denied access to information available in classified bulletins and was controlled as to what it could discuss.[88] They criticized what they wrote as being unrelated to readers' concerns, made of "half-truths which do not actually explain anything,"[89] and being "silent about many topics . . . because, if a journalist comes up with critical material, he is considered a malcontent"[90] or accused of writing things which would aid the enemies of socialism.[91] They did this without dealing with the question of who put up the information blocks or allowed only weak criticism.[92]

Most journalists were concerned first about the specific problems they had with their chief editors and within their staffs. These included working conditions and relationships within specific newsrooms. Journalists went on to stress that chief editors neither respected them[93] nor supported the SDP and its activities. Some journalists criticized the lack of "a collective spirit in the editorial office" when, in fact, the staff as a whole "should discuss things."[94] Finally, journalists directly and indirectly advocated the recognition and encouragment of "famous name" journalists.[95]

Their solutions to these problems centered on strengthening the professional association. They charged the SDP with researching and organizing studies of how journalists could work more effectively. They charged the SDP rather than the government with granting awards to leading individuals and providing journalists with resources for their writing. Finally, journalists criticized the leadership for not advocating their financial and material interests more actively. Some even pressed the SDP to explore the possibility of transforming itself into a union for journalists[96] although this was rejected out of hand as being impossible by the governing board.

The Congress' response to the issues was limited. The transformation of the SDP from a political to a professional organization began with no opposition when membership requirements were lengthened to two years and changed so no one could remain in the organization if he or she did not "do journalism" for more than six months.[97]

Those left to run the association as members of its governing board were, at best, a new breed. The board was expanded to thirty-six members in the face of protests by those outside Warsaw that they were ignored by the profession. Regional journalists and "new names" got far more support than the former executives of the SDP.[98] Of the non-journalists nominated, two were chief editors who were not members of the Central Committee, two were both editors and Party leaders, and only one was a purely Party official. He listed himself, this time, not as Deputy Director of the Central Committee Department of Agitation and Propaganda but as a "publicist".[99] The rest were representatives of establishment journals: *Trybuna Ludu* and *Życie Warszawy* each had four members on the board. Radio and popular journals, fledgling media, had some minimal representation. But, youth and literary journals involved so few professionals that, even though they were just beginning to lead in the public liberalization, they were not represented.[100] The concessions to both the new demands and the old strictures left this governing board, most of whom would not be elected in 1956, with little "real influence on the profession" and also without the "moral honor" their positions supposedly gave them.[101] What happened in what has come to be known as the "Polish October," then, happened earlier in the editorial offices and swirl of events outside the offices of the SDP.

Radicalization process: from professional to public concerns, 1955–1956

The activism and critical posture of the journalism profession on issues of public and professional policy began to explode soon after the National Congress had ended. Changes occurred in the political environment, professionals' opportunities and mobility, and the internal dynamics of the profession. As journalists were able to act openly as professionals in politics rather than just microphones for the establishment, the pressures for change in the profession multiplied.

As Poland's leaders and its population began to make previously unthinkable demands, journalists were immediately involved. As Party members or "agents of the Party," almost all of them increasingly had access to Party documents. As links to the population, journalists were subjected to more and more open criticism of their work by readers. As members of the new Communist intelligentsia, journalists were either involved or close to activists in intellectual circles. They felt trapped. Poland's economic situation was becoming more and more chaotic and people asked questions journalists were at a loss to answer. From Party sources and their own contacts with Hungarian journalists, many knew the Soviet leadership was increasingly involved in the internal affairs of the Hungarian Party and was pushing parts of the Hungarian leadership to develop some popular support. But, even as this went on in Hungary, the Polish leadership refused to move toward liberalization until the death of Bierut and the "Secret Speech" of Khrushchev in February of 1956. Many in the Party advocated backing away from Stalinist political control while maintaining close ties with the Soviet Union. In line with this, Władysław Gomułka was released but not reinstated. Polish society pushed for even more rapid liberalization. The revelations of secret police defector Josef Światło on the secret police and the life of the Party, broadcast by Radio Free Europe, swept through the society. These revelations put the profession in a particularly bad light. Discussion groups challenged journalists to match their writings to the critical discussions that were going on everywhere. Beginning in mid-1954 and escalating rapidly after the death of Bierut and the "power struggle" within the Party, external controls over the media became increasingly unstable.

Material situation

The rules of the game for the media system itself were transformed. On the one hand, the media system went through a period of rapid expansion from 1954 to 1957. Sporadic publications became weeklies. Beginning with student and intellectual periodicals like *Po Prostu, Student, Nowa Kultura, Przegląd Kulturalny,* and *Życie Gospodarcze* and ending with the dailies, the press went from being dry, dull, and conservative to being major voices in liberalization filled with popular, critical and sensational articles.[102] Staffs changed. Political appointees were pushed out. In their place, journalists with writing skills and flair were hired.

New journals were planned. Regional Party leaders encouraged proposals for new journals modeled after Western journals. Some popular regional journals were moved to Warsaw. National Party leaders sought to establish journals to satisfy popular demands and indirectly represent their individual views. Most of these journals were not organized until Gomułka took over. Then, they were opened rapidly. These new options encouraged journalists "to make a name for themselves" so they could move to these more desirable journals. This also emboldened journalists by giving them a sense that, should they lose their jobs for being too critical, there would always be new and better journals to work on.

Even as journalists revelled in the growth of the media, they were faced with the reality of the adjustments that were required when the government subsidies to the press ended.[103] The euphoria of the new system was short lived. Cuts affected middle and low level journalists as well as political appointees with no professional competence since, on some journals, nearly half of the staff had to be fired. This left a pool of excess professionals ready to fight over any available positions.[104]

Other moves were made as well to make journals' production costs equal their earnings. First of all, the policy of institutional subscriptions was ended. Without having at least half of their circulation guaranteed, journals suddenly had to rely on readability to sell. Next, prices were increased for most journals to match production costs. This made the press more expensive and cut down on casual readership.[105] Because these decisions were made by the central publishing house, controlled as it was by the Party, the price increases and the pressure to get readers were much steeper for the Catholic and highly critical press than for the less controversial publications. The prices of Party dailies and other Party organs simply did not increase.[106] Yet, readers continued to buy critical journals and ignore other, cheaper ones. Journalists did perceive of these changes as attacks on their profession but, as individuals, they counted on their popularity to protect them.

The third phase of the economic rationalization process was discussed in Party circles between 1954 and 1956; but it was not acted on until 1958. This phase involved limitations on circulation and the consolidation of journals. Initially, journalists saw this as a move that would hurt the propaganda media that were not read and were continually in deficit. This they did not find objectionable. But, when the policy was carried out, critical journals such as *Po Prostu* were closed down and other journals, such as *Nowa Kultura* and *Przegląd Kulturalny*, were consolidated into new journals, like *Kultura*. Other journals also faced massive cutbacks in paper allocation, restricting the kind of reporting that they could do and the size of the audience they could reach.[107]

Finally, a new pay scale for journalists was established in 1956. As had been the case in the past, journalists were not involved in the decisions. Nor were they particularly interested. The pay scale was based, in large measure, on a piece work rate that ultimately would not be favorable to journalists, given the cutbacks in the size of the media. But, given their involvement in more substantive changes in professional life and the immediate increases in their opportunities to publish and make a name for themselves, journalists did not treat this as a major problem. It was merely an incentive for them to write the more critical articles editors sought. The middle and lower level journalists who did feel the impact of the regulation immediately were not influential enough in the profession to make a difference. So, they were ignored as being poor professionals who were underpaid because they could not write.

Professional life

As the material situation for the press changed dramatically between 1954 and 1956, so too did journalists' entire world. There were no authorities and no rules. Whatever faith journalists had in the Party was destroyed by its internal divisions; the rehabilitation and reappearance of people who had been vilified and jailed in the Stalinist purges;[108] and, in February 1956, the revelations on the Stalinist era of Khrushchev's "Secret Speech" read at Party meetings and circulated among journalists in Poland.[109] Furthermore, editors were no longer filters that kept journalists from knowing the "dirt of local politics." Journalists now heard about the machinations of local Party organizations through their own contacts. Individual Party officials either acted directly against the press or came to journalists as partners. Newsrooms and offices were filled with constant discussions of the new revelations and the changes in the Party. These were led often by young, unestablished journalists. In all of this, journalists who had been purged returned to haunt their former colleagues. Each day's events were simply so consuming that few thought of the future.

Criticism of the situation in Poland had begun in the literary journals[110] so journalists were not in the forefront. Nor were many entirely in agreement with these views.[111] At the same time, the swirl of events stimulated journalists to talk critically among themselves and to seek more and more information. By mid-1955, journalists were convinced that they had to get some authority as professionals. In Warsaw, this sense of their unique role and mission was supported by the reliance of the new Party leadership on them as consultants to draw up policy and present it. This meant that journalists came to see themselves as power brokers.

When they began to make their criticism public, however, the public had already turned to attack the press. So, journalists' own criticism first focused on themselves and their profession. However, their sense of the tenuousness of Poland's political situation as well as their new sense of importance as power brokers weighed against public demands for complete freedom to write and to break with the Party.[112] What this meant was that their focus was on

> the aspiration for making attractive articles by increasing the range of information, particularly in the daily press, and invigorating discussion through battling with whitewash and schematism [but also] a push to present a succession of injustices in important areas of the society which had been passed over up to now.[113]

The socio-cultural weeklies were to be "the rostrum for distinguished publicists to discuss burning social issues."[114] At the same time leaders in the profession advised that:

> The painful and costly experiences of the last few years taught journalists once and for all that the pen should never be dipped in rose oil because that makes a sugar-covered lithograph. That same experience warns that pens should not reach into barrels of pitch for those results are not any better than others. The road from whitewashed schematizations ought not to be frequent lines of gloomy schematizations.[115]

Journalists kept the Stalinist notion of the press as a mobilizer. As professionals, they saw it as their responsibility to

> develop the political world view of a citizen through giving him the facts and presenting the society with all the motives of a decision, revealing all the causes that brought the Party and government to take a step, enlightening citizens on all of the difficulties, and referring to the patriotism of the society in commanding, for the moment, their interest in the review and in the development of the nation.[116]

This professional role restrained them from acting as standard bearers for a reader controlled media.

Journalists' relations with the Party and Party factions varied in this period. Those in Warsaw, both young and old, were often called to participate in Party discussions. In the transferral of power to Gomułka, a small group of journalists on *Trybuna Ludu* were informed of the decision by those Party leaders involved and asked to prepare the edition announcing his election secretly so it could be sold just as the decision was formalized. In this way, they were told they would be blocking a conservative coup. This, along with the roles some journalists played as emissaries to Gomułka, convinced them they were keys to Gomułka's power and that of his allies. Later, upon hearing of the Soviet invasion of Hungary, a small group went to the Politburo and requested that Poland not support the Soviet Union in the United Nations on this issue. They were told that, should the demonstration they were planning against the invasion be carried out the next day,

Poland also would be in danger of Soviet attack. The delegation returned to the university to dismantle the demonstration.

The situation outside of Warsaw was much different. Journalists had been attacked and tried for their reporting of the Poznań worker revolts. In June 1956, some seventeen journalists were fired for their articles and involvement in the post-riot events and discussions. In all but one regional journal, the editor would not allow journalists to "publish from the heart." Instead, they were forced to publish statements that were not true.[117] When some local journalists protested "over the radio wires," one local *województwo* committee of the PUWP punished them.[118] The censors' office only further inflamed them: one censor said that he agreed with them but could not countermand his orders by allowing them to publish articles their editor and the Party Committee had not approved.[119] In the early fall, even as the national leadership changed, journalists were limited still in their coverage of the trials of demonstrators in Poznań's summer disturbances.

All of this made journalists feel the need for leadership within the profession. The traditional leadership was discredited. Many had withdrawn voluntarily because of "the changing political situation." Other prominent journalists left the country. The only group left who had not publicly sinned during the Stalinist years were journalist educators. They became the new leaders of the profession in 1956. But, although they were able to lead the profession publicly and had the time for the weekly and sometimes daily meetings of the association leadership, they were not models for professionals. They could not set an example for writing or editing nor did they have the connections within the profession to direct it. Nor were these educators able to solve the daily problem of the lack of editorial leadership without which journalists had no way to plan their work: as editors changed so did the possibilities of publication. And, with the increasing economic pressures, the professional staff wanted to keep their journals from economic disaster.

As political men who had lived through the terror of Stalinism and who were aware of the invasions of Hungary and the attempted Soviet intervention against Gomułka in Poland, professionals coming out of the Stalinist era were concerned about the long-range consequences of these political gains and losses as well as their appropriate roles. They were equally concerned about the potential of readers who had begun to take journalists to court for libel when they were displeased with their writing. They became concerned about protecting themselves from intervention then not only from the top and the Soviet Union but also from the bottom.[120] This made direct contacts with readers uncomfortable. The old shelter of the censor's office folded. Even before the censor's office disbanded itself in 1956, censors were unwilling to act because they knew the Party line would change in hours and they risked being attacked for their decisions.

Editors were fired or shifted to other journals. When they stayed on a journal, they had no power over staff members' actions. In addition, most journal staffs were so riddled with political differences and filled with new, unknown people, that journalists were not entirely comfortable in their own offices. Nor were experienced journalists impressed with the new entrants into the field. Stories were published of young journalists stealing and misusing professional privileges.[121] While most "older" professionals respected the work of journalists on *Po Prostu* and the like, at the same time, they felt these staffs were either being used by some group or should control themselves.

Journalistic education and the SDP itself collapsed. By 1956, the education program existed in name only. It had been discredited and its remaining faculty moved into the SDP even though many people were also involved in setting up conferences and new proposals to save the journalism school. Classes were not held; students were all involved in writing or political activities. Although student journals like *Po Prostu* were leaders in the moves for more criticism in the press, professional education became pointless. At the 1956 convention, the convergence of dissatisfaction with the program itself and the shrinking of the profession made it clear: "We should eliminate fictions after October like a department that produces graduates for nonexistent jobs. What we need is a program open to humanities graduates limited to 10 people so we maintain some influx of fresh journalism blood."[122]

The formal Governing Board sessions of the SDP had no authority. The best they could do was propose organizing studies of the effect of press criticism and the changes needed "to better the situation."[123] Out of this came the establishment of a press research center in Cracow (The Center for Press Research) in 1954. It was staffed by newly trained scholars and funded by the main publishing house and the SDP [124] For this center and the Research Center on Polish Press History in the Polish Academy of Sciences, formed at the same time, funding was no problem. As one scholar pointed out: "That's simply where the money was. Anything even slightly related to the press we proposed to research got swamped with funds. We were simply able to tell them what to do." Out of these institutes, then, came the research agenda, methodology, community of scholars and publications that were essential to making professional education an academic discipline.[125]

In spite of having this new legitimacy for the research they had long sought to do and the real movement toward journalistic freedom and openness that had been unthinkable before, the formal SDP leadership attacked itself: "We think that the problems are products of the failure of the Governing Board to make ties with the terrain; the ineffective work, to this time, of the Governing Board; and its failure to excite journalists outside of Warsaw to consider various issues."[126] Ultimately, then, the elected leadership simply stopped functioning.

New *ad hoc* structures of internal control were set up before the National Convention of 1956. Work was begun on a code of professional ethics.[127] A Press Review Board of journalists and some political figures invited by journalists was set up to monitor the media and, after articles had been published, to advise editors and journalists if they had exceeded the bounds of what the profession considered acceptable. This board called in the editors of journals like *Po Prostu* to convince them to use editorial restraint. Specific articles were discussed. When their advice was not followed, individuals went personally to talk to the offending journalists and tried to persuade them of the necessity to use restraint, given how tense the situation was in Poland and with the Soviet Union. Although they felt they had no impact on *Po Prostu*, with other journals they were able to exert some influence.

A largely self-selected leadership did meet almost daily after the Poznań riots to discuss the situation, advise the political leadership of the profession's feelings, and make plans for the forthcoming national meeting. This they did largely in isolation. Between the Plenary session of the governing board in January 1956, and the National Convention of November, events and leadership changed so rapidly that there was no time for formal or informal contacts with the bulk of working journalists. The leadership met daily and was too involved to go outside Warsaw.[128] Regional groups acted on their own.[129] Groups specializing in various areas called meetings and held discussions without any direction from the leadership.[130]

By October 1956, the situation was entirely different. When one regional SDP branch protested to the *województwo* committee that their chairman was "too conservative," they were notified five days later that he had resigned.[131] In less drastic ways, similar changes were made elsewhere. Not only did the journalists who were involved get a sense of power; but, *Prasa Polska* in November 1956 (controlled then by the new, self-appointed Board of the SDP), published an extensive discussion of journalists' actions against the editors who had restrained them in the past all over Poland.[132]

Journalists also felt they had power in the Party and with the population. In some communities, journalists headed Party committees, were dominant on the regional government council (WRN), and were the leaders of newly organized intelligentsia associations. The isolation of journalists from writers disappeared. In some cases, a leader of the "new SDP" also became a leader in the more prestigious Writers' Union. Journalists even began to talk of electing "their own" members to the parliament because they were both authoritative and popular.[133]

Within the profession, divisions between conservatives and liberals emerged in open warfare. In one case, radio journalists who had attacked writers in a liberal Party paper were censured and sent to the new Journalists' Court.[134] All over, the changes in the regional SDP executive boards were almost total. In seven regional SDP units, no members from the 1954 (and, in Bydgoszcz and Poznań, the 1955) boards were returned. In all, only two were returned. Their voices were muted because of the expansion of the boards by one or two members.[135] Local meetings were forums for discussion of the issues the sixty-seven regional delegates were to bring to the SDP National Congress.[136] Journalists advocated the dissolution of the national publishing house and the establishment of smaller, independent publishers.[137] Some pressed for the SDP to prepare a draft press law controlling censorship in Poland. Others felt that any such law would lead to too much external control over the profession.[138] Members suggested that the SDP become both a professional club and a union organization. Their criticism of the SDP for not concerning itself enough with the regional units[139] was muted by the presence of national leaders at these final local meetings.[140] Finally, regional journalists focused on developing the specialty clubs as significant forces in changing Party–press relations and raising the level of information among professionals.[141]

These regional demands, published in *Prasa Polska* the month before the Convention, and the discussions at the more divided Warsaw meeting served as the basis for the National Convention. But, because of journalists' involvement in the political events of the time, these specifically professional issues were not discussed in full until the second session of the National Convention was held in March 1957. At the first session, held in November 1956, journalists attempted to sort out the issue of Party–press relations and to evaluate Władysław Gomułka. Many felt that he was the hope of the profession and that middle level Party officials were trying to turn him against the profession.[142] His relationship with the press was considered crucial as journalists recognized that the selection of editors would still be "ultimately up to the Party."[143]

Events in Hungary set the tone for the Convention. Journalists collected money for Hungarian refugees. They were preparing to provide refuge in Poland for exiled Hungarian journalists and their families.[144] However, they were cognizant also of Poland's tenuous position. Not only did journalists speak about how there could be no "criticism of brother socialist parties"[145] and how Poland's economic situation was so bad that the populations' expectations had to be controlled;[146] but, they also sent a delegation to Gomułka with their plan for serving as a refuge for Hungarian journalists. When he advised against it by warning that such an act would surely bring on a Soviet invasion not only of Hungary but of Poland as well, they accepted his position without question.[147]

Journalists were primarily concerned with developing regulations to keep unskilled and unethical individuals out of journalism.[148] Other professional issues were not discussed as fully as they would be in the follow-up session in 1957 simply because the future of censorship and publishing houses was not clear.[149] They recognized that their ultimate goal of making the SDP a strong union organization required more information than they had at hand. So, the meeting was adjourned until March 1957.[150]

Denouement: 1957–1960

The continuation of the 1956 Convention was the beginning of the end. In the three months between the two sessions, the euphoria had disappeared and reality had intervened. Even before the closing of critical journals like *Po Prostu*, journalists were aware of limits on their possibilities. And, by 1957, the profession was so fragmented by its political involvement and so weak that it could not regain its momentum.

Reality hit hard and fast. Those who went to the initial meeting of SDP leaders with Gomułka after the 1956 convention said, after the five hour talk, they were "unclear as to the results." Gomułka, they reported, had focused on making sure they understood the necessity of controlling themselves so that he could continue his fight against "conservatives and revisionists" in the Party.[151] National union officials told journalists that demanding a separate union for themselves was impossible and "elitist."[152] The Ministry of Transportation simply refused to meet with journalists to discuss their demands for reduced fares.[153] In addition, journalists, once they realized the difficulties they faced, split over what was the best course for them to follow.

On the issue of membership, there was an underlying agreement among the convention delegates on the need to have an exclusive organization. But, conditions had changed so drastically that the precise boundaries of professional work were unclear.[154] Journalists could not be verified as members of the SDP until a statute was passed to establish a verification committee and that statute could not be written until it was clear what the SDP was to be.[155] If there was to be a creative organization and a separate union for journalists, then membership requirements could be far stricter. If there was to be a union, then membership would have to include all those working in journalism.[156] Furthermore, in 1955 and 1956, many journalists become "freelancers." To include them would allow for the inclusion of the political propagandists the SDP did not want. To exclude them would block membership of a large number of professional "stars."[157] So, decisions on what had been the critical issue for the profession were put off until 1958. In addition, the press law that was to have been drawn up by this second session was said to require at least one more year's research before any concrete proposal could be made.[158]

For all of the profession's enthusiasm for change and for its role in the politics of the "new Poland," activism in the SDP had declined already in 1956. The head of the newly formed "Self-help Fund" reported in 1957 that journalists were unwilling to contribute one zloty a month for the fund to be established.[159] The apparent unity within the profession at the 1956 convention also visibly dissolved with the collapse of journalists' earning power. Significant numbers of journalists were unemployed, fired in the staff cutbacks the association had orginally accepted.[160] This meant that professionals were in competition with each other for what few positions remained. Attempts at negotiating with editors whose firing of journalists in 1956 had been brought up at the first session were reported to have been unsuccessful. The SDP leaders had to admit that the current regulations did not give them a real voice in the hirings and firings of journalists and all they could do was try to help those who had been fired find jobs.[161] The association also attempted to set up an SDP press agency to employ the unemployed professionals, but, for this, there were simply too few funds and too many applicants.[162] In addition, there were about 150 graduates of the journalism program who were looking for work.

Whether or not journalists were aware, as they met and heard these negative reports in the first days of March 1957, that Gomułka was preparing to attack his "revisionist" allies in the press and the Party is not clear. At the very least, journalists were increasingly aware that the leadership changeover was not going to mean a change in the middle level bureaucrats with whom they had to deal. The March Party Plenum was the beginning of an attack by Gomułka on "revisionists" within the Party and the press. The press was the first stronghold to fall. In the months that followed the Party plenum, new editors were put in charge of virtually all of the Party dailies and a warning was put out that freedom of the press did not mean working against the Party leaders.

The leaders of the SDP increasingly lost their commitment to transforming the association. They could find no allies to help them make the gains that had been mandated. As they saw membership commitment to the association and its activities drop, they felt stranded. They had come into leadership positions on their own volition when the SDP was a political platform. They were, on the whole, less committed to financial gains than to political change.[164]

Therefore, when *Po Prostu* was closed in October 1957, along with the School of Journalism, the leadership made a statement of protest to Party leaders that went unanswered. Journalists from *Po Prostu* were helped on an individual basis in getting jobs elsewhere or in finding other means of support. In fact, the closing of *Po Prostu* was not a major issue for journalists. At this point, they were concerned mainly with their own finances. They did not feel strong enough as a group to protest because their own journals were hardly secure. Furthermore, *Po Prostu* had been a renegade journal of student or unknown journalists with few links to established professionals. It had refused to accept the suggestions of the journalists' own Review Board. Journalists knew staff members often warred with each other and turned to various Party allies for support. Finally, even the *Po Prostu* staff had expected to be closed down much earlier.

Until 1958, that Press Review Board continued to exist. However, journalists realized, as Party authorities ceased to attend, that it was a doomed institution. Journalists themselves dropped out and the institution became moribund. As individuals, they were increasingly involved in censoring themselves to protect their jobs. For them, the whole issue of censorship remained a murky one: they had tried to censor themselves and were not fully successful and there had never been a sense in the profession that censorship could or should be abolished.

What the closing of *Po Prostu* and other liberal journals (like *Przegląd*

Kulturalny and *Nowa Kultura*)[165], the collapse of the Press Review Board, and the reports at the SDP meeting in 1957, did indicate to journalists was that the world in which they worked had stabilized. With it came a reestablishment of authority structures both within and outside the profession and a clear depoliticization of the profession. Journalists turned to protecting their professional lives.

The character of the profession itself did not change significantly. In spite of claims at the 1958 and 1960 Conventions that the profession had been purged of its "revisionist" elements, journalists who had been active in the 1956 period and remained in Poland stayed in the profession and often were active professional leaders.[166] Only 153 members of the SDP out of 3000 were removed in the "verification" of credentials carried out in 1957–58 to root out revisionist elements. Some hard-line Stalinist journalists left the profession permanently in 1955–56; but many returned to positions in the profession or in press control organizations. Interwar journalists who were permitted to return to the profession after 1956 did not do so in significant numbers: they had either found other work or were too old to return to full-time journalism. Finally, there were few new entrants into the profession after 1956 because there were few openings for them.

The professional's concerns changed. The consolidation of the press, the pressure on journals to be self-supporting, and the competition for positions on journals heightened journalists' concern with regulation. The cuts in individual incomes also had an impact on the process of professionalization. Individuals were forced to concentrate on increasing their individual productivity and decreasing their political commitments. Financial pressures also made administrative blocks and citizen interference (through time-consuming court cases) major professional issues. It was these issues and not the decreased power of the profession that were the topics at the 1958 Convention and that remained the prime foci of conventions until 1980. Political statements were, on the whole, limited in 1958. This continued until the profession got embroiled in the disputes of 1968.

The Polish October and the subsequent stabilization of the rule of Gomułka was and has remained a watershed in the life of the journalism profession. For professionals, this transition from the Stalinist period to a new, less controlled journalism was a time to experiment with political power and lose. For the student of professional behavior, it is a demonstration of the impact of the collapse of political control on professional behavior. The time seemed unique. It was a flashpoint of professional life for the next twenty-five years until the Solidarity strikes liberated journalists to raise the same issues, develop new journals, and rise to lead the population. All of this was done with a concern not to follow the same path that had been followed in 1956 and which had led to weakness and defeat then. For, although many students and young workers joined the reform movement like their predecessors in 1956, the leaders in the transformation of the press were veterans of Stalinism, the Polish October, and the uneasy truce years of the sixties and seventies.

The profession in 1956 was never truly revolutionary. It did not reject censorship or Party control completely. Therefore, as the Gomułka elite institutionalized itself, the profession was easily drawn in. It was weakened by the simultaneous collapse of the highly politicized Stalinist structures and the external controls on the profession. The pressure and rapidity of political events, the profession's own involvement in filling the void in political leadership as well as the euphoria of professional power did not leave journalists time to set up viable institutions and substitutes for those that had collapsed. Nor did the profession, in the heat of the Polish October, see the tenuousness of its position and the inherent strength of the political structures that remained. Finally, changes in the economy of the press and the profession, originally perceived as logical, left individuals in a position where economics rather than politics had to be dominant. Thus, 1956 strengthened the sense journalists had of their importance to society as professionals and weakened their interest in taking the risks of being political actors.

For the professional journalists of contemporary Poland, the Polish October was also a period of establishing themselves as names in society. It was a learning period too: journalists saw what was possible and what was senseless, euphoric politicization. A myth of the profession's importance grew up and would last for the next twenty-five years. Journalists would remember what the profession was able to do and what were the limits on the profession. In the years that followed, they stressed that they had learned that the profession was only as strong as it made itself and as the political leadership was weak. Finally, the 1956 period was the formative period for the history of journalism simply because it was an experience shared by most of the profession and it was the period when the journals and the journal staffs of contemporary Poland were established and stabilized.

The Gomułka years

Although "normalization" followed rapidly on the heels of the liberalization of the Polish October that brought Gomułka into power, the press policy Gomułka instituted was far from the policies of the Stalinist era. His own experience of being attacked in the press and jailed as a nationalist made him reluctant to allow the Party to control culture.[167] It also meant that few journalists in the existing press establishment had any personal relationship with him.[168] Instead, he kept them at a distance and neither drew them into the inner circles of policy-making nor pressured them to join and support the Party.[169] His position was, one journalist explained, that "He disliked sycophants and liked critics, those willing to take the risks of disagreeing with him. But, he always said that he could tolerate journalist critics only a distance – the press was just far enough."

This posture meant that Gomułka was willing to tolerate the independence of, and criticism from, the media by basically ignoring it. His toleration of criticism from the media and disinterest in it was reinforced by the fact that he really did not control his own elite. As a result, he had to accept criticism and negative reports championed by those in his own leadership who did not support him.[170] The variation he allowed in the media was further facilitated by the fact that he had little interest in doing more than ruling the nation as it was. He did not want or try to modernize and transform the economy or the society so he did not need the press as a mobilizer or inspirer.[171]

From Gomułka's perspective, journalists were to provide information, a positive view of their nation, and "criticism of some real, essential and visible errors in our everyday life."[172] In doing this, he said:

> the factual and deepest argument of propaganda for our Party, is to present positively the problems of the development of our country, to respond to the issues concerning public opinion, and to enlighten the public broadly as to the difference between socialism and capitalism as well as the battle of peaceful forces against imperialism and unsafe aggression and war.[173]

Simple and traditional as this definition of the press' role was, Gomułka and his allies did not see the press as performing it well. Their experiences with the media of the Polish October and what seemed, from their perspective, to be the failure of the Press Review Board proved that journalists could not be trusted, and that, as Gomułka told a group of journalists in 1956: "You want to have it all too easily. You want clean hands and for me to do all the dirty work. That's why journalists cannot govern themselves, much less the nation. You behave like romantics not realists." Not only this but journalists, to his mind, failed to develop the dialogue with workers and peasants required to block their dependence on Western news sources.[174] Furthermore, when journalists were "to serve society and respect Party politics,"[175] what they did was to become too little involved with the life of the country and too enamored with Western consumerism. As a result, the press "too rarely ran stories about honest working people, their differences and troubles, and the toil that they put into everyday life."[176] And, although Gomułka and his cronies never treated journalists as important elements in society, they made it clear that they caused low-level Party and government leaders inordinate and unjustified problems.[177]

All of this meant that, for journalists, leadership consisted only in being attacked for what they did if and when it came to the attention of the Party elite. This gave those who were attacked an unintended "star" status and made opposition of value to the profession.[178] This "hands off position," in fact was initially a matter of pride for the Party leadership: "We all know that the Party, which directs the country, abstains from petty involvement and blocking of initiatives by journals, that it does not lead the press by the hand, and that an editorial staff has broad possibilities in selecting problems and carrying out the craft of journalism in all its forms."

When Gomułka and his regime were attacked directly and indirectly through the press in 1968, his loyalists responded with a stance that gave increased ideological and political significance to the profession of journalism and its work. They made it clear that the media, underfunded as it was, was to be under the direction of the Party organizations.[179] Critical discussion was to be generated within the Party and only then expressed to the outside.[180] The role and limits of this criticism were similarly redefined, making the press not simply a necessary evil and an entertainer, but a propagandist as well: "Above all, we care for the content, for the character of the arguments and only then for better forms, and our main concern should be for the cadre of propagandists."[181]

The Gierek years

All of this was too little too late for the profession and for the Gomułka regime. The contrast between the benign neglect that had been the *modus vivendi* in the sixties, the involvement Gomułka's enemies had on an individual level with journalists, and Gierek's promises for the whole profession, set the stage for journalists to welcome Gierek in 1970. He had, after all, assiduously courted the press since the mid-sixties while Gomułka ignored it.[182] He offered to treat the media positively both materially and ideologically.[183] He also offered a situation where journalists would be included in the policy process when he sought the social and economic change most journalists had come to favor as they became more and more frustrated with the system's stagnation.[184] The trade-offs for this involvement were less than clear. Few journalists knew anything about the reality of Silesia and the Silesian press.[185]

The Gierek program of rapid socioeconomic modernization required that support be based on promises of long-term rewards. It also brought with it an entirely different pattern in relations between the media and the leadership.[186] As he brought with him men with whom he had worked closely in running the Silesian media, Gierek also instituted a new system of media–government relations. It went almost full circle away from the system journalists had come to know under Gomułka. The prime elements of his new model were control, involvement, and consistency. His ability to impose this model was increased by the control he had over his own elite.[187]

Instead of satisfying "mass demands," as it was supposed to do in the Gomułka period, the "great role" of the mass media in Silesia when Gierek ran it and in the nation as a whole after he took over in December 1971, was to "shape the consciousness of the masses through a constant, systematic influence on the working people . . . by reaching them with the Party's work, indicating the goal and the roads leading to it through the concentration and mobilization of all of the society around the Party."[188] In doing this, journalists were "political activists who fight with their talents and abilities side-by-side with all the Party for the implementation of its goals."[189]

For the profession, this meant they were no longer marginal actors. Journalists at all levels who supported Gierek were rapidly and quite publicly either inducted into the Party elite or consulted by it. Gierek initiated and gave major play to press conferences and meetings with journalists and editors to draw them into activist roles.[190] Party meetings and ideological statements were devoted to raising the status of the profession by finding ways to train journalists to be "multiskilled social activists."[191] In keeping with their changed status, journalists' incomes were raised and they found themselves beneficiaries of massive investment in the media and its technical potential.

At the same time, the profession was restrained. The old system of "star journalists" was attacked and journalism was redefined as an anonymous profession instructed to be members of an "editorial collective, shaped with the party's help."[192] Finally, journalists ceased to have their professional work defined simply by their writing and production: they were expected to be community activists sponsoring entertainment and festivals, participating at various levels in the party leadership, and leading community projects.[193]

Initially, the convergence of journalists' support for Gierek's policies to modernize the country and improve the economy and Gierek's willingness to publicly involve journalists and give them credit as partners in change worked well. But, as Gierek's economic policies began to fail in the mid-seventies, journalists' role came to involve a "propaganda of success" and a denial of the realities of the world around them.[194] Press criticism was no longer an acceptable way to point up faults in the system, no matter at how low a level it was aimed. The call of the final Gierek Party Congress in 1980 was for the media to fill the "Party's great needs":

> to make clear to the society national and international affairs, develop active ideological postures, inspire the actions of the party, through positive images as well as criticism of negative characteristics, and initiate citizen's discussions of current problems of the nation and the world.[195]

To do this, Gierek's policy of the "propaganda of success' required that criticism be closely supervised and limited to issues that could be easily resolved and that would "present the Party's goals on a broader scale."[196] The focus was to be not on the problems with the policies, or the problems in the goals of policy-makers, or, for that matter, failings of the policies themselves but on "the negative elements of society" which influence the functioning of institutions, waste, laziness, and the lack of social discipline.[197]

Ultimately, the Gierek ideological position on the media and its roles as well as the unity Gierek was able to create in the top elite and the institutional centralization carried out at every level gave journalists very little opportunity to write critically or have an impact on the policy process. As the economy began to fail, the involvement journalists had been promised in policy-making and evaluation became symbolic.[198] The relationship between journalists and their sponsors was broken by the control of instructors from the Press Department. The dramatic difference between the reality of everyday life and the success the leadership claimed as the only tolerable inspiration for the population made honest writing about national or even local events difficult at best, and criticism virtually impossible.[199] When journals or journalists did try to discuss issues that came to them from the population, they found themselves accused of "blackening the vision of socialism."[200]

Even the role of journalists in producing the media was reduced, although the public's image of their involvement was not. Journalists and editors were pressed to leave the ideological presentations and theoretical discussions to official party propagandists.[201]

Ironically, from the mid-seventies on, journalists were trapped in the Gierek system. They lost control of the dissemination of information and criticism not only because of the Gierek limits on them but also because of his regime's failure to limit the "uncensored" press.[202] In response to the "propaganda of success" and the spread of repression after the workers' demonstrations in 1976, dissidents established the Committee in Support of the Workers (KOR). That group and others that followed it focused their action on developing an alternative press that publicized political repression and dealt with issues censored in normal press. In part because of an increasing isolation and, in part, because of a desire to buy off intellectual disaffection and Western creditors, the regime allowed this press to exist virtually in the open. The result was that journalists' own position was further weakened since the contrast in openness was easily visible to intellectuals in Poland's major cities.[203]

Solidarity and martial law

The spread of strikes and work stoppages that accompanied the announcement of price increases in December 1980, cast the death knoll on Gierek's regime and its use of the media to put forth a "propaganda of success"[204] just as Gomułka's isolation and the price increases enacted in December 1970, had brought down his regime. Even before the Gierek leadership had been pushed out, the media was a target of attack from all sides, one of the strikers' major demands being the publishing of divergent views.[205] Gierek's closest allies in the media were charged with personal corruption on a massive scale.[206] Workers' demands were responded to with public admissions of an economic collapse that disproved the "propaganda of success."[207] Even those who had been in the Gierek regime chimed in to attack the "propaganda of success" as having done "great harm."[208] At the Party Plenum that followed the signing of the initial accords (which included a promise to draft and pass a law on censorship allowing for discussion from all sides), the "propaganda of success" received much of the blame for the disruptions:

> From the time when the successes were less and less, such propaganda, objectively speaking, made the society opposed to the party,

> deepened the crisis of authority, and created disbelief in even rational arguments. As a result of the propaganda of success, there was no space for criticism, for true evaluations and opinions. Facts that showed the worsening economic situation in the country were trivialized or went unspoken. The society's moral code or its sense of justice were not mobilizable because of this fight to ignore the negative conditions in the society.[209]

From the advent of Solidarity through the "normalization" and reestablishment of control that began with the declaration of martial law, the elite was so torn by its own internal battles and its inability to get support from the population that its stance on the role and position of the mass media was inconsistent. There was clearly a sense of betrayal when "regime" journalists turned into radical critics of the polity, and also a sense of the need to control the explosion of criticism and honesty in the media. At the same time, it was acknowledged that the restriction of the media had helped bring on Solidarity. There was a willingness to allow the failings and crises of the past regime to be attacked but an unwillingness to have journalists turn on the remaining Party and government leaders. There was the claim of a "varied" media and a willingness to allow the media to make clear the problems of the present just as there was a tightening of the reins on journalists, and on the media's ability to propose options and be treated as a "loyal opposition party."

The final reality of martial law was, for journalists and the population, far from symbolic. It demonstrated that the Jareizielski regime's ideological statements about the press and the media were no more benign than Gierek's "propaganda of success" was connected to reality. The ultimate reality was a return to past patterns. As Stanisław Kwiatkowski, head of the government's opinion research center characterized the situation in 1984: "In the areas of ideology and propaganda unfortunately we are returning once again, and this time for good, to the philosophy of past years: we offend, teach as though we know everything and, in our sense of mission, we order people to support socialism in Poland."[210] This, even as the Polish press has remained, even during the martial law period, the most free and critical in Eastern Europe.

The evolution of both the new elite approach to the media and, ironically, the clear return to past ways are far more than a simple reality. They are a demonstration of the impact of social change on both the profession and the political elite. They are also a part of the reality with which professionals have had to deal and which they have had to constantly reevaluate in forming new professional roads and preserving their old professional system and values.

Journalism history and the Polish media system

The Polish media system itself has been as much a product of its history, the myths of power that it has generated, and the shifting demands that have been placed upon it as it has been a product of the Soviet model of the ideal Marxist–Leninist press. The Marxist charge for the press was to serve as a "collective organizer, agitator and propagandist" for the masses, raising them up through education and images of correct behavior. The tradition of the Polish press, however, focuses on a limited intellectual audience since, historically, there was little local capital for an extensive and permanent mass press, especially given that there was a high level of illiteracy in Poland, as elsewhere in Eastern Europe, until after World War II.[211]

These same financial strictures, coupled with European press traditions, led to a press which pushed the concerns of political groups. In Poland, the legitimacy of this focus on addressing the media to the "best and the brightest" was further reinforced by the role of the press as the voice of national interests during the partition of Poland and the lead it took in advocacy during the interwar period and in the liberalization of the mid-fifties.[212] The Polish media system, in both its structure and emphasis, has reflected all of this in its focus on discussion, analysis, and culture addressed primarily to the *intelligentsia* and, only secondarily, to what the mass of the population wants to read. Furthermore, whenever possible, press names and images harken back to their noncommunist, prewar predecessors. Even the writing award of the Association of Polish Journalists is named after a leading Polish *publicist* of the Partition period.

In the late forties and early fifties, the Polish press was different. It was directed to be written primarily for and by workers and peasants. The prewar journals of noncommunist political groups, religious organizations, and intellectual or professional associations were closed down as power was secured by the communists. But, with the liberalization of the Polish October in the mid-fifties, "normalcy" returned to the Polish press, a "normalcy" that has remained and reflects prewar patterns. Journalists and journals moved to specialize in various subjects and approaches. In doing this, the press they created ceased to be a faceless mass press spouting a universal ideology and became a press in which individuals were "stars" known for their individual approaches and concerns.

A media hierarchy, divided both in terms of readers and professional advancement, also developed. Its components were not to be changed until some journals closed and others appeared after the imposition of martial law. At the top of the hierarchy have been the socio-political weeklies (*Polityka, Kultura, Życie Gospodarcze, Życie Literackie, Literatura,* and *Prawo i Życie*) that address intellectuals. Writing for these journals confers high status.[213] In addition to these prominent national weeklies, there emerged, after 1956, a Catholic press representing pro-regime and independent groups as well as the Church hierarchy. These journals were weeklies and monthlies. Professional associations, real and paper intellectual organizations, and various special interest groups, each have had their own monthlies or, in some cases, weeklies. Most of these have very small staffs and limited circulations.

For the broader population, there are some hundred journals with foci ranging from peasants' and women's interests to management, labor unions and chess. Many of these have large staffs, develop their own regular topics and campaigns, and provide special services for their readers. Most have their roots in the prewar or Stalinist press.

The daily press is divided. There are popular afternoon papers based on prewar traditions of the "yellow" tabloid press that exist in the West as well. There are also communist dailies, sponsored by the Polish United Workers Party, that were established in every region in Poland as the communist forces came. These are headed by the national Party daily, *Trybuna Ludu*. The two other legal parties, the Democratic Party (addressed to the small class of artisans and private owners) and the United Peasants Party, also have dailies and periodicals for their constituencies. Even the names of these stress their continuity with the prewar predecessors of these parties. Even more tied to prewar press traditions are the so-called "readership" dailies. This small group of papers has been, at least ostensibly, independent of any group. In the early years after the war, it was designed to appeal to the reluctant, non-communist intelligentsia. Since then, it has retained its orientation to the more educated sectors of the population and has, therefore, veiled its ideology and followed traditions of the past.

The final element of the mass media system to develop in Poland was the broadcast media. Radio began in a limited fashion in the ruins of World War II. Little money, however, was available for its development so it remained a stepchild, used primarily for blatant propaganda addresses or for quick news circulation. Television was similarly underfunded at the outset by Władysław Gomułka, given his reluctance to buy new technology. Only with the Gierek regime in the seventies was there a program of modernization and development of the mass media. Much of this concentrated on expanding the reach and quality radio and television. Two radio channels expanded to five, which included some channels dedicated to intellectual audiences, and one primitive television channel became two stations with national reach and local programming as well.[214]

3 Living and learning journalism

The world of Polish journalists is a world of conflict. They learn to be professionals, to judge their own work, and to cherish their specialness as a profession, from their training and experiences as working journalists dealing with the demands and pressures of fellow staff members and readers, from the directions they receive from the Party and government elite, and also from those who edit and publish the media. None of these demands, pressures, or directions are the same nor do the practical constraints of production – deadlines, space restrictions, and resource limits – allow journalists even to come near fulfilling outside expectations. So, journalists are caught, as professionals in bureaucratic structures, in a web of constraints they cannot possibly fulfill. It is these impossible cross pressures that create in journalists a sense that they are professionals.

Like other professionals in bureaucratic settings, journalists live in two worlds. They must be responsive to and loyal to the nonprofessionals who run and fund the hierarchies where they work, even though journalists know they were hired and are needed for their special knowledge and skills. On the other hand, their values are explicitly their own. And, although they recognize that they have to work in a bureaucratic and political context, journalists resent interference. They struggle to create a work and professional world where they do not have to deal directly with the outside – however much they accept the reality of its interference. And, given the fact that journalists – like their colleagues in the West – do not have a real "unique" body of knowledge to gain in order to be journalists, the workplace establishes their professionalism. Their identification as a member of the staff is what makes them "journalists". Therefore, faced with heavy pressures from the outside world and the lack of an identifiable barrier for entry into the profession, being "on staff" becomes a jealously guarded line of defense between journalists and the unappreciative and unwelcome "outside." Afterall, it is that "outside" which seeks to regulate and manage what they regard as their very creative and essential professional work.

What happens inside an editorial office – whatever the medium, whoever the journalist players – is the "business" of the profession. Most of the time, orders and criticism that journalists tolerate come from within the office. The structures and procedures journalists have evolved from practicing journalism in a bureaucratic setting that is beset by changing and conflicting demands turn the newsroom into a fishbowl with visible outside pressure refracted and diluted before it reaches journalist-practitioners. For journalists, this is their world. They protect it as the major bastion of their professionalism. So, as researchers from the Central Committee reported, "Journalists are quite willing to talk about their work but are unwilling to deal with the possibilities of organizational change."[1]

However focused journalists are on their own world and their own insulated professional bureaucracy, the very nature of their work requires them to deal with the outside world. There are clear institutions of control and direction established in both the government and Party. Individuals throughout society look to the media and expect different things from it as readers than they do as targets of media reports. Most of their demands, though, are not put to journalists directly but are simply "in the air," well veiled, or presented through intermediaries. This creates a web so complex and shielded that even the most experienced journalist often loses track of how and from where he is being controlled or manipulated. Given the political leaders' interest in having a positive image portrayed in the media and readers' and most journalists' interest in a critical media, there is no simple and comfortable balance for journalists. The conflicting pressures have been further heightened in the post-Stalin years when journals were pressed to be at least self-supporting, if not profit-making enterprises, even though paper and printing time as well as air time, have been allocated, in part, on purely political criteria.

However conscious or unconscious journalists are of interference and control over their work, journalism is not only a very professional process but also the major force making journalists act like professionals. In essence learning to be a journalist is basically a product of the natural pressures of work on the media, not of any "higher politics" or explicit teaching. The "rules of the game" are barely hinted at in journalism programs – whether academics dominate the program or politics do. The rules of being a professional journalist are learned, instead, only when journalists start to work as professionals. Then, too, competition for the occasional jobs that open up on any journal allows editors and their senior staff to control who enters the profession. Low salaries for those in entry level positions and the long years of journalistic training cull out those who are not committed to the life or work of journalism and who would otherwise see it as simply a way to make money.

Finally, journalism is so time consuming that, even though most post-fifties entrants did not experience the Stalinist educational system that created senior professionals' peer group, most journalists in every generation make their closest and oldest friendships with the men and women they know from work.[2] After all, their irregular schedules and their role as critics isolate them from most of their counterparts in other fields. Journalists interact and talk so often with each other, almost to the exclusion of all others, that they and their journals take on profiles. These profiles can only be slightly modified by chief editors brought in from the outside. For journalists, then, the editorial office was and is "an administrative unit, but also a circle of friends and a base for people coming with pleas and ideas."[3]

Particularly in the sixties and seventies, this solidarity was intensified by the stability of most staffs – virtually no one came in or left. The public saw individual journalists as representatives of the journals where they worked and it saw journals as a singular and unified chorus singing the same tune. Even when there were new or expanded staffs or, as happened in the eighties, when some journalists shifted to Solidarity papers or more active political roles, these long-time human ties were not severed by this mobility and political differentiation. Rather, until martial law, the web of personal ties merely expanded.[4] Ultimately, this meant that, in the aftermath of the declaration of martial law, journalists cared about each other even if they disagreed and fought bitterly. They monitored each others' fate and helped each other, particularly when they had worked together. So, even with strictures against any gathering, journal staffs gathered in the initial days of martial law to discuss the critical professional and political question of "What next?" Most then responded with some unity to demands for verification or the threat of firings. And, those who took other paths into the political leadership still felt some responsibility for those in their profession or, at least, felt stung by their criticism. Finally, as professionals lost jobs and moved to new posts, new jobs were found by friends for those who had been forced out by the authorities or who wanted to move into more marginal and less visible positions as a sign that they did not condone the declaration of martial law.

Far more than this sense of professional community grows out of the worklife and, to a much lesser extent, the education of the sixties and seventies. A sense of distance from the rest of the society also develops. Whatever their position in the community and whoever their friends, those who are not journalists most often complicate journalists' lives, criticize their work, and limit their earnings by blocking their access to information or keeping them from publishing what they know. And since many individuals approach journalists to solve problems they cannot solve themselves, contact with them teaches journalists that the system and the people in it are not rational. They are buffeted first, as new entrants, between professors and practical journalists and then, as working journalists, by readers, editors imposed from the outside, government and party officials, and censors. Journalists come to see their professional work as assailed by the contradictory demands from outside. For them, their professional milieu is the only safe and rational haven they have. The lesson that journalists have learned from all of this has been that only they can and should determine how and what they do and write. And, since they are paid largely by how much of what they write is actually published, protecting their professional autonomy becomes more than a matter of principle. It is a matter of economic survival.

The panopaly of forces that affect journalists' lives make simply conceding to any one group and serving as a "mouthpiece" impossible. The demands are never consistent, so pleasing one master at one point in time only means displeasing another. Journalists react to this as individuals and as a group in intentional and inadvertent actions. Their work styles are intended, explicitly or inadvertently, to give them stability to do their work peacefully and profitably. The sum of their actions gives professional life its character and its isolation.

Training for journalism

For those who entered the field in the sixties and seventies, the road into all but the least attractive regional newspapers and the one or two positions that opened on Poland's most prestigious intellectual journals began with a two to three year masters program at the school of journalism that followed a five year initial university degree. Or, for those who had come into journalism without a university education, the professional requirements of the seventies forced them to make a detour in their careers for an extension course that would grant them a university degree. All of this made formal professional training an "agenda item" for those who entered the field after 1960, when the program reopened. But, it did not make professional education more relevant to the needs of the newsroom. Nor did it create quite the same intense professional community that the Stalinist program had inadvertently created.

In the sixties, formal journalistic education was as academic as possible. Led by a close friend of Prime Minister Józef Cyrankiewicz and designed on the Columbia Journalism School model, it was dominated by the faculty's research interests rather than those of either the political elite or the profession itself. In the end, it was essentially irrelevant to life outside the "ivory tower." Media investment was so low, in fact, that graduates were hard put to find work in journalism itself. Instead, they found they were outsiders in the very profession they had trained well into their mid-twenties to enter. Even the practical education that had linked school and newsroom, however marginally, was hard to implement. Professionals saw the program only as a public symbol that they were a serious profession like law and medicine. But, the program and its students were so irrelevant to their professional lives that they were unwilling to deal with its students.

From the point of admission on, academic interests dominated. In selecting students for this less than popular program, the school's faculty and director invited political activists and professional journalists to be on the admissions committees. They knew, though, that the decision would ultimately be theirs. So, on their entrance examination, students were asked to deal with sensitive political questions only to be judged primarily on their grammar and writing abilities. Calls for recruitment from among technical school graduates and workers and peasants were easily ignored because students were evaluated and scored on their cultural knowledge. The program students took once they entered was a very theoretical one that only provided marginal political and professional training.[5] Ideological courses were tacked on but not taught by regular faculty or counted in students' overall evaluation. And, while professional experience was required, it was taken less than seriously by students, faculty, and the journalists with whom they worked. Those who took the courses given for working professionals without university degrees found them equally irrelevant. Busy with their own careers, the forty-five students who registered each year "did" courses by doing a minimal amount of work and coming to the school of journalism as infrequently as possible.

In the end, students learned important but untaught lessons from these programs. Few of them formed real peer groups since they knew that, for jobs in journalism, they were in competition and would have to push each other aside. The forty-five students who came into the program each year were also largely middle-class university graduates who lived at home and had their own old friendship circles. Professional education for them was just another hoop to jump through to get into journalism. What they learned were not the facts and theories of press history or of public opinion but the almost total irrelevance of the education they received either for finding jobs or for their work as professionals.

For them, course work was to be done as symbolically as possible just to get a job. Ultimately, for the graduates of the sixties, education did not work: it did not prepare them for the real professional world, and the jobs they were educated for did not exist, any more than the visions they were to put forth in their writing made any impression on reality. Those who were lucky enough to find jobs came into the world of journalism in their mid-twenties, having completed seven years of university education only to be hired as poorly paid apprentices with two years more to prove themselves. Graduates from the sixties resented the less educated Stalinist generation for holding secure and well-paid positions in the media. This created a ferment that led to a generational split that bubbled over into professional ferment in 1968, and to demands from political leaders that students in the program be given more political training, even though they were the political loyalists of the university community.

The same lessons were learned in the journalism program of the seventies, even though, after the expansion of the media under Gierek, there was a real need for these graduates, and also, the Gierek leadership explicitly directed that the program be politicized. Little really changed from the sixties. The Gierek agenda for training journalists as political agitators, at first, resulted in more funding for the school and more visibility for its faculty. But, by the mid-seventies, increased funding brought with it a loss of autonomy: the school of journalism was taken over by the department of political science and made only one of a number of training programs for "political activists." In effect, however, the pressures on the school were shuttled aside by the determination of a faculty whose cohesion had been built over years of working together or training each other. As a result, even when laboratories were built for practical professional training in a new building on the outskirts of Warsaw, the program's faculty refused to move from its rundown, downtown offices in the midst of the university. So, students could receive no more supervision and practical experience than they had in the sixties and the political lessons learned were given primarily through theoretical courses designed by scholars on public opinion formation, press structure, and press history.

Students learned, again, that ideology was presented as a necessary thorn in their side, not a critical issue for the professionals. The division of the school into press, radio, and television specializations and the presence of new journalism programs in three other universities meant that students never had to study far from home and establish new friendships. The new variations in programs – postgraduate degrees, doctoral programs, and undergraduate concentrations – also meant that students did not develop a sense of belonging to the program or to a professional group. For the profession, this professional education was an embarrassment: it was clearly no longer an independent field of study and was tied to the very political training and agitation that journalists had resented in the fifties. What made the program a "non-issue" for the profession was that it was marginal for everyone. The few students who did come onto journal staffs could be retrained. For politicians, this focus on academic interests and research did not spell better political education for entry level journalists. Young members of the faculty studying public opinion, media use, and international communication often got results that were very negative for the regime's image. Most shared these results with their students who, although hardly dissidents, soon were not afraid to challenge regime representatives and members of the faculty. And, while they did not move to open dissent, students joked and grumbled together about the failings of the very regime they were being trained to support. All of this helped create yet another generation of cynics who, like their counterparts from the Gomułka era, had little commitments to each other or the leadership's promises.

Little changed in the journalism school with the advent of Solidarity. New and more liberal leaders were elected but, for most students, however cynical or conformist they might be, the real world lay well beyond their classroom walls. If, in the midst of the turmoil, they actually went to class, what they heard was no more relevant to the new situation than it had been before, nor was it much different. And, only a handful of new students applied to the program. Workers and intellectuals from all fields simply began professional work without professional education as the media and its options exploded in Solidarity's fifteen months. In the program itself, only a few overtly political courses were changed and some students were involved through their research in discussions of a new censorship and press law.

Only in the aftermath of martial law did journalistic education become a force for professionalization. While the program and its faculty changed very little, the spaces created by journalists who resigned or were blacklisted made the school of journalism a real hiring ground for the profession. So, for the first time since the fifties, journalism school graduates have entered the profession not as lowly apprentices or cub reporters but as full-time professionals with real opportunities to report and make money. And their contacts with the profession during their training have grown: professionals who remained in their positions and some few who had left journalism work supplemented their income by teaching at the Institute. So, journalism students were able to have personal ties with leading professionals. Finally, the public disgust for journalism and the media, that emerged after Solidarity's criticism and the repression of martial law, brought students in the program closer together. Even though most students were from Warsaw and lived all over the city as had their predecessors in the sixties and seventies, the social life of the students was more focused around the school and less on friends from other programs. In these years of public opposition, after all, many found that only with other students in the journalism program were they safe from criticism for going into what was unpopular and unrespected work. All of this meant that, while students still learned the professional rules of the game on the job and little that was necessary to professional work from their formal education, they learned from their training to be part of a loyal and coherent peer group not unlike that of their predecessors from the fifties. Ironically, too, like their fifties counterparts, they have not only taken on leadership roles but they have felt safe enough to push the boundaries of the system in which they work.

Lessons of working in journalism

Whether or not journalism education was ever or could ever be the archetypal professional education of medical schools and law programs, journalists have learned from it and from their experiences "on the job" to see themselves as special and deserving of protection from the bothersome interference of those outside their profession. The very irrelevance of academic lessons and political claims has made them all the more committed to professional work and the lessons of their jobs. They know that the boundaries of journalistic work, however much they may try to expand them, are clearly set by the agendas of journalists' clients (readers, bureaucrats, and officials) and the Party and state institutions that hold those agendas in place. Not only do these boundaries influence professional work but the impact they have on journalists' lives teaches indelible lessons about the status, needs, and roles of the profession. Within these boundaries, journalists work in mini-bureaucracies, interlocked with other institutions, but styled by the imperatives of producing a newspaper, or a journal, or a program within the everyday strictures of equipment, staffing, and time. The very structure of the media bureaucracies in which journalists work has evolved so that it serves as a mechanism to allow journalists to feel that they work as professionals and also to maximize their power. Finally, the very experience of "making news" or preparing a program enforces professionals' sense of themselves and of their hold on special skills even as it is a reflection of their determination to be "professional."

External influence and control enters the newsroom through several doors. Journalists' awareness of it comes less from formal directives than from cumulative experiences and observations. As one leading Polish journalist stated:

> Sure, we read all the papers. What happens to any one journalist is an indicator to all of us of what we can do and how far we can go. That's the way we keep track of changes in the rules of the game. We, Warsaw journalists, are much better off because we know what's happening in between the lines – who did what with whom.

The political elite outwardly treats journalists as professionals and manages them by manipulating their professional interests, both directly and indirectly.[6] When the elite is open about its interference, professional journalists express clear frustration – this then turns to ferment at the first sign of political leaders' weakness. So, the political leadership's most effective control is carried on through indirect channels.

Under these conditions, external control occurs at three stages: topic selection and information gathering, pre-publication preparations, and post-publication reactions. State and Party institutions and individuals are in constant conflict over how much should appear at all levels. This allows editors to appeal the decisions coming from advocates of one group to its contenders. In addition, Party and state institutions need different things from the media. State institutions seek to restrict the critical information given out about their activities. The Party seeks a press active in supporting its policies and in acting as a check on the state bureaucracy.

Normally, individuals and departments in the Party and the state apparatus do not try to order or request explicit articles on specific topics from journalists. Where this kind of direction has occurred, though, it has been directed not at the journalists themselves but at their editors, or it has been presented in such a veiled way that no orders are given. For major national and international events in the Gierek period (Party Congresses, the American Bicentennial, the Helsinki Conference, the Pope's visit, and the construction of the Nowa Huta steel plant) explicit directives were produced by the Central Committee and sent out to top editors.[7] For most, these were merely written indications of the posture Party leaders were taking. They were not imperatives. They were presented to and seen by journalists as just that: information about Party policy, not orders to them. The specific directives that were given as to the extent and location of coverage clearly were never observed.[8] Instead, journalists set out, on their own initiative, and wrote all they thought was feasible. Other less explicit modes of direction are also used frequently. Editors or leading journalists in a specific field are called in to press conferences with officials who not only answer their questions and give them the facts but also suggest how issues should be covered.[9] Or, individual journalists or editors are sought out by officials who either wish to scold them for what they have written or who want to encourage positive coverage. And, although journalists regard accepting payment or rewards as unethical, Party and state officials either facilitate or hamper journalists' coverage or they may aid journalists in getting scarce goods or privileges. These have ranged from the military's provision of helicopters and airplanes for Polish television news reporters' trips in order to encourage positive and visible coverage of the army, to easing journalists' access not only to cars and apartments, particularly in the provinces, but also to factory stores for pottery, glassware, and clothes that are normally difficult to buy.

At the same time, although both Party and state institutions and leaders try to get the press to report what they think is appropriate and in their interests, they are more able to discourage or eliminate than they are to force journalists to report positively, since most journalists think such reporting is unethical or improper. Journalists and media institutions, in fact, often simply refuse to present an issue about which they can not print what they see as the truth. So, in 1968, when provincial journalists found themselves caught between demonstrating students and the demands of local and national politicians that they condemn the students, many simply published agency reports and statements by local political leaders without commentary.[10] The same reaction was characteristic of the response of many papers and journalists' to government demands that they downgrade or criticize Solidarity or, later, that they attack Solidarity and support martial law. In both cases, they distanced themselves either by publishing nothing or by publishing only political leaders' statements or news agency reports without commentary. In most of these cases, whatever pressure is exerted for publication is generally exerted on the chief editor by his political friends rather than on journalists.[11]

In more general moves to change the emphasis in journals, the results have been similar, although less a matter of deliberate action. A study was done in 1974 of the use of the increased paper supply given to twenty-seven journals to increase their concentration on areas of interest to the PUWP. Although there was a great deal of variance between the journals analyzed, the researchers concluded that: (1) areas of interest to the journalists and their readers (use of illustrations, analyses, advertisements, information on youth, cultural and artistic presentations, and information on sports) increased at least as much and usually more than the areas sought by the Party directives, and (2) that the only area of PUWP interest in which there was significant change in the proportion of space used was the area of information on other socialist countries. This did not fully redress the inequity that had been discussed extensively in the press and by the Party: that other East European countries were not raised in the minds of the readers to the same level of significance and knowledge as Western Europe and the United States.[12] In fact, reporting on other socialist countries continued to be negative in comparison with reporting on capitalist states.

Party institutions

The Communist Party touches journalists' professional lives, directly and indirectly, from personnel policy to circulation controls. At almost all points, the Party directs rather than controls. Its involvement is more intense for party sponsored journals, than for non-Party journals since, on these, other sponsoring organizations give more immediate direction. But, for no journalist is the Party a nonentity. At the least, journalists make themselves aware of Party statements on the press – what they are and whether there are indications of divisions within the Party leadership on the press or policy in general that might signal changes for the media.[13] Individuals' contacts with the Party and with Party media policy vary, however. Top level journalists are involved with individuals and issues at the very top of the Party hierarchy. Lower level and regional journalists are touched mainly by regional or low level Party officials. The rest pales in its insignificance for them. Over time too, there also have been shifts. In the fifties and sixties, the Party was a "watcher" – an institution of appeal and last resort. But, in the Gierek era, the Party became an active leader and director of what was to be said and by whom.[14]

Party members are far more involved than are non-Party members since they are expected to attend regular Party meetings at their workplace. At these, problems of the staff and the journal get some hearing as do internal Party documents and memoranda. On large staffs, Primary Party Organizations (POP), made up of all the Party members on the staff, may serve as alternative avenues for the exchange of unpublishable information. When the editor is inactive or the staff very divided, these can also be forums for discussing the issues readers have brought to journalists' attention. Journalists in the PUWP are also encouraged to go to special Party ideological schools for short seminars or year long programs.[15] But, normally, journalists do not treat these ideological programs or the POP meetings and the access to information they offer seriously. The most influential journalists have their own personal channels for information and pressure. Many journalists, particularly in the seventies and eighties, actually belonged to the Party only in order to satisfy the political requirements to advance in their work, since Party membership was a prerequisite for most editorial positions and for interesting but sensitive political reporting. Effectively, then, POP meetings were held because they were required not because the POP had any real role to play in guiding or training the profession.[16]

For most, "the Party and its involvement" is funneled through the Press Department of the Central Committee. This, even though, at the top levels, journalists are aware that media policy is not what is printed or said explicitly but is made by individuals on a case by case basis. So, if they can, they often go to or are called in by Politburo officials to talk about an issue. It is, however, the Press Department that is charged with providing directives on appropriate press coverage and treatment; evaluating and coordinating central and provincial journals; supervising appointments to all key positions; giving general guidance on appropriations for the media; controlling presentations of the PUWP and its elite; and, in the Gierek era, directing and coordinating all censorship decisions. The Central Committee Press Department also commissions studies from media research institutes. In the Gierek era, too, the Press Department initiated public and "off the record" press conferences to let journalists ask questions and also give directions. And, at the same time, in this era, the number of positions that had to be appointed through the Press Department expanded. And, so, for journalists and papers outside the view of the top leaders, the Press Department is a main force.

Under normal circumstances, the Press Department has an impact on journalists, as professionals, in a multitude of ways. The head of the Central Committee Press Department may speak publicly about what they should be doing at a meeting of the Association of Polish Journalists (SDP), at Central Committee Plenums, or in special forums such as interviews in particular journals. Directives, distributed either by the Central Committee Press Department or through the censor's office to editors, are often well known to journalists who hear about them or see them in the course of editors' discussions of what should or should not be covered.[17] Whatever they cover formally, though, these are not treated as orders to be followed, they are merely indications of who the internal Party winners and losers are.[18]

Most importantly, the Press Department watches over the working of the media. Usually, this is based on "off-the-cuff" contacts and appraisals of what has been published by instructors in the Press Department each of whom is charged with monitoring or managing a set of specific papers or programs.[19] These appraisals take on real power because the people who make them are also major actors in the appointment process for all editorial and journalistic positions on the *nomenklatura* lists. In the Gomułka era, for those outside of Warsaw, the ten Press Department instructors had little further contact. Management and interference in journalists' work went on through the editor's membership on the regional Party committee, personal intervention by individual committee members on specific issues, and general directives that were sent out from the center. Most provincial journalists were affected and felt very constrained by them because local leaders were always trying to make sure that the local concerns journalists knew well were presented only in a positive light. For journalists, this unduly limited their role in monitoring local institutions and influencing the public's agenda as they felt they should. The pressure to represent local interests also meant that too little national news could find space in their press.

In the Gierek era, local Party organizations lost power to the, by then, fifty-instructor Central Committee Press Department. After the 1975 territorial redivision, regional journals served not one *województwo* but a number of the smaller governmental and Party units. As a result, they had no single local boss but were supposed to work with a local committee made up of the heads of each Party committee served by the paper, representatives of local civic groups and institutions, and the editorial board of the paper. The committee's job was to aid the paper's Central Committee instructor by giving him a sense of Party and community leaders as well as a sense of local needs and what the paper was and should be providing.[20]

Journalists treated these meetings, as they had treated earlier Central Committee directives, as a resource and not an order. They reported, in interviews, that they prepared carefully for these meetings in order to use them to get information about future local issues, events, and options even though the increased powers of the central Party authorities forced them to orient themselves more toward the interests of the center. For both local papers and the media in the rest of Poland, this meant that journalists were less harassed by special local interests and more tied down by the national Party leaders' demands. In addition, pressure was increasingly placed on journalists to restrict themselves to "nonpolitical" discussions and to have Party leaders and agitators write "political articles." Ultimately, the shift from supervision by local officials, with whom journalists and editors were often friends or long-term opponents, to "visiting firemen" from Warsaw limited local journalists' field of maneuver. It also meant that rules and reactions, predictable and contestable in the regional context, became less negotiable.

By the end of the seventies, even for journalists on central Party papers and programs with editors who were a part of the Central Committee itself, Press Department instructors were ever present, not as friends, but as constant nuisances. In fact, top journalists, whose editors had politically powerful positions, felt they were threatened and ordered about by Party bureaucrats as though they were fledglings. It was these leading journalists who served as role models for others and who saw the profession as the most trapped and limited in the late seventies.[21] Their only option, however, seemed to be to retreat to "safe subjects" until the workers' movement came to change the balance of forces.

The Press Department's role remained constant in the turmoil of the Solidarity era. Even when liberal Józef Klasa ran the Press Department,[22] the staff of instructors continued to put out orders, give formal approval to staff changes, and review and criticize the media. The difference was that, from the Solidarity Weekly (*Tygodnik Solidarność*) to the Party daily, there was a clear sense among journalists of the Party's powerlessness and, therefore, of their own ability to ignore or circumvent the orders given them. This defiance kept the contacts between journalists and Party bureaucrats bitter. It also meant that, with the imposition of martial law, the old mechanism, albeit with the new personnel that had been brought in to replace Gierek's disgraced press moguls, was ready to begin, under military guidance, approving or appointing editors, deciding what papers should be published, sending out orders on coverage, reprimanding and threatening recalcitrant staffs, and pushing behind the scenes for printing delays, distribution limits, and assaults on the sponsors of daring journals. However, even with the force of martial law, Party orders were something journalists were willing to use but not totally follow.

State institutions

For journalists, however, the real, daily interference in their work and their autonomy has not come directly from the Party. It has come from the various government institutions charged with producing the media and from the various government officials and institutions whose affairs it covers. Not only do journalists see themselves as checks on the government but they also live and work in a society and system where virtually every aspect of life is touched or controlled by some government agency. So, at every turn, journalists are reporting on an official government institution.

The attempts by government and economic institutions to manage the news is often much more bothersome to journalists than are the various Party attempts at direction. These "government" attempts at management involve, not suggestions or hiring for high positions, but individual journalists' access to information and their ability to publish that information and be paid for their work. For journalists and government officials at all levels and in all areas, the battle is over coverage; no official wants to have his own failings or those of his institution or his profession made public. So, the law and periodic directives from the Prime Minister as well as instructions by the Party formally protect journalists' right to information and a response to their criticism.[23] But, for most journalists surveyed in 1976, getting information that they wanted to use was their most acute problem.[24] Interview data indicates that, although far more was publishable in the Solidarity era, this battle for information did not change.

Even with legal sanctions against keeping information from journalists, most journalists appeal not to the law but to whatever patron they feel can be played off against government bureaucrats to get information. Individual government officials, at the same time, use whatever powers and connections they have to prevent the publication of information or criticism, be it with calls and threats to the journalist and his editor or, more directly, in attempts to get a ruling by the censor's office.

For journalists, the lessons are all too clear. Journalists assume that institutional bureaucrats and managers consistently hold back all but positive information. As a result, they try, to the consternation of managers, to speak privately with workers or patrons of an establishment or to use their personal contacts with officials and specialists to get information. In fact, for the overwhelming majority, these indirect channels are their prime information sources.[25] For established journalists in all areas, this problem of information access and the need to have connections are an additional impetus for specialization on a single topic. In this way, journalists simply become their own best sources for information and guidance in understanding problems. They build up personal libraries as well as personal expertise. They weave an entire network of connections with other journalists working in the same area. This allows them to circumvent institutional authorities and to rapidly summon up information. In turn, even as bureaucrats and professionals bristle at and try to block any criticism from the press, they also see it as an aid in promoting their work and praising their successes. This is done most often by flattering journalists who work in their area and not by criticizing them. Their responses create, in journalists, a sense both of power and of the need to guard against being coopted. However, at the same time as institutions flatter journalists, they also alienate them by simply refusing to deal with their criticism, making them feel unjustly ignored and belittled.[26] Even government and Party regulations encouraging bureaucrats to respond are regularly ignored. So journalists see themselves all the more as unjustly treated by bureaucracies and are more and more convinced that, if it is possible to change bureaucracies or protect their sources,[27] this will happen only because of their own power as professionals. For, neither they nor the bureaucrats they criticize think press criticism really moves top leaders.[28]

Another governmental institution that makes an impact on journalists' lives is the publishing house. The impact of their control over personnel and staff allotments; salaries and benefits; access to permission for funds for foreign travel and cars; tape recorders and cameras, as well as their power over paper allocations; the assignment of printing presses and printing time; and the circulation and distribution of a paper can – as journalists are well aware – allow a paper to grow or kill it.[29] But, other than the formal hiring and firing of journalists and editors – seen by most journalists as ordered not from some publisher but from political powers – the publishing house remains an unseen framework for most professionals in their day-to-day work. Only a very few journalists, men whose professional lives and power had been squeezed by the tactics of publishing houses aimed directly at decimating their particular journal,[30] mentioned the publishing houses as significant in their individual careers. Ironically, while most journalists sense little guidance or interference from their publishing house and generally do not think about it as one of their problems, many, particularly those who had been editors, feel strongly, as they pointed out in the Solidarity era, that journalists, as professionals, should be party to publishers' decisions – whether they were political or administrative decisions. So, in the Solidarity period, SDP activists pressed for the publishing system to be broken down into small cooperatives which would compete with each other. Commercial publishers, journalists felt, would make fewer politically based decisions on key issues ranging from paper allocation and budgetary support to the distribution and sales of the media.[31] This would let journalists and their journals make gains for solely professional reasons. But, this proposal was never allowed.

Censorship organs

For journalists and editors, the final and undeniable boundary of their work world is the Main Office for Control of the Press, Publications and Images (GUKPPIW). Although few journalists in the profession as a whole actually claim to have been censored, for virtually all journalists who were interviewed or who wrote or spoke about their experiences the institution of censorship and the potential it held were significant, if symbolic, limits on their professional rights and autonomy. Most journalists simply consciously and, eventually, unconsciously avoid censorship by watching to see what their colleagues can publish. In this way, journalists develop an internal catalogue of issues not to even consider. This socialization has been so pervasive, in fact, that even those working for the Solidarity press unconsciously avoided subjects from this unspoken list until virtually the final days before martial law when old unconscious strictures had been worn away by popular ferment.[32] Censors' directives further illustrate this: even in the years of explicit directions, major national and international issues were never on the list of bans because "just living, we [the censors] knew how they should be handled and so did journalists. So, the problems never arose."[33]

The process of censorship in itself veils many of the specifics. The Main Office for Control is an independent government agency which is, in reality, directed and intertwined with the Press Department. By law, it reviews at least the proofsheets if not earlier drafts of everything printed and the scripts or tapes of all that is broadcast.[34] Any censor can require that words, sentences, pictures, entire articles or even entire pages be changed or cut. Editors can sometimes argue their case or appeal against these decisions. But, the odds weigh so heavily against winning that most editors simply try to avoid points of conflict.

For individual journalists, the threat of censorship, as most know, is far greater than simply the hassles involved. Since journalists are paid by what they publish, being censored is a real financial problem, particularly when a major article on which a journalist may have invested months is cut. It is also an image problem since journalists are known and get status from what they publish. Not to be able to publish creative and critical articles is essentially a loss of professional prestige and visibility in the wider community. With this comes not only a drop in status but often a drop in lucrative and rewarding invitations to lecture to community groups or in the willingness of sources to volunteer information.

At the same time, to be censored is to call attention to yourself among the political elite. The censor's office does regular reports on what is censored and what appeared that should not have. These are classified documents for the censors and the top political leadership.[35] In some cases, being reported in them has a positive effect: censored articles circulated by the censor's office often come to the attention of government and Party leaders more quickly than if they had appeared in one of the myriads of journals or programs the leadership never monitors. Often, journalists who see themselves as a check on the administration consider being reported by the censors as a way for their criticism to be heard and problems solved. (One journalist even reported having received a thank you letter for raising an issue and a number reported that they were paid for these articles, "published" as they were in the censors' press.) At the top ranks of the profession, too, some individuals termed the censor's office a "safety net." Its presence meant that they did not have to think about the political sanctions for what they wrote. The censor would take the initial fallout if publication displeased the powers that be. In other cases, journalists reported that being censored had a negative effect: some were blacklisted or called to task by their editors because of complaints about what they had published and what they had had censored.

When censors did act to block articles, these actions often were shrouded by the censors themselves and, sometimes, even by editors who were embarrassed at their own weakness in the face of this professional *bête noir*. Formally, large numbers of specific directives from the seventies on what should not appear were marked "for the information of the censors only." The intention was that no editor would be told specifically that a given regulation existed. This would insure, apparently, one of two things: (1) gossip would not begin and spread on potentially professionally or socially objectionable regulations that, if they were known, would bring pressure to drop the regulation or (2) editors, not knowing that a given topic could not be discussed, would continue to have journalists work on it and, thus, generate information that the leadership could use.[36] This secretiveness as to why things were removed was, clearly, intolerable to the profession since the key provisions that journalists included in their 1980 draft law on censorship insured that only specifically defined information could be kept out of the press and that journalists were to have an explanation as to why something was censored.

Structurally, too, deliberate barriers have been set up between censors and the journalists whose work they review. As a result, journalists do not normally deal directly with the censors. To establish this distance between journalists and their censors, censorship normally occurs, with the exception of the closed office of the censors in Polish Radio and Television, in the printing plants where papers and journals are sent for preparation.[37] Time too separates journalists and censors. Journalists' individual articles are seldom, if ever, submitted to the censors before they have been edited, placed in the paper and set in type ready to print out. Even costly television tapes are completed and given through a slot in the censors' office door at Polish Radio and Television to be reviewed just before being aired. This gives the censors less time to play with articles or broadcasts since they know that it will be costly to replace or rework them and that there is a clear and looming deadline that must be met. On the other hand, the censors are able to deal not only with specific words and ideas but also with the messages conveyed by the placement of pictures and articles, the overall emphasis of an edition, and the headlines and graphics.

This means that, in the case of dailies, the only contact is between the member of the editorial staff designated to see the paper through to publication on a given night and the censor working on that paper. By the time any argument takes place, most journalists are no longer in their offices. Battling over the censors' decisions requires contacting the chief editor to call higher officials in the censor's office or powerful individuals in this "stable of friends." Given the problems this causes, neither the censor nor the night editor seek confrontation. In effect, when changes must be or are made, the editor responsible for getting that issue printed and out often simplifies his life by presenting the request to the author whose article was changed or dropped as a *fait accompli* – as something required by the censors or as an editorial request. In most cases, the issues are mute when journalists return to their offices and the paper is on the streets.

Discussion and participation by journalists is more feasible in the case of weeklies or monthlies. Marked page proofs (with words, sections, or whole articles crossed out) are picked up at the censors' office and the staff has a day to make the changes or seek support to override a prohibition. This too, though, happens so fast that few people, if anyone at all, outside the top editorial staff get involved. The "bleeding" copy, covered with the red marks of the censors, comes on the day one issue has "gone to bed" and the other is not yet begun. Here again, attempts at intervention are made by the editors through their private contacts or through the formal hierarchy but these protests and discussions often require more than a day to resolve. Most journalists, then, come to know of all this and get involved only indirectly if at all.

Censors are not only kept away from journalists by their own regulations, their location, and the timing of their work but also by the fact that they are constantly shifted from journal to journal. Only on highly specialized media or the Catholic press are censors relatively permanent. In these cases, although most of their contacts are by phone, censors and editors come, at least, to have personal contact and often a jocular relationship.[38] The most common pattern, however, is for censors to move often enough so that no one censor comes to identify with any journal or its potentially censorable ideas.[39]

The specifics of censorship are further clouded for journalists by the unpredictability of the rules and regulations. In the Gomułka era, rules were made and canceled on an *ad hoc* basis. Officials called and demanded at one moment that information just collected be blocked and then others called later to order it published.[40] In the Gierek era, rules and regulations were made and coordinated centrally so they were more consistent.[41] But, spoken and unspoken differentiation in their use and interpretation has continued. In part, over the fifteen years to 1989 this unpredictability has been a product of changes in the leadership and their political postures.[42] In part, too, this instability is built into the system. Some journals (particularly those with small and specialized audiences) are allowed to give coverage or more coverage than others to specific issues. In fact, this is not only a "given" of the system but is specifically provided for in some of the censors' regulations. Furthermore, some topics are blocked for a period and then, when the topic is no longer timely or sensitive, allowed.[43] This too, like the rest of the work of the censors' office as well as the battles that go on between editors and censorship officials, is shrouded in secrecy and, so, it is seen by journalists only through circumstantial evidence.[44]

It was this very combination of secretiveness and unpredictability, particularly on minor issues, that made censorship a force not only in the media and in journalists' ability to act but also in journalists' sense of the need for professional autonomy and their sense of living in a political world that is costly and unpredictable. Were it not so unpredictable, journalists would simply unconsciously self-censor their work to avoid topics that had never been publishable. Were it not so secretive, journalists would not need to rely on themselves and on protection from fellow professionals, or to use their editors and even the Association leaders, to whom they go periodically to have a specific decision overridden or to get some relief. After all, no one is taught what will be censored, so everyone must ultimately work on suspicion.

The other side: readers

For journalists, it is their readers who are their most important constituency. While they know they are hamstrung by institutional demands and expectations, they also know that to do their work and be read they must deal directly with and be supported by their readers. They meet them on the street and see them in stores. They must contact them to do reports and get material for articles. Their sense of themselves is measured in part by their contacts with readers.[45] In doing their work outside the confines of the traditional media, journalists go to meetings with their readers and face their questions and their comments. In the end, after all, although the political leadership demands that they be loyal and accurate presenters of the ideology, they are also expected to be read and believed, treated and seen as respected professionals.[46]

Their readers, journalists know, see the profession as a part of the political establishment. They think of journalists as being constantly involved in personal gains – solving personal problems, going abroad, getting sought-after theater and music tickets, and focusing on their own needs and names.[47] At the same time, their status is lower than that of professors, doctors, lawyers, engineers and teachers in Poland. They are also classed in public opinion surveys as intellectuals – the most respected and high status group in the society –[48] and rank higher on status lists than do journalists in West Germany and the United States.[49] Also, from the public perspective journalists at one and the same time are both the most visible part of the political establishment and a profession that is made up largely of anonymous individuals – with whom, in fact, fewer people have contact than even with miners or engineers.[50] Their most "known" and recognized colleagues are, in fact, those who work on television – the least trusted and respected of the media in Poland.[51]

For journalists, the reality of this mixed picture comes home not simply in their proclaimed status or their ranking in popularity surveys, although, for those involved, these surveys are important. It is seen in the reliance of readers on journalists as the last, most reliable, and most effective point of appeal. Even in periods of the greatest repression when there is a dramatic increase in the number of readers who do not even trust journalists enough to sign letters to them, when they write to request help or report problems, journalists remain "the only institution of intervention independent of local power intrigues." And, even as some 30 percent of one survey group thought the press did not provide enough accurate information on events in the country and 37 percent thought the situation in Poland was presented as better than it was in reality,[52] readers in the sixties reported they used Polish radio and television to air their complaints because: (1) it has influence on other institutions (51.0 percent); (2) they want publicity (30.3 percent); (3) it is interested in their affairs and problems (26.1 percent); and (4) they fear the local authorities so radio and television are the only safe sources of support (25.5 percent).[53] This respect for journalists, however mixed it is, comes to the fore in periods of crisis when prominent local and national journalists, on the one hand, are scorned by readers for their cooperation with the regime and, on the other hand, are often the only visible figures with enough name recognition and credibility to lead.

Journalists know too that Poles do not use only one journal nor do they view only one program but rather they use a variety of different Polish and foreign media. This, for journalists, is seen as a sign of the problems they have with getting and maintaining credibility and respect just as they do not take comfort in the fact that readers have a propensity to turn to the media to intervene. It was, after all, the media users among workers and intelligentsia who called out "The press lies!" in 1956, 1968, 1970 and 1980. For journalists, the comparison of foreign and Polish broadcasting, so often made by Poles, is one which makes them "objects of public ridicule because we are so much slower and more limited in our reporting of national and international events than the foreign news sources broadcast into Poland and our own rumor mill."

The position of their profession, from the journalists' perspective, has been further complicated by the fact that, while most individuals in the sixties and seventies, thought that the media "always or almost always prints the truth," there has been a general sense that not everything is published.[54] At the same time, barely half of one group surveyed in 1977 said reading the papers was important and only one-third said using radio or television was important.[55] And, more critically, certainly in the eighties (when much work was done on perceptions of the media) but also in earlier years, using the media did not necessarily involve having a positive feeling about its messages. In fact, Polish television was not only the least respected and credible source of information for the population in the eighties – although it was the most used – but use of it cast a negative pall over users' impressions of all media.[56] Even for weeklies like *Polityka*, readership support has never been complete, as yearly readership surveys have shown: "most regular readers agreed with its positions although some criticized it for having incompetent opinions."[57] In the case of press criticism which, for 35 percent of Polish media users in 1977 was the most important thing they sought from the media and also the most important part of journalism for journalists themselves, the data journalists received showed that readers' perceptions were equally negative. For most, it neither satisfied them by explaining "why" nor dealt sharply enough with problems.

All of this has resulted in journalists seeing themselves as a special group able to use their professional expertise to solve problems with which others can not deal. It also has demonstrated to them the significance of their profession and its work. And, finally, given the sense they have of being needed and respected but also subordinated and unjustly distrusted because of their political connections and political interference they can not make public, journalists sense that they must eliminate the interferences and insure that the distance between the profession and the political forces is maintained. After all, their trust with their clients is reduced by what they themselves feel is uncomfortable interference from the outside.

The bureaucratic setting and its lessons

Like the making of the media in the West, far more goes into publishing a paper or producing a program than simply the sum total of all the staff members' work. Not only is each article filtered through layers and layers of outside controls, but each journalist must function within the bureaucracy and practical realities of his office as well. A journalist's work is weighted by his publisher's expectations as well as by the evaluations of professional colleagues. His ability to do his work and the horizons of his paper are part and parcel of his editor's powers and commitment. In all, whether or not journalists are aware of all the controls under which they work and the institutional strictures on them, their work and their output are clearly affected by the bureaucratic structures and leadership under which they work. So, even though journalists have clearly tried to control their own work world, they have never been able to achieve full autonomy as individuals, nor, given the realities of journalism itself, will this ever be possible.

For the profession as a whole, whatever the medium and whatever the focus of their coverage, the bureaucratic structures in which their work is carried out differ little. Television and radio are linked to the print media. Dailies and periodicals have more in common in communist media systems than in Western systems because information and discussion and not speed are the critical factors: not only can journalists move from one medium to another or appear in a number of different formats but it is also possible to talk about the "journalism process," the actors, and the external controls, without having to make many distinctions between print and broadcasting mediums, elite and mass audience targets, and daily or periodical publications.

The outer rim: sponsors

In the battle for information and the right to publish critical material, journalists often find themselves directly or indirectly at odds with or tied to their "sponsors." Since most papers and journals are formally under a social, economic, or political group and are supposed to serve the interests of that group, journalists often focus in on a particular area of specific interest to the group that sponsors them. Their editor sits on the board of that sponsoring organization under all but the most unusual circumstances and both joins in their discussions and takes direction from them. As the staff and the editor to these things, they find themselves raising issues and problems for the group or organization that publishes them. Some even find themselves called upon to criticize or stand apart from their sponsors.

The results of these connections between journals and sponsors are varied. Most often, the officials who are most a part of journalists' lives are from the paper's sponsor, whether they be the propaganda bosses of the PUWP who, in the seventies, hung around the offices of what was then their prime organ – nightly television news – or the head of the Blind Artisan's Cooperative who, in the initial period after martial law, shared his office with prominent journalists by making them editors of the Cooperative's journal both to help them and in the well founded hope that their presence would catapult his journal to visibility.[58] In this way, explicitly or implicitly, some journalists and sponsors become entwined. Journalists also find themselves typed as representatives of their sponsors; or, they feel some unspoken personal pressure not "to rock the boat."

At other times, though, journals or programs are far from their sponsors. This sometimes occurs because the sponsor is politically weak (as the Polish Lawyers Association was in the sixties) and the journal editor politically strong (as the editor of their journal, Kazimierz Kąkol, was then). So, as in this case, the sponsors had neither real sanctions nor real rewards to use to bring the staff into line. It has also occurred when the sponsors' goal is to develop a magazine that gives them visibility, challenges the status quo, or poses an option that will increase their position in the political game. This was the case for the Polish Engineers Association's use of its liberal and critical journal, *Przegląd Techniczny* in the seventies. Their tolerance and their active funding (including increased allocations for purchasing the best paper, graphics, and staff support) continued even when *Przegląd Techniczny*'s reform policies far outstripped the interests of the Association's leadership.

Once they had established this pattern, however, there was little that could be done to stop it, short of closing down the journal and ousting the old staff. Even after martial law was declared, the old staff members who stayed on continued to push pro-reform articles against the will of less skilled but more conservative outsiders who were brought in as editors. As a result, in the Solidarity period and, to a much lesser degree, as the situation was "normalized," *Przegląd Techniczny*'s staff was one of the initial leaders in the fight for reform even as its sponsor has blocked and battled many of the reform's critical proposals.

In other cases, the interrelationships between the sponsor and the staff of the journal are so tight that many journalists' hold dual positions and see their interests as closely linked to those of the sponsor. In these cases, journalists are involved personally and professionally with the internal and external politics of their organization. And, since most of these cases involve organizations that are often under siege – Catholic organizations, the minor parties, and even Solidarity groups – the unspoken restraints and pressures of "group interest" are strong forces.

These relations all pit sponsor and professional interests against each other. This was true even in the case of union activists working on *Tygodnik Solidarność*, the union's own weekly, who were forced, resentfully, to change their articles in the interests of Solidarity and who were treated as activists of Solidarity, not as reporters for it, when they were interned. Whether because they find themselves called to account by their readers and friends as representatives of an organization for which they are not responsible or they find their professional fate determined by uncontrollable political factors, journalists' ties with any sponsor are never completely comfortable. Instead, they lead journalists to protect themselves – however unconsciously or personally they support their sponsor – by saying "I am a professional. I work for this group. Even if I share their goals, I must be judged as a professional."

The chief editor

The editor-in-chief is the main link between a journal or program and the external political world. Editors are formally appointed by the organization that sponsors a journal. So the trade unions formally appoint the union paper's editor, the League of Women formally appoints the editor of its journal, the Catholic Church and the Club of Catholic Intellectuals formally appoint the editors of their respective journals, the parties each formally appoint the editor of their papers, and publishing houses formally appoint the editors of other journals, just as the Committee for Polish Radio and Television formally appoints the directors of various television and radio shows. Only editors of socio-political weeklies are ostensibly appointed with no direct sponsor. Their positions, though, come with high level PUWP approval.[59]

All editors' appointments though are subject to direction and pressure from the PUWP. Any group can be blocked by the Party if it tries to appoint critical and controversial editors. When this happens, sponsoring organizations are forced to either leave a position unfilled or take an appointee selected by the Party. So, there are stories of controversial editors who have had to fight with PUWP officials for their appointments on a whole list of publications. This list includes many prominent journalists from the sixties and seventies who objected to martial law and moved on to the Catholic Intellectual Club's monthly, and other specialized journals. In other cases, unqualified editors were appointed to head the long unfilled chief editors' position on such journals as the Association of Engineers' journal, *Przegląd Techniczny* (Technical Outlook). The ability of the PUWP directly to intervene and block the appointment of editors who are unacceptable to them or force the appointment of "their men" is augmented by the fact that editors are also servants of the major publishing house, RSW Prasa, which, in addition to publishing more periodicals than any other, controls the production and distribution of all journals published legally in Poland.[60] Contentious editors can thus be countered, even if their appointments have been agreed to by the Party, by RSW Prasa decisions to limit access by their journals to printing presses, paper, funds for reporters' expenses, or adequate distribution channels. In this trap, editors are then called to account for the fact of their journal not being self-supporting when their sales potential and costs are actually determined by what RSW Prasa sees fit to allow them.

These processes of appointment and budgetary control insure that most editors are tolerable to the political leaders and acutely conscious of the rules of the game for them. This affects their relations with staff journalists. So, even though most editors compensate for their lack of professional experience by joining the SDP and stressing their prior journalistic work experience, they are seen by their staffs as being politicians and administrators rather than journalists. This is not unrealistic. After all, it is the editor's job to be the link between his paper and the outside. Only a few editors actually write for their journals; most others edit only in terms of what is politically tolerable and what is simply too risky.

The duties of an editor-in-chief tend ultimately to involve responsibility for internal supervision, external administration and organization, and the coordination of staff.[61] The focus of most editors' supervision has tended to be on departments of prime concern to the PUWP: "culture, economics, party, local, foreign, agriculture, education and science, and ties with the readers,'' departments that actually control the political direction and image of the paper.[62] Their direct supervision of at least some departments is also used by editors to make contact and get loyalty from their workers as they ''direct new staff members, evaluate subordinates, aid staff members with problems, and activate the staff. Through this low-level contact, it is possible to deter any staff actions against an editor.''[63] The editor's more administrative functions usually include the ultimate responsibility for hiring and firing of employees, distributing bonuses, enforcing discipline, and providing or allocating resources for travel and special projects.[64] The underlying assumption in manuals on editor–staff relations is that it is ''the atmosphere, the initiative of journalists, their desire to work, and their production that depend on the relations of the editor-in-chief to the staff.''[65]

Even as he manages his staff, it is the editor who has constant contact with Party and state elites on both formal and informal levels. He is expected to make himself visible and cultivate friendships with industrial managers, government officials, Party leaders, and other local ''notables.'' Formally, he is a member of the executive board of his sponsoring organization and attends the meetings of the board. In this role, he gathers information about the sponsor's concerns and policies and also barters information about journalists' contacts and ''finds.'' Some of the information he hears through these meetings becomes his currency to share with his staff just as the personal power he garners from the information he provides to the executive board members allows him to advocate for his journalists. This linking role is played even by the established editors of socio-political weeklies who, by and large, identify themselves as ''professional journalists active in politics.'' Their relations with their staffs have been much closer than those of most other editors no matter what their political roles. But, even these self-styled journalist–editors active in ''journalism work'' are evaluated on the basis of their political ties and power. Quality editorial leadership is measured, then, by editors' ability to protect and advocate for their journalists and journal.

Chief editors also appear before citizens' groups as representatives of their organization's leadership and of the paper or program they edit. Often they are asked to discuss issues or answer questions at Primary Party Organization meetings in various firms and factories or in meetings or gatherings of local citizens. They also meet with the administrators of their publishing house on administrative matters. In the Gierek period, many of these editors were likely to be invited to press conferences with Gierek and other high officials (or else they were able to "honor" a staff member by delegating him to attend). They were also summoned to meetings with the censors to hear of new prohibitions and be instructed on the coverage of forthcoming events or warned about their journal's sins. And, in some cases, editors were included in Central Committee sessions. They were usually then expected to disseminate what they had heard or were told to their journalists.

Worker attacks on the mass media in the eighties triggered the removal of editors who had been political appointees and who had made their journals conform to an unpopular political line. These editors were attacked from the inside and outside for their failure to advance the interests of their journal and to take risks in what they published. Those who replaced them were, on the whole, no less politically connected and attuned. At the same time, they were usually also committed and experienced journalists. For, it was still inherent in their work, even in these heady periods of political freedoms, that they perform the same administrative functions and serve as links and advocates in the same way their predecessors had. As Solidarity gained power, journalists followed the model of other professionals in demanding that they be allowed to select their own editors. This actually occurred in only a few journals. But, where it did, the outcome reflected journalists' realism about the need to have a good representative to the outside. Established journalists with political allies were elected as editors by even the most "liberated" staffs.

Ironically, the tensions between editor and staff were no less on Solidarity's weekly, *Tygodnik Solidarność*. Tadeusz Mazowiecki took on the project of staffing and running Solidarity's first legal newspaper while he was serving as Lech Wałęsa's personal advisor. He continued to try to combine these roles throughout the life of the paper. Because of his role as Wałęsa's advisor, he struggled to insure that the journalists and intellectual and worker activists who filled his staff did not use the paper to advocate any special interests. Instead, as Wałęsa directed, Mazowiecki used his powers as editor-in-chief to insure that *Tygodnik Solidarność* served the goals Wałęsa set out by limiting itself to providing a public record of union activities and serving as a forum for reporting key topical subjects not related to Solidarity itself.

With the advent of martial law and the regime's attempt to reclaim the media by purging it and imposing, whenever necessary, new and reliable media managers, the old patterns of the editor torn between his institutional "bosses" and his staff were magnified. However, editors became much more circumspect about discussing the orders they were given and their personal connections with their staffs. Journalists' cynical perceptions of their editors as nothing more than "just hacks" were also magnified. Furthermore, established journalists felt threatened by the imposition of new and often suspect editors. So, they withdrew into a group on their own, forcing these editors to function more than ever as outsiders able to rule their staffs and mold their journals only by rejecting articles, commissioning costly but safe articles from their friends outside the staff, or firing journalists. These antics only further reduced the editors' ability to lead and to determine what they actually produced.

The extent to which journalists are an editor's prime concern depends on his personal interests and the nature of his staff as well as on the traditions and role of the journal.[66] The more an editor knows and has worked in journalism, the more he is involved with and treated as a fellow professional by his staff journalists. And, the smaller and more exclusive his staff, the more an editor tends to be drawn in. His willingness to discuss his arguments with the censors and other officials or to reveal confidential conversations to his staff depends on his feeling of strength *vis-à-vis* both his staff and the political authorities with whom he must deal officially and personally.

In all of this, he is caught in a vice. He needs to give his staff information about how the political wind is blowing, yet, to get some respect from them, he must keep them from seeing his weakness and inability to protect their stories from censorship. Therefore, even long-term professionals assume that editors often lie to journalists about why their articles do not run. So, rather than admit the censor's power, editors blame journalists' incompetence. This, they hope, will cover their powerlessness. If they look strong, they reason, professional journalists will trust them enough to share information that might be unpublishable but is the inside "dope" their political bosses will find useful.

Editors who were both personally and politically strong, on the other hand, most often were reported by journalists to have been open with information and to have made it clear to their staff when an article or a program was criticized or censored. This has tended to create a sense of the editor and his staff as skilled, independent thinking professionals embattled against the outside authorities. These patterns of honesty versus glossing over problems have held in times of control and of liberation since, no matter what the political realities; an editor remains the link with the outside who must guard the staff, and his own position with both the professionals he tries to direct and the outside sponsors and publishers he has to serve. All this he must do through his connections and his personal power.

Editorial board

Editorial boards vary in size and in character. Among them these basic patterns exist: communal decision-making; fragmented decision-making by each actor almost independently; and a hierarchical system. On a few small journals, the entire staff is the editorial board. As a group, they meet to plan and discuss upcoming issues of the paper. This puts most decisions and problems in the hands of journalists and those assigned to various administrative tasks. Problems and reactions raised by earlier articles are argued through by the whole group. What the paper might or might not do is hashed out. Out of these meetings often comes the sense of a common political orientation that cements the staff on socio-political weeklies like *Tygodnik Powszechny* and *Polityka*. On *Polityka*, in the sixties and seventies, with its staff of twenty-seven and Mieczysław Rakowski, a prominent political actor committed to journalism, as editor, staff meetings, *qua* the editorial board, took on even more significance. Individuals from the political or economic elite and other experts were summoned from time to time by the staff to discuss subjects and policies about which they wanted to know more. These discussions were either published or used by the staff and speakers to make their positions clear and explore leadership positions. In these situations, Rakowski, and others like him, functioned not as directors but as one among equals.[67] These small journals and some larger journals where the chief editor is well established and at least close to leading staff members, function as though the professional staff and the editors' work and fates are closely intertwined. Both know that how a journal presents issues can make or break an editor's position as well as their journal's image. They benefit from an editor's strong political position since he often uses it for the journal's benefit. But, there is a tradeoff: for him to keep his strong position as a political force, the chief editor must have enough staff support to get information from journalists about what they see around them and to be able to generate the articles he needs to protect his political position. At particularly sensitive times, journalists may even have to restrain themselves from writing critically so as not to sabotage their editor's political position. This meant, for instance, that journalists on *Polityka* felt, in the late seventies and the early eighties, that they had to choose between compromising Rakowski's political position and restraining themselves in the hope that he would, ultimately, be strong enough to push their policies in the Central Committee and protect them and their professional autonomy. This restraint and sacrifice, however, ultimately fragmented and frustrated the staff since it left them outdistanced and questioned by other journalists who used the liberty of the Solidarity period to explode forth with criticism.[68]

Direction has been much less communal on staffs in the rest of the media. Staff members work either on their own or, depending on the chief editor's style, under his strict guidance. They seldom gather together as a decision-making body. On some, the editor runs a "tight ship" and gives out very clear directions. On others, like *Kultura*, a weekly published in the sixties and seventies, the chief editor has been so involved in his own political activities that he either disregarded the paper or he treated it as an extension of his politicking. Ironically, under these circumstances, journalists and department editors often have been free to make their own decisions about all but politically key articles and programs. So, in spite of the prominence of its chief editor, *Kultura* staff members often used his office only to get paid or to drop off an article. Department editors made their own department themes irrespective of the editor's formal plan and the chief editor was left to simply skim over each finished edition before it was sent to the censors. Or, if these editors wanted to present a political line or a policy, they simply wrote their own articles or commissioned outsiders to write what they wanted.

On most large and medium-sized journals, the editorial board (*kollegium*) has served as a tie between the chief editor and individual journalists. Board members participate with the editor in making long and short-range proposals. They also filter editorial instructions and confidential materials and information back to the staff, including the classified press agency bulletins normally available only to them. Meetings of the managing editor, assistant editors, and department editors are usually held after each edition comes out, be it daily or weekly. There, they evaluate the previous edition and plan the next. Although the editor-in-chief is technically responsible, he normally follows the board's advice since he cannot monitor everything and also handle outside contacts. He, therefore, relies on his assistants to alert him to issues and articles that are potential problems.

On many staffs, the potential for cohesion even of the editorial board has been limited. Even the full editorial board becomes a cumbersome structure so coordination is more random or more formally managed.

On *Życie Warszawy*, for instance, the week's articles typically have been planned by the editorial board on Monday. The managing editor then is responsible for fulfilling that week's plan; he approves articles as they are turned in; and, if there is time, also has them approved by the assistant editor responsible for that subject. If there is no time, an article is read by an assistant editor only after it has been dummied up, printed, and submitted to the censor. For the 20 percent of the paper covering imperative but unplanned local and national events, approval is more haphazard.

> If the article is submitted by the managing editor by one p.m., it can be approved by the daily editorial board meeting. But, there are also times when the author takes an article directly to the managing editor or, even late at night, to the wire service processor who works the night shift. He then tries to contact the department editor, but if he can't find him, he must make the decision on his own.[69]

For these huge staffs, general meetings are infrequent. Journalists deal with their department editor or the managing editor, who reports the chief editor's views to them second hand.[70] The world, for these journalists, centers around colleagues working on the same beats. Direction comes from their experiences and contacts with fellow staff members and with their news sources. The editor-in-chief fades from their professional world. As a result, even when the central Party daily, *Trybuna Ludu*, was a major propaganda tool under Gierek, journalists on the staff felt cut off. In one department, journalists even reported that, in the seventies, they tried to figure out what Party policy might be, but, since they got no explicit directions, they simply worked on their own because no one ever told them what the paper's line was. Their sources, like those of other journalists, had to be others in the profession and their personal contacts. As a result of this pattern of direction, even those on the chief party organ were more involved with their profession than with the political world they were supposed to serve.

The deputy editor-in-chief on all but major political organs, such as *Trybuna Ludu* where there are a number of deputy editors all of whom are political appointees, is a professional journalist. He normally has moved up from managing editor to be deputy editor on "his" journal. This is not, for journalists, a professional honor. But, deputy editors with journalistic backgrounds still are seen by their staff of journalists as comrades who represent the last level of professional control.

While the assistant editor or editors fill in all the spaces left by the editor-in-chief, it is the managing editor (*sekretariat*) who does the daily balancing and direction. To journalists, this is the most difficult job on a paper, it is an administrative post requiring extensive journalistic training and experience but also involving talents in management and political negotiation. The managing editor is the "gatekeeper" for information that goes to press. He lays out the paper, corrects and approves copy, selects what will be used for each edition, coordinates with the publishing house, and manages the paper's finances.[71] He is the one who accepts or rejects journalists' work and thereby regulates their earnings.[72]

Through his role in the production of the journal, the managing editor is acutely aware of patterns of censorship, even though he is usually not the one to argue for the publication of articles blocked by the censor. That responsibility normally falls to the editor-in-chief and his assistants since they have the external authority to give themselves some leverage. If he can, the managing editor tries to catch problems before they happen; he refers anything he suspects is sensitive to the editor for approval. If an article slips through only to be fingered later by the censors, he is held responsible for it and he is the one who must do the scrambling to fill all the gaps left by what is censored. Managing editors thus become strict censors, particularly if the editor is not interested in what appears or willing to fight for publications. To staff journalists, however, the managing editor usually explains his decision to remove an article in terms of its quality and shortages of space, not political pressures. All journalists can then do, under normal circumstances, is suspect that they were censored. Only on socio-political weeklies with powerful and committed editors or independent Catholic journals, are managing editors and chief editors consciously willing to let things slip. In these cases, they know their editors will fight to keep articles. Therefore, as the censors' statistics on the number of articles questioned on socio-political weeklies and Catholic weeklies show, there is less prior censorship by the editors and the censors have more to question.

The changes in 1980–81 did not fundamentally alter any of these patterns. True, there was a shift from carefully planned and orchestrated articles to a heavy emphasis on quick and comprehensive news coverage.[73] But, the desire of journalists to publish critical articles made their editors' jobs all the more difficult as they were caught between shifting censors' regulations and impatient and hardly subservient journalists.

The imposition of martial law did not change these structures. What it did was force a major shift in personnel. In the initial weeks and months of martial law, staffing of editorial positions was done or overseen by military personnel. Later, even those journals allowed to reopen and able to get enough politically tolerable and willing staff to function had to work with a truncated editorial staff. Editors served more as writers than they normally had and large sections were dependent on outside contributors, news agency reports, or reprints. This meant that, initially, little reporting on real events and problems was done. Much of what there was to publish was canned news. Or else editors found themselves faced with a staff that submitted articles that were barely tolerable so they had to make do with these articles or spend extra money to buy articles from outside contributors.

As the retrenchment continued, more and more journals filled their staff positions with new recruits to the profession. Articles written by staff members reappeared. But, deliberate editorial planning was hampered largely by usually undeclared but clearly visible divisions between editors, who served at the behest of the martial law authorities, and their staffs, who were anxious to reestablish professional credibility through critical articles. The result of the conflict was a draw. Staff journalists needed to publish to survive financially. Editors were often political appointees shifting from post to post who did not remain on one journal long enough to establish control or earn the respect of professional journalists. So, editors, when they had the connections to do so, turned to a stable of freelances. This cut into journalists' salaries by making it difficult for them to print their quota, based as it was on a piecework pay scale.

Professional staff

The typical general circulation journal has a staff of about fifty fulltime journalists. This varies, though, from over a hundred journalists on the Party's national daily, *Trybuna Ludu*, to less than twenty-five fulltime staff on socio-political weeklies and two or three on the small, specialized publications of various special interest groups.[74] Some of these tiny staffs have been marginal enough to be havens for journalists blacklisted in the seventies and those blacklisted after martial law. Beyond full-time staff, most journals have a well-established coterie of freelances and contributors. Also underpinning professional journalists' work is a group of administrators whose jobs range from secretarial assistance to organizing press actions and managing often quite large departments for contact with readers and intervention in the various problems that readers bring to the press.[75]

Whatever the staff arrangements, journalists are the working professionals in the Polish press. They normally do not come to their work as political appointees. Many who came in the sixties began as freelances who proved their professional skill by trial and error in order to get what few full-time positions became available. Others who came into the profession in the seventies were able to enter as full-time workers after having served as freelances while they were in the school of journalism program or were working in other professions.[76] Established journalists, although they are formally channeled through the personnel offices of publishing houses, move through personal contacts. But, reinforcing staff cohesion and identity, particularly on small and medium sized staffs, has been the inability of most journalists to move from one city to another or to find work in other journals. Long staff tenure has, thus, been the norm in Poland or it was until martial law. Finally, less established journalists are hired by interview and through presenting portfolios of their work. Provincial journalists still tend to be recruited through individual contacts: so few graduates of journalistic programs are willing to move to the provinces that prior training in journalism is not required. Young applicants simply apply to the editor for a job and are approved by the personnel office of the publishing house.[77]

On Communist Party dailies and in the broadcast media, successful members of staff are encouraged to join the Party after two or more years of work. However, even when Party membership increased overall, the Party was unable to force that same level of growth in the ranks of working journalists. In fact, the failure of the Party in the Solidarity and martial law period to keep its members was magnified among working journalists. Cases of individuals fired from their jobs for political errors being rehired, often in more prestigious positions, in another region or after the intervention of the editor, give further evidence of the dominance of the editorial board and professional norms rather than political requirements in staffing decisions.

Cohesion and a sense of community among professional journalists were particularly striking on visits to editorial offices done for this research. By the end of the seventies, on small and medium-sized staffs, most journalists had worked on one journal for their entire careers. They were on a "first name" basis with other professional journalists ranking above and below them and knew intimate personal details about the lives of their colleagues. Most seemed to feel free to arrange spontaneous social gatherings with the other journalists with whom they worked. Journalists appeared comfortable about talking critically in front of their colleagues. This they did in the same tone and same vein as when they talked privately. And, journalists often anticipated their colleagues' comments and criticisms. Furthermore, journalists in their small units were known to their chief editors as people and as professionals.

On large journals, even between established staff members and their editors, this level of familiarity seemed absent. Journalists often talked about whether they should move or work part-time elsewhere. Few actually moved, however. For those outside their immediate office space or department, formal contacts were the norm, particularly with older and younger colleagues or those from other departments. They were more inclined to know about specialists in their field than about members of the staff working in other departments of their own paper. They were more likely to limit their discussions to private conversations with trusted friends. So, they were less likely to make contacts or spread news among fellow professionals on their own journal. In fact, social events had to be formally organized and advertised by an appointed committee since there were few spontaneous contacts. Finally, chief editors were more aware of staff statistics than they were of individual journalists. Their personal ties were usually only with department editors. Even the managing editor ran a much more formal office than his peers on smaller papers: journalists were not seen chatting with him. His office was much more isolated. On these staffs, instead, there appeared to be a heavy reliance on formal, organized meetings.

On major socio-political weeklies, the staff ethos has been strengthened by long histories of cooperation. For instance, many of the old time professionals had been on *Po Prostu* and *Sztandar Młodych* in 1956 and then moved into positions on various leading journals.[78] The staff ethos was strong enough to insure that, when individuals were blacklisted, there was often a conspiracy of journalists on a staff to see that they were paid to write and publish under assumed names until the blacklisting ended.[79] This practice continued even when the profession split over martial law. Working colleagues brought blacklisted friends whom they respected as professionals into their journals or funneled blacklisted journalists' work under their own names so they could earn some money.

For those who remained in the press after martial law, staff connections were a buffer against a hostile outside world. Journalists gathered with those who also elected to remain in the profession. Some, where they could, served as links and screens for journalists who had been completely blacklisted. Their hope was to get some legitimacy from these alignments even though they were considered collaborators by many former colleagues and readers.

In addition to this basic staff of journalists with full-time, tenured positions, each journal has a group of individuals who work part-time or who submit articles and are paid directly for their publication.[80] This is intended to facilitate the publication of articles by non-journalists; but, in effect, it allows editors to circumvent the blacklisting of journalists. It also allows, in normal times, more discussion and coverage than small staffs of journalists can provide. When the editor and his staff members are at odds, it allows editors to limit the control held by established staff members. Its use, though, is limited by the financial burden it places on a journal since full-time journalists must be paid their base salaries even if others write stories on a freelance basis.[81]

The typical staff is divided into departments based on themes (economics, culture, politics) and divisions of local and regional news, national, and international news reporting. In addition, each journal has divisions which process and investigate readers' letters, and departments to handle Polish Press Agency articles.[82] On a few journals, the staff is divided, instead, according to specializations in writing styles and target readership groups.[83] Additional departments focusing on women and youth groups, who are often alienated and seen as not interested in the normal fare, have also become common.[84] Large journals also employ staff columnists or news analysts (*publicists*) who work independently of the four to six-man departments.[85] These posts were added in the seventies to provide advancement for skilled senior writers and political propagandizers who did not move into administration. They have been used to honor established journalists and encourage journalists to write advocacy and criticism.

In spite of the fact that these departments are made up of specialists with assigned areas of responsibility, journalists do not think it is necessary simply to write about daily events on their "beats." Most feel this reporting is a job for novice journalists: In 50 percent of the editorial offices studied, the provision of information is an obligation for the thematic departments only when the information is "broad," illustrative of a general "problem," or "regional" (in cases where the local department handles city information and the regional departments handle local level information).[86] For established professionals reporting current news was seen as "wasting a lot of time and not providing too much without allowing journalists to properly use their creativity."[87] This attitude changed only slightly when local events became heated national battles under Solidarity. Even then, the reporting journalists wanted to do was investigative, not simply descriptive.

For all but a few central journals with funding for international correspondents, the news agency is the only permanent source of national and international news. It makes decisions about what news should be highlighted, what treated tangentially, and what limited to confidential backgrounding for top journalists. Once the agency stories are written, daily news bulletins are published (or sent out by telex) in various categories depending on their subject, target audience, and assigned level of secrecy.[88] Newspapers almost always can select from the non-secret bulletins whatever international and national news they want to publish. Infrequently, agency stories are rewritten to fit the journal's audience. News agencies also provide articles on specialized or national subjects to provincial journals without the resources to assign journalists to these articles. All of this makes it clear to journalists that, at any level, news is not their business and that, as professionals, they are divorced from reporting actual events and facts – divorced in reality and in responsibility.

This news agency system was replicated by Solidarity and, again, by the opposition under martial law. A number of Solidarity news agencies sprang up to provide local Solidarity papers and foreign correspondents with international and national news and Solidarity statements. In addition, many expanded to challenge establishment news agencies reporting on national and international news. These operations, like their establishment equivalents, though, were not the work of visible professionals. They did what the profession of journalism does not consider skilled professional work. They recorded the facts or transferred the government or Solidarity position.[89]

The journalism process

The charges given journalists by the ideology, the political leadership, and their readers, as well as journalists' own sense of their professional responsibility and the realities of their work with readers and officials, are to do far more than simply report events as they happen. They are to analyze, criticize and make news understandable. Journalists, as a result of these roles and the requirements of their work, have come to see themselves as apart from and above the rest of the society. To work, they need the respect of information sources and the freedom to criticize with impunity. This they do not often get; yet, they are on the front lines seeing and having to explain the failings of policies. And, as rapidly, they have learned the power of their words. Whether these words are knit into press criticisms, discussion articles, proposals for actions sponsored by the media or simply reports of events or interventions, journalists know that, if they do not change things, they can at least get problems acknowledged or get a response from readers, their journalist colleagues, and their targets among policy-makers and administrators. The lesson for them is that they are critical to the society, doing professional work that may be uncomfortably and unjustly interfered with, but that is so special that only they should control it. Their sense of distance and of isolation is further created by the many layers of the bureaucratic structure in which they work.

Journalism in Poland and in the rest of the communist world is seldom, if ever, merely a product of the flow of events and the practical demands of staffing, transportation, and production deadlines. Instead, since news is not the paramount focus of journalistic writing and reporting, much of what appears in the press, radio, and television is planned in advance or is a product of the ebb and flow of the concerns of both the leaders and, at times, the larger population. Even in the Solidarity period when events could be reported as they occurred and journalists were caught up in the drama of previously unimaginable changes and crises, this sense of the need for a planned press remained for both old and new journalists. Even on *Tygodnik Solidarność* events were not simply reported. Their coverage was planned to handle themes that the editor, Tadeusz Mazowiecki, and his co-workers felt should be covered as a result of formal and informal consultations with Wałęsa and other Solidarity leaders. So, while plans were constantly submerged by events and the barrage of explosive and long-taboo topics, the tradition of long-term commitments and planned coverage remained.

Normally, a plan of broad themes is drawn up by each editorial board for a full year. It is then discussed, revised, and approved by the Party's press bosses and whatever group actually sponsors the paper, magazine or program, be it the Radio and Television Committee or a publishing house, a union or social organization, or a ministry or party. Campaigns for activities to involve readers are scheduled. Broad themes and issues to be raised are listed and apportioned in meetings of journalists and editors.[90] More specific plans are drawn up for six months and then broken down for each quarter of the year. These plans outline specific topics to be covered and which department or departments will handle then and when. Based on these plans and their own discussions, journalists make their own long-term commitments to individual topics.

This planning process minimizes the expectation that established journalists under normal circumstances will remain "on top of things" and gear their reporting to events except, perhaps, in international news.[91] Events, for journalists, open doors or close doors for analysis or criticism. They may trigger re-planning when they permit or require new avenues for discussion. But, the expectation of journalists and editors alike is that a "good" journalist will be able to chart the flow of events before they happen and be able to anticipate and explain them rather than be directed by them.

Still, while journalists work very hard to fulfill their plans, they are not unaware of the world around them. In 1976, most cited "readers' pressure" as a source of their ideas for both long-term plans and also their more immediate coverage.[92] For leading and politically prominent journalists, far more ideas come from contact with readers than from elite requests or direction. At the same time, most journalists interviewed said their own ideas and editors' suggestions were the primary sources of their articles.

When story ideas come from outside, journalists maintain some distance. They seldom admit to being told or requested to write a story or cover a topic. Nor do they admit to being conscious of being watched. Readers' input seeps in through their personal contacts with regular sources, "on-the-street" observation, letters from readers in need of help, and speeches journalists give to various groups. Elite pressures and requests are normally given and received in the same way. Journalists go to meetings and meet personally with administrators and politicians as friends, colleagues, or fellow activists. They also keep track of bulletins, statements of the elite, and other journalists' reports of the "doings" within the elite. In all of these encounters, whatever they are asked to do or ask of readers or political actors, journalists have the sense that they make their own evaluations and do not simply follow directions. They made clear, in interviews, that ethical journalists do not parrot politicians' words – only hacks writing with pseudonyms do. They also clearly distinguished between press criticism that was "real," based on journalists' ideas, and that which was "artificial," sought and manipulated by some leader for his own interests.

Journalists also select and process information and demands as specialists.[93] Even if criticism and discussion of issues they write about are embargoed by the censors, journalists keep up with what is going on through attendance at press conferences, contacts with leading individuals and practitioners, the use of press offices in institutions and ministries, and their own observations and research. In addition, as they become known experts on a subject, sources seek them out to tell them what is going on behind the scenes or to ask their advice.

Journalists also create their own information sources; they keep their own private libraries and their own coteries of experts who have become personal friends. In the SDP, clubs for specialists hold discussions and invite experts and policy-makers to meetings to provide background information and be grilled about policies that concern journalists.[94] There is a continuous dialogue going on among journalist colleagues about gossip and events in any given area.[95]

The lack of pressure for a "scoop" and the restrictions on information make working with one's colleagues critical and fights for a "scoop" far less important than they are in the West. Journalists perceive writing style and skill as far more important as the source of their popularity and power than getting an exclusive story.[96] For journalists, the fact that others have reported on the same story is a demonstration that it is safe to write about. What is important is how they can best present the idea: be it in a narrative style, an essay, an interview, a straight presentation of information, or an argumentative analysis. Most often, this decision about how to say things is made not only on the basis of what will give an article power and popularity but also what will best camouflage its intent and allow it to pass through censorship and still be understood by readers.

The actual writing of an article depends on the individual. All journalists seek some solitude. This draws them away from their newsroom and the bustle of discussions with the fellow members of staff and other members of the intelligentsia. After all, writing schedules are often far more erratic than normal professional work schedules. Those who rank high do long analyses and critical articles and most are well enough off to have room to work at home. As a result, many prominent journalists virtually never work in their offices. They go into their offices basically to socialize and trade gossip with colleagues. Lower level journalists (those on regional papers and in middle and low ranks on national staffs) do not spend long periods of time working on a single article, do not have the space to work at home, and are without the connections and resources to research for articles on their own. They work in crowded offices, producing more articles in less time. They engage in constant discussion about all they do and write. As a result, they receive more guidance from their editors and senior journalists, often without being really aware of how much direction they are receiving.

In the process of initiating and writing an article, most journalists do check informally with their editors about whether it is a publishable topic and approach. To do this, they cultivate their department and managing editors. Those who can also attempt to increase their latitude by developing their own style and reputation so that, if their writings disappear, it would raise questions and create a scandal.

Finally, once an article is written, journalists give it to their managing editor or, if they work on larger staffs or are at the bottom of the ladder, to their department editor. Those who are invited often willingly participate in the initial editing discussions. Then, they wait to see if what they have written will be published. Those who do not have close ties to their editors often do not know, if an article is not published, whether it fell victim to space limitations or to the censor's pen. Those journalists who are well connected with their editors and Party insiders are much more aware of the fate of what they write. They are, therefore, far more concerned and sensitive to controls on their work than their less daring and less well connected colleagues. They, ironically, are the ones who are most aware of the limits, even as they have the most power to push those limits. Ultimately, though, knowing why an article did not appear makes one far more powerful professionally because it is a signal of what journalists can and should do next. Even if an article appears, the journalist is not finished. Many journalists anticipate, with dread or hope, a response from their readers. These come in angry calls to the journalist or his editor or they come in policy changes or readers' praise. Other journalists are targets of political leaders' venom either privately or publicly for what they have written. And, at the same time, journalists expect and receive responses from their readers informally and in formal conferences to which they are invited. All of this, then, sets the stage both for journalists' attitudes toward their professional problems and responsibilities and their next writing project.

In effect, journalists have done their work and performed their roles within a hierarchy that molds their options and their results. The reality of the work world and its strictures is clearly a major force in journalists' lives. It, more than any other force, sets them apart from both their political alliances and the rest of the society. They are ideologically charged with challenging and criticizing those around them. Their work is either openly blocked by administrators or visibly but indirectly limited by the Party and state bureaucracies on the leadership's unpublished orders. At times, on the other hand, these leaders and their personal connections in the bureaucracy can "free up" information or overrule censors' regulations. As a result, journalists come to see politics not as a system but as a game they play and to see Party leaders as more useful if no more effective than administrators.

The conflicting demands and realities of journalists' work world, like those of their educational experience, professionalize their sense of themselves and their role much as do the more consistent realities in the lives of Western professions and professionals. Journalists are expected to be critical enough to be read but not critical enough to cross the constantly shifting boundaries of the permissible, an impossible task for all but the least active. They are expected to respect the very administrative and political norms and actors that they know complicate their work and their earning potential. They are given veiled guidance but little sense that they can really protect their prerogatives. Finally, they are specialists in their fields, knowledgeable and involved, even though, on questions of what and how their specialties should be presented, nonspecialist censors and politicians have the deciding voice. All of these factors both determine their values and concerns and also their drive and ability to do what they regard as a part of their professional work – their investment in policy decisions.

These countervailing pressures and restrictions, coupled with the relative permanency of most staffs, have made the staff hierarchy of individual news organs the prime focus in professionals' lives. It is a world that, internally, professionals control and one that is intentionally designed to exclude outsiders even as it is controlled by the outside. At the same time, it is a world and a work experience that creates a professional community and sets that community apart from and, in journalists' minds, above the rest of the society and the very hierarchy in which journalists – by virtue of the technical requirements of producing and funding a media – must work. It is furthermore, one that, on the whole, supports individual professional work. And, it is one which acts as a buffer between politics and professionalism.

4 Professional associations and professional politics

The professional life and world of Polish journalists does not end as they leave their offices and finish their day's work. Nor are their editors and the leading journalists on their staff their only protectors, mentors, and role models. Like Western professionals, Polish journalists' lives are embedded in a web of informal and formal organizations, gatherings, and information exchanges.[1] Their relations with the world outside their profession are brokered not only through their editors and their personal connections but also through their informal and formal professional organization and the example and power of their own professional elite. Finally, their professional training and work experience as well as the demands and the realities imposed on them by their readers and the political elite are not their only basis for the development of group history, myths, and heroes. The professional community and the profession's formal association serves as a forum for the creation and maintenance of this history and these group myths and heroes – even when there is clear political pressure against them.

Ironically, many working journalists in the sixties and seventies publicly scoffed at the idea of the association being any more than a building, clubs of journalists working on the same topics, and services ranging from medical care to a good restaurant with subsidized meals. But, when the Solidarity movement forced journalists to take stock and clean house, it was their organization, the Association of Polish Journalists (the SDP), that they turned to immediately.[2] Most of the old SDP leadership then left of its own accord as the storm in the profession brewed.[3] Old, well-known professionals – some of whom had been blacklisted under Gierek – seized control of the association but changed none of it. In fact, even after an Extraordinary Congress had been held and almost went on record condemning the past SDP officials, the new executives asked a former official to stay on since he knew the ropes.[4] Then, as this new leadership swept into more and more political battles, it tried to differentiate its professional role from the personal political activities of its leaders and members.[5] As the press came to be something written and printed by virtually everyone in the society, journalists also made it clear that there was a line: they were professionals and others had to earn their credentials to enter their profession.[6] And, as professionals, the members and leaders of the SDP focused on the traditional problems of the profession from salaries to censorship even as the political euphoria and battles of Solidarity's fifteen months competed for their attention.[7]

However, the litmus test for the role of the association came with the declaration of martial law and the explicit suspension of the SDP as well as the attempts to intern all of its leaders – even those personally connected with former journalists in Jaruzelski's government.[8] When martial law was declared and the telephone lines were cut, journalists went from house to house to see who had been interned and who needed help. They rushed to the SDP building to see who controlled it, and those involved in the leadership tried to save their archives. They collected news of each other's fate and the events going on around them by gathering at the church identified as the "writers' church." In doing this, many formed new and tighter bonds of friendship. They sought as well to make sure professional journalists responded as a group. A code of ethics, complete with procedures for enforcement, was drawn up to respond to the contingencies of martial law.[9] Relief aid for those out of work or in difficult straits was collected.[10] Those few who got out of Poland took their stories to international journalists' organizations in a search for help and support. SDP leaders who had had personal ties to political leaders like Rakowski, *Polityka*'s former chief editor and the deputy Prime Minister under martial law and other lesser figures in the political sphere, pushed constantly for the association to be reinstated and some were even ready to select a new leadership and drop the SDP's most controversial leaders.[11]

More significant even than the formation of such a temporary underground association mirroring, as much as possible, old organizational patterns, however, was the response of both the politicians and professionals to the old association. The SDP had been such a strong, independent force, particularly, but not only, in the Solidarity period that its name alone was synonymous with independence. Its leaders in 1980–81 – whether or not they were in official positions – were the most respected professionals from the past decade. All of this made the entire postwar journalists' association a threat to the government during martial law, and to the acceptance they sought. So, the SDP was disbanded. In a sleight of hand, a gathering of mostly journalists who either supported the new regime or thought the SDP had become too political met as soon as the disbanding was announced to form another association, the Association of Journalists of the Polish Peoples' Republic (SDPRL).[12] In its structure and its proclaimed goals, the SDPRL was no different than the SDP was in the years before its Solidarity era transformation. Although none of the founders of the SDPRL were professional stars, a large number, in fact, had been in the second tier of the SDP leadership in 1980–81.[13]

However, for journalists, the disbanding of "their" organization was a direct assault on the profession. They could not but respond to it. No amount of cajoling or promises of economic benefits, including access to the retirement funds collected over years from SDP members and then made available only to members of the SDPRL, could stop a large-scale boycott of the new association. Simultaneously, the old SDP leadership continued as an informal professional community claiming to be the rightful leaders. This self-proclaimed leadership did studies of the media and of the recent history of the profession and published them underground or circulated them privately. They created an award for outstanding journalism in the establishment or underground press. They have continued to speak to Western colleagues about the repression of the media and to get food and clothing for journalists in need. They hold informal group meetings; exert quiet pressure on those who would return to the establishment media or join the new SDPRL; and, have even sought meetings with political leaders as well as foreign representatives to argue their case and oppose the restrictions imposed on their association and the press.

The story of both the SDP and SDPRL in this period of liberalization and repression is a part of the complex story of the profession itself told in chapter 6. But, because the structure, goals and most of the actions of the SDP and the SDPRL are similar, both associations will, where appropriate in this chapter, be treated together as one example of the life of professional organizations.

As Western students of communist systems have assumed, professional associations, including the journalists' association, in communist societies always have been the regime's "transmission belts" from the political elite to groups of professionals. They provide continuing political education for their members. Their leaders often are closely tied to the party leadership and, at times, even selected by it.[14] However, the associations have never functioned simply as transmitters of elite orders.[15] Both deliberately and inadvertently, associations have encouraged individual professionals to see common interests and problems.[16] They have pressed for professional interests both as a "private government" of the profession and as lobbyists with the national government.[17] Even when professionals have been drawn into political battles, the SDP has restricted itself to resolving professional issues and problems. And, when the national government will not help its members with their problems, the associations have set up their own autonomous structures, programs, and funds to provide this assistance.

In serving the interests of the profession, the organization creates a base and forum for the profession. Formally, any professional association is drawn to try to satisfy its potential clientele to insure that the eligible professionals will join it. Members make demands on the leadership to represent their interests and serve their needs even when the leaders themselves are imposed from above on the association.[18] Members also use the association and its facilities as a base for informal group interactions. These are a key in the life of the profession and in professionals' sense of themselves as part of a group extending well beyond the newsroom.[19] Finally, the associations, in providing long-term education for members, also serve to bring journalists together and to facilitate their contacts with experts and policy-makers from outside.

At the same time, as the sudden emergence of journalists who had been blacklisted, or outside the association leadership in the seventies, into professional leadership in 1980 demonstrated, the association and its leadership are not the only professional elite. In fact, as with Western professions and professional organizations, the professional association serves basically as a link between the profession and the outside government and as a base for voicing and handling professional concerns;[20] but, it is not the only professional center. Its officers are, as in the West, seldom leading professionals. The most outstanding professionals do not get involved. They have too much invested in pure professional work and have no need for a formal organization. The officials of the association, like those of Western groups, are less successful professionals who lose nothing by making a career out of advocacy and administration for the profession.[21] However, outstanding professionals also play a role. They form an informal professional elite that leads by example and that will, from time to time, lend its name or its power to the organization on causes it feels warrant its involvement.[22]

In dealing with the outside world, both the Association of Polish

Journalists (SDP) and the Association of Journalists in the Polish People's Republic (SDPRL) as well as those who take on tasks of political advocacy function like their peers in the West. Journalists, like other professionals working in bureaucratic settings, are primarily concerned with protecting professional prerogatives and lobbying for professional benefits. So, for them, the ethical code they enforce is only one part of their regulatory activity.[23] They also try to regulate the interaction between professionals and bureaucrats.[24] In dealing with national and regional governments and bureaucracies, the associations tend to act when a policy is introduced that contradicts their normal values and interests. Again, like Western groups, they do this typically by using professional expertise to justify their demands.[25] Unlike unions, these associations, like most professional associations in the West, do not use strikes and work slowdowns. Those are considered unprofessional. Effectively, most of what they do, although tacitly approved by the profession, does not involve the membership directly.[26] The main goals of their lobbying attempts have been to insure the profession's exclusive right to select, train, and police their own membership and to protect its right to handle its own work.[27]

The formal professional organization: the SDP and its successor

Polish journalists' interests were legally represented by two institutions, the trade union for journalists and other media workers and the professional association itself. Ostensibly, the National Union of Professional Workers in Publishing, the Press, and Radio and Television represents journalists, along with everyone else involved in the media, from printers and maintenance workers to editors and directors, in all negotiations about salary and on all decisions about work rules and working conditions. And, the associations (SDP and SDPRL) are to

> (1) assemble professional journalists in a creative organization cooperating in the building of socialism and in all areas of development of the Polish People's Republic; (2) care for the state and the development of the profession of journalism in Poland; (3) protect freedom of the press and press criticism in the interests of socialist construction; (4) regulate the ethics of the journalism profession; and (5) act together with the professional union in representing the interests of the profession, both moral and material.[28]

The SDP also supervised, at least on an advisory level, admission to professional training, the training itself, the behavior of professionals, and contacts between the system and the profession. The SDPRL has moved to do this as well. In addition, although the union is supposed to deal with questions of journalists' salary and work conditions, the SDP and SDPRL have publicly participated in these battles. They have lobbied for, taken credit for, and, in part, distributed the gains they succeeded in obtaining to journalists. All the while, they made it clear that journalists are a different and special group separated from the rest of "media workers." To a greater or lesser degree, these organizations have also taken on the responsibility of lobbying for professional autonomy with the Party and state leaders and providing members with special benefits like a good restaurant with subsidized meals, tours, language lessons, medical care, and stipends for research or long-term writing projects. They also facilitate and provide a forum for discussion on an entire spectrum of special topics.

Organizational structure

In performing all of these functions, the SDP and its successor organization have served the conflicting needs of a variety of constituencies. For their members, they have provided special material, social and educational benefits. All of these are intended to be an inducement for professionals to join the organization by enhancing the position of dues-paying members *vis-à-vis* others in the field.[29] For the profession as a whole, both members and non-members, the SDP and the SDPRL are assumed to be the main lobbyists for their salary, benefits, and work rules. The associations also advocate the professionals' right to control their work and champion the prestige of the profession to the public.

Polish journalists have been primarily concerned with protecting the profession from the outside rather than championing the "free press" idea common in the West. They are, therefore, more willing than Western journalists to have their organization involve itself in regulating the profession and in supplanting the government in professional affairs.[30] They worked as omnibus organizations, doing what is often done by a combination of unions, fraternities, and honoraries in the West. To carry out the varied and often conflicting tasks that are required, the SDP and the SDPRL work at a variety of levels with their power and authority centered on the national body. At the lowest level, there are delegates in every workplace responsible for persuading individuals to join, collecting dues, joining the editorial board in discussions of working conditions and pay rates, and distributing information as well as intervening in work problems. In doing this, particularly when the editor relies on them rather than on the trade union appointee, they duplicate the role of the assigned trade union representative, who is supposed to be a labor mediator for everyone connected with the media at all levels. Often, too, they are more important information sources than the Primary Party Organization.[31]

Outside of Warsaw, there are regional organizations that provide a forum for continuing education, work to solve local professionals' problems, and bring in and monitor new members. The central association, since it is located in Warsaw, plays these roles for Warsaw itself even as it advocates professional interests nationally; so, it funds Warsaw-based activities and partially funds other local groups, sets up national activities for members, and speaks for the profession as a whole. Members, as individuals, participate in national and local activities.

At regular intervals, delegates from the local units are chosen to attend a national convention. Normally, a list is proposed by the officials who head local bodies and is ratified by the members. However, the explosion of local pressure for a special congress in 1980 and the dominance of delegates elected directly by the local members both in 1980 and before, in 1968, is proof of the possibility for independent action to be triggered by members' dissatisfaction.

Delegates at all of the SDP conventions, no matter how they are elected, discuss issues of concern and review the activities of the national and local organizations. Parts of these discussions are made public through formal channels. Others are informally reported by delegates to their local chapter members and colleagues. At the conclusion of the session, the delegates vote on the slate of candidates proposed by the leadership for the governing board and three standing committees. Normally, more candidates are listed than there are seats on the board and on various committees. So, there is some choice. Since 1954, this has been increased by the fact that candidates have been nominated and elected from the floor.

The governing board that directs the work of the association normally has about forty members who are organized into committees which handle specific concerns. A twenty-member presidium of the governing board meets regularly and prepares for general meetings of the whole board. Finally, the governing board selects officers from the presidium to run the association's administration.

This administrative staff and, less directly, the elected officials are involved primarily in serving members' needs. They direct the various services provided to SDP members: clinics, a library of domestic and foreign press, association records and books on journalism, a restaurant, and various special language classes, films, and social events. They are also responsible for training programs held through the association and for regular contacts with regional delegates and foreign journalists' groups. Finally, and most importantly for their members, they service the various clubs of specialists whose programs of panels, trips, awards, and prominent speakers are the lifeblood of the association.

Two other national institutions have enhanced the leaders' contacts and control over the membership. A small staff selected by the governing board edits a national professional journal, *Prasa Polska,* which provides information for professionals and promotes communication on issues of mutual concern. It is given to all dues-paying members of the SDP and to government institutions dealing with the media. The second is the national journalists' court which enforces the profession's code of ethics.

Membership

Not all working journalists partake of SDP activities and services as members. SDP membership has never been required for employment. So, for example, "in 1960, 24 per cent of journalists on daily papers were *not* members of the SDP. In 1970, 27 per cent of radio and television journalists were *not* in the SDP."[32] Before the disbanding of the SDP, in 1982, however, some journalists did not belong either because they had begun work very recently or worked only part-time. They, therefore, did not fulfill the requirements for membership. Others did not belong because they lived in regions so distant that they could never partake of the association's activities. Only a few refused to belong as a matter of principle or because they felt they were too prominent to be in a professional association. The association was then dominated in "normal" times by middle-level journalists and their needs for advocacy and support in making contacts with policy-makers and other experts. Yet, in crisis periods, most of the "stars" aligned with both the establishment and with dissidents, came back into the organization.

Ironically, the members have sought to have as selective an organization as possible so that membership would be an honor and not simply an identity card. At the same time, there is a practical pressure to involve and touch the profession as fully as possible in order to support the claim that the association represents the whole profession. So, in the immediate postwar years when the shortage of experienced professionals and the expanded needs of the media brought in large numbers of new recruits, the newly reconstructed association felt it had to decrease its candidacy requirement from three years to three months to get enough members to be a force in and for the profession.[33] This reduction in qualifications was pushed even further under Stalinist leaders: membership involved, to journalists' mind, "only broad and loose connections" with journalism so political agitators, institutional press monitors, and even self-proclaimed writers could join.[34]

This lowering of membership requirements for those who had entered in the Stalinist period was a major reason, in the opinion of journalists, for the lowered quality and status of the profession.[35] Therefore, as a part of their newly extended freedom, in 1957, the association set up strict standards for membership. Interwar journalists were welcomed back.[36] But, to block political appointees and part-time professionals, membership was limited to those who worked full-time on journals that appeared at least weekly.[37] The position of "full member" was further limited to those who had served a two-year candidacy in the association.[38] Some acknowledgment of changes in the character of the profession was made, at least, with the admission of some radio and press agency journalists. But, the new postwar group of mass journals published less than once a week was ignored because the association did not want to include journalists working on occasional publications of Party propaganda.[39]

At the 1961 National Convention, the criteria for admission were further tightened to include only "professional journalists, citizens of Poland, whose main source of income is work in journalism (the press, radio, television, press agencies, and film chronicles). Those who do not fit these criteria can be admitted if they give evidence of actual work in *publicystyka* or press research, backed by a long period of earning in one of these areas."[40] However, membership still was not merely a matter of being in a media position. It remained dependent on the recommendation of the regional association and the National Admissions Committee.[41] National Convention delegates actually rejected a proposal to end the candidacy period.[42] In fact, opposition to reducing entrance requirements was so strong that the drafting committee was actually forced to lengthen the candidacy period to three years.[43] Only in 1968, as a result of the internal ferment in the profession and the sense that the profession and its association were aging, was the two-year candidacy reinstated.[44] Association membership also has required continuous work in the profession: trained journalists have not been able to maintain their formal association position if they work outside the profession. The only exception has been made for those summoned into Party work on a full-time but temporary basis.[45]

The significance both of these requirements and of the act of belonging to the organization was critical in the eighties. Initially, with the rise of Solidarity and the sudden inability of the regime to control the independent press, anyone with access to a typewriter or mimeograph could "do journalism." Journalists responded by increasing their news coverage to remove the *raison d'être* of this new press. As a formal Solidarity press emerged, staffed by young workers and some former writers from the opposition press of the seventies, professionals found themselves working as equals with and even, at times, under newcomers. This they accepted as the "challenge of change." But, even when Solidarity raised it, membership in the association from outside the normal channels was not considered. Instead, as one former association official reported, "the issue for us is schooling them not admitting them." So, although the SDP headquarters became a center for open public meetings, professional journalists were not willing to give up their exclusivity.

With the formal disbanding of the SDP and the formation of the SDPRL, membership itself became an issue. Since the SDP was closed down because of its leaders' political activities during Solidarity and their refusal to condone martial law, joining the new SDPRL – however much it claimed to be the rightful continuation of "their" SDP – was considered anti-professional even by many who remained in the establishment press. By March 1983, in comparison with the figure of some 9,000 members of the SDP in 1980, there were 5,376 members of the SDPRL, 70 per cent of whom, according to the SDPRL, had belonged to the SDP. Most of those were from the younger generation of journalists – those with the least commitment to the SDP and the most real needs from the SDPRL in terms of its programming and services.[46] For the 30 per cent who came as new members, joining was facilitated by the drop in association requirements so that one only had to have worked in the media or some media related profession for two years to join. The candidacy period was simply dropped.[47] Health and financial services were clear inducements against any boycott, since the major move to join the SDPRL came, not with its founding but, with increases in the services it provided and the denial of those services to non-members in a period of economic crisis.

Membership services

Using their own and outside funding,[48] the associations have provided their members with some exclusive benefits. Association members receive special health care; aid for widows, orphaned children and those with disabilities; aid for further education and research; loans to buy apartments, pay debts, buy furniture or cover emergency expenses; and possibilities for subsidized vacations and professional exchanges abroad.[49] Members also have their own retirement fund, their own vacation resorts, and the right to eat cheap meals from well-stocked restaurants at the SDP buildings in major Polish cities.[50] In addition, SDP membership entitles individuals to reciprocal rights in the use of other intelligentsia and professional club facilities. Yearly monetary rewards and formal awards – publicized in the media – are given to members for professional excellence.[51] Even in the seventies, in fact, when the SDP leadership was relatively politically restrained, these awards were periodically used to aid individuals who were being blacklisted. This tradition has been so important that it has been continued not only in the SDPRL but in the dissident SDP. When these awards have been given to non-star journalists or journalists who are unable to publish, they have allowed these individuals to survive in the profession.

The association programs and publications provide information about the position and work of professionals; government and Party decisions about media and propaganda goals; and new political, technical, and professional developments. While these "educational activities" are perceived by the political elite as a means of transmitting information and mobilizing the profession into correct political involvement, they actually have helped increase the internal strength of the profession. Journalists simply use them selectively for their own purposes. For example, "professional communications" stimulated by the political elite, such as reprints of political speeches on the media, tend to go unread by professionals. Required courses on political, as opposed to professional, problems sponsored through the "Journalism Center" are not well attended. Instead, members press the center for short courses in professional and technical areas and for more speakers to be brought to the clubs.[52] In *Prasa Polska*, "political" and "educational" articles are ignored by journalists who avidly read all the sections which provide "professional gossip" on promotions, personnel changes, and professional awards as well as "professional criticism" (found primarily in a regular "Free Tribune" column of controversial opinions by individual journalists).[53]

While membership involvement and support of the association as a whole dropped with the creation of the SDPRL, *Prasa Polska* was turned into a journal that aimed for a broader audience. It was hoped this would give some power and visibility to what was seen as a political and quisling organization. It initially published new science fiction, the conversations of a leading Nazi war criminal and an underground fighter who were jailed together after the war, and large numbers of historical reports from the early postwar period. Along with these features came more ideological reports, discussions on the problems and the gains journalists had achieved in their salary and benefits negotiations under SDPRL leadership, and comparisons of the SDPRL with other East European journalists' groups as well as the usual chronicle of the profession, announcements of contests, and discussions on professional issues. *Prasa Polska* became both an important public vehicle and such a draw to the SDPRL that the founder and head of the SDPRL retained and focused on its editorship, which he had begun in 1981 under the instructions of the activist SDP to "jazz up" and popularize the magazine.[54]

The most popular function of both associations has been the specialist clubs that developed spontaneously in 1957.[55] They served ostensibly an "exclusive membership" of those "who seek information and an exchange of views and who organize meetings themselves to do this."[56] The clubs represent specialties of professional work (editors, managing editors, photographers) and of topical interest (social policy, international relations, economics, law, sports) within the profession. They are organized independently by journalists who share common interests and professional experiences. The specialist clubs' membership depends largely on the need journalists have for information and a forum in a given topical area. In 1961–64, 2,307 out of 4,406 SDP members joined; in 1964–68, as publication possibilities were limited under Gomułka, 3,672 members out of 4,802 belonged; in 1968–71, after the turmoil in the profession and during the Gierek era honeymoon, when information was more accessible, 3,589 out of 6,055 belonged.[57] Changes in membership in the clubs are directly proportional to the availability of information in each of these periods. So, for instance, when information access decreased in the later half of the Gierek era, attendance increased. The Solidarity era was the exception. Then, discussions were very critical and pitted groups against each other so even some of the more exclusive clubs felt forced to open their meetings and found them packed with members and non- members.

Clubs are officially seen as a way "to raise the status and authority of the profession."[58] For officials and agencies, they are a way to seek public support for their programs and to distribute positive information as well as to get a sense of public criticism before it is published or has to be censored. So, policy-makers have been willing to aid clubs by sponsoring trips, exhibits, and speakers to increase journalists' support of them and their work.[59]

Journalists active in clubs, on the other hand, are melded even more into a professional community since work in the clubs gives them a clear sense of having a special body of knowledge and of being part of a professional hierarchy. They see the clubs as a way to influence policy, get information and force reaction to their criticisms. One journalist explained: "These are *our* organizations. They are the only forum where we set the agenda and get what we want from policy-makers." The clubs are especially useful to non-elite journalists, particularly those from outside Warsaw. For these provincial journalists, they are a primary source of first-hand information and direct contact with policy-makers and top-level administrators who are centered in Warsaw, as well as with the leaders in their fields.

Most active clubs concentrate on bringing in outside speakers and panels to discuss issues their members consider significant. In order to encourage speakers and members to be forthright and to give those who come to the meetings regularly an edge over others, most meetings are held in closed sessions and "off the record." They seldom focus on purely ideological and professional questions but rather are designed as the basis for key stories. In addition, clubs provide professional evaluations and incentives for their members through the awarding of annual prizes to journalists in their area.[60] Some even maintain their own international contacts and international travel and exchanges. They also take it upon themselves to act as hosts for international guests.[61]

The level and nature of the activity of individual clubs depends on the interest and the connections of their members and leaders. Clubs with topical specialities in "political" areas like law, social policy, economics, education and international relations tend to be the most active and exclusive. They also tend to be more "Warsaw-centered."[62] The Club of Economic Affairs Analysts and the Legal Affairs Club have been the two most active SDP clubs and have often been cited as models for others. Their frequent discussions and programs are often highly critical of political events. In one of the more sensational cases, for instance, the Legal Affairs Club, when it became clear that the Gierek leadership was pushing through constitutional reforms to institutionalize Party power and the role of the Soviet Union as well as to increase citizen responsibility to and control by the state, invited the drafters of the then secret amendments to address them. At this meeting, the amendments, known to leaders in the club from their own personal connections, were sharply criticized. Demands for specific "inside" information on the reasoning behind decisions and support for them were made. This, in turn, created a sense among the drafters that their amendments were going to create far more public furor than they had expected. This was one of the key considerations in their modification even before their introduction to the parliament.

At the height of the economic crisis and the censorship of it under Gierek, the Economic Affairs Club brought individual speakers and panelists representing different points of view together to discuss the effectiveness of current policy, the problems encountered by journalists in their attempts to do economic reporting, and their proposals for policy changes. So, too, in the Solidarity and martial law periods, this club, along with the Association of Economists, became a center for critical economic reform discussions. The early forum it had provided for economists paved the way for journalists to be included with economists in public discussions. For, in the seventies, officials, unwilling to talk openly with individual journalists or to go formally before economists, were often willing to attend a journalists' club meeting. At these meetings, journalists not only took up policy questions and criticism, but also pressed for greater access. Growing out of these discussions was a consensus as to the problem areas in policy and a sense among journalists of the stand individuals and journals took on various issues as well as a sense of comradery with others in their area. As a result, these groups and their meetings, along with those in other specialist clubs, played a particularly active role in shaping press campaigns and creating "a profession."[63]

In expanding this format in response to the Solidarity movement and the ferment that surrounded it, a group of Warsaw journalists established "Forum." By doing this, they took their professional club format public in a series of debates on a wide range of critical topics from interwar history to Party leadership. To these, they invited speakers who took both sides on critical issues to talk not only to journalists but also to the public or, at least, members of other professional and intellectual groups. Coming out of these debates, they hoped, would be a published series of discussion transcripts that would further broaden public discussion and knowledge. Journalists' groups all over Poland held similar debates, serving often as a town hall to standing room crowds of SDP members and non-members and subjecting establishment figures to bitter attacks.

Local chapters of the association

The local chapters of the association serve as administrative agencies for the national organization; facilitate interaction among regional journalists and between journalists and other local professionals and administrators; and sponsor discussions on topics of regional interest. They are not, however, small-scale models of the national organization. In fact, because of their traditional isolation and the high status of and concern with the central Warsaw media, local organizations have basically been left on their own. They are connected with Warsaw by meetings with official delegations from Warsaw and through individual members' participation in Warsaw-based specialist clubs. Normally, they do not get direct instructions from the national organization on what to do nor have they been of much interest to the national leaders.

Local organizations are further cut off from the central organization by the very realities of their existence. Much of their funding comes from local sources, supplemented only sporadically with grants from the national association. Most are so small that they run activities for the entire local intelligentsia so that, everywhere but in major intellectual centers like Cracow, Wrocław and Lublin, journalists' meetings always have been the center of local intellectual life, just as they were all over Poland in the heydays of liberalization in 1956 and again in 1980–81. The provincial units also sometimes jointly organize activities with local officials aimed at, from journalists' perspective, putting forth journalists' own interests. All in all, though, while these activities served "to liven up the social and cultural life of the regions," they never bridged the gap between journalists and their intelligentsia peers.

The relations between Warsaw and other media centers have been repeated issues of concern in national meetings. Local organizations have felt dominated by Warsaw and the national organization since the Stalinist period. To remedy this, they have demanded and received increases in their representation in the national bodies. They pressed to have national leaders attend local meetings and to have national meetings held outside of Warsaw.[64] Regional journalists have complained bitterly about differences in opportunities and living standards between their members and Warsaw journalists as well as the lack of financial support to underwrite their local activities.[65] These concerns and this tension were very much taken into account in 1980 when journalists formed the slate of the new governing board and selected full-time officials of the SDP carefully to include regional journalists in order to insure that all groups felt involved. To do this, they initially even passed over Warsaw-based stars they knew well. The SDPRL then followed this lead – especially since they could not find leading Warsaw journalists to officiate – and involved many regional journalists.

The Warsaw group, on the other hand, is an exclusively journalists' organization since it has its own building and basically dominates national clubs and meetings. Essentially, Warsaw is integrated into the structure of the national organization. In effect, it is so separate from the rest of the regions that, until 1974, annual reports listed Warsaw as a section apart from the other regional associations. The Warsaw steering committee of twenty members and a full-time staff meets with delegates from the Warsaw journals to discuss professional problems. It also organizes formal ideological and professional meetings for the Warsaw membership as well as periodic open sessions for them on subjects of current interest. But formal meetings of the entire membership are much less frequent than those of other regional bodies. The journalists' association in Warsaw is ultimately based around informal contacts in the lounge, the library, or the dining room and specialist club meetings as well as in homes and cafes all over Warsaw.[66] The role of these informal meetings in melding a professional community and facilitating professional life is clear from the emphasis placed by journalists on getting a good cook for the restaurant so that it was not only profitable but good. It was also clear in the seventies from the number of formal and informal meetings that took place in the building that Warsaw shares with the national unit.

Non-membership specific activities

At the same time as the associations have worked to serve their members, they also have spoken for the entire profession. But, in deference to an unspoken policy that has existed since the interwar years, the national body remains inactive in national politics and avoids most proclamations of support for the regime. So, since the Stalinist period, national leaders have, on the whole, dealt with political events and changes in terms of their professional ramifications and made only token bows to ideology, as required of them. This, even though there are individuals who, as members of the SDP leadership, privately have supported groups and ideas within the Party and, in doing so, have used these connections to help the profession's interests. Stefan Bratkowski, the head of the SDP in the wake of Solidarity, was the prime example of this duality carried to an extreme. Although others in the SDP leadership drew sharp lines between their professional role and private political commitments, Bratkowski became a presence in negotiating and advocating in battles that were only indirectly media related but were highly charged politically.

Whatever their personal politics and commitments, Bratkowski and his colleagues and predecessors in the leadership of the SDP, though, have addressed the same three basic issues for the profession as a whole since 1958. These have been the issues of salary, control, and education. They are, effectively, what journalists are troubled by and expect their own leaders to address.[67]

Salary and living conditions have been the issues of prime concern for most journalists and in the professional leadership's public policy actions.[68] After this, journalists and the leadership have focused on the issues of legal and ethical regulation.[69] Training professionals to raise their qualifications has been the chief job of professional associations according to political leaders. Journalists, though, generally have considered this far less crucial. As a result, it, in fact, received only marginal attention from association leaders.[70]

In achieving each of these goals, the SDP and the SDPRL have taken the same posture as professional associations in the West even though what they have attempted to achieve has clearly been limited by their sense of the political environment.[71] Whatever the political leaders' posture toward the media, however, professional leaders have stressed the unique needs and public service value of the profession. Throughout all their negotiations they have also made it clear that they are the only leaders of what, they emphasize, must be a respected and very autonomous professional group. This has meant the association leaderships have exerted pressure to institutionalize their role in negotiations, to establish new work codes for media workers and to institutionalize provisions for professional representation in any decision affecting journalists.

On professional issues, the pressure has been to deal with immediate problems in the most effective way possible. Most often, the public statements of the associations' leaders frame professional issues so they are palatable to the public. For instance, while salary was always a basic concern of journalists, their representatives have pushed for increases in benefits by talking not about salary but about the heroism of journalists, plagued as they are by poor health and high mortality, and the failures of the media to achieve its full social role because of journalists' own sufferings. (This, in turn, has had the unintended effect of raising professional journalists' concern about their own health.)[72] When and how any issue is presented to the government generally is calculated by internal association pressures and representatives' perceptions of feasible gains. When the political elite has been receptive to aiding journalists, specific demands have been made and lobbied for by the leadership. This was true in the case of "Work Code" discussions in the early Gomułka and Gierek periods and, to a lesser degree, in pressures to revise the proposed Law of the Press in 1983. When the political elite has not been receptive, the leaders have focused on private compromises and on securing for themselves a position as the controlling force in everything affecting the profession. At such times, the leadership tried to get support from journalists by publicly advocating gains they knew were both popular and possible or by developing their own substitute programs to help journalists with association monies or other aid. The following case study of lobbying for material benefits illustrates this interaction between the willingness of political leaders to move and professional lobbying efforts as well as the, at least limited, ability and determination of the professional association to act as an advocate and not simply a transmission belt, even when it looked to those outside as if it was doing little or nothing. Finally, it illustrates the ability of members to "punish" association leaders who fail to satisfy their needs and represent their interests.

Case study: the ongoing battle for material benefits One of the major concerns of the profession of journalism has been how little they earn. Until 1972, journalists, unlike other professionals, were paid almost totally on a piecework basis even if they were full-time staff members. Because of this, only a few were able to earn high salaries. Others were trapped into competition for what limited space there was for their articles. In the sixties, when the Gomułka leadership did not move to increase earnings in general and those of journalists in particular, various natural "coping mechanisms" were developed. The editors used funds for outside contributions to increase staff earnings by paying them not only their salaries but the monies set aside for freelancers. In this way, the percentage of individual journalists' salaries based on piecework went from 37.5 per cent in 1955 to 80 per cent in

1960–62 without any salary code change.[73] The SDP officially sponsored research on journalists' needs and problems and used it to lobby for salary increases.[74] The national professional leadership, when it was unable to get the government to increase investment in the media, attempted to augment journalists' salaries by establishing large money prizes.[75] Individuals also turned to quickly researched and quickly written articles to maximize their earnings. In doing this, they also avoided doing critical articles since they were both time consuming and, sometimes, hard to get through censorship. But, the real long-term solution clearly required that the external authorities provide state funds for increased salaries, early retirement provisions, and longer vacations. These provisions and the overall increases in investment in the media, when they were finally passed under Gierek, opened up opportunities for journalists to change jobs and for new people to enter the field.

In 1955, the first post-Stalin pay regulation had had a clear Stalinist heritage: pay for journalists was based on the political nature of journals, quality and appeal played no role. Journalists and journals were divided into seven groups based, primarily, on their closeness to the Party and, only secondarily, on circulation. Journalists were paid for the number of articles they published beyond the minimum established for their rank. The result was an over 200 per cent variation in pay not only between journals of different classes but, also, within most staffs.[76]

This salary base was not officially revised until 1963, in spite of a 115.2 per cent cost of living increase between 1955 and 1960 and the 148.7 per cent increase in the average salary of Polish workers.[77] But, individuals, when they could, worked the system to improve their earnings. Individual journalists took advantage of the "Work Code" provision and submitted articles to journals other than their own.[78] This increased the earnings of journalists with unique specialties and wide contacts; but it did not help low and middle-level journalists.[79] The "Work Code," though, provided journalists with few other benefits. The SDP was explicitly excluded from staff decisions. Journalists were given tiny expense accounts for travel. Vacation time and retirement requirements were no different from those of the other professions.

As the political situation stabilized, in the sixties, the SDP leadership and membership focused increasingly on doing something about material benefits even though the SDP did not legally represent journalists on benefit issues.[80] Meetings were held with the Ministry of Labor and with trade union representatives to argue the case for journalists.[81] When a new pay scale was devised in 1963, the leadership of the SDP pressed for specific modifications in it and for it to be more comprehensive. Although the SDP was allowed to sign the 1964 "Work Code" as a party to negotiations, this did not mean it was formally acknowledged as the representative of journalists' interests.[82] And, its leaders also made it clear in *Prasa Polska* that this was not "an ideal law and no one will see it as such."[83]

This 1964 salary scale raised the salary of those who were hurt most by the piecework system: the administrators who did not have the time to write and journalists on the lowest ranked journals. It also shifted the basis for ranking journals from political significance to circulation and frequency. Editors' salaries, while clearly differentiated by journal, were specified and increased. A position of "applicant" or "apprentice" was demarcated to give this lowest stratum some minimal wage guarantees. Salaries of journalists on the smaller journals, which had become increasingly rare as the press was consolidated, were also raised.[84]

In the 1964 negotiations with the union and The Ministry of Labor, the SDP leadership had attempted to modify the salary scale provision limiting journalists' piecework earnings. The SDP maintained that this would diminish journalists' earning power. In addition, the SDP objected to the fact that work norms for provincial and radio journalists had been increased when their salaries were increased. A partial concession from the union was won: piecework payments were not limited to any percentage of an individual's earnings. The work norms of regional and radio journalists, though, were only changed through informal agreements between the leadership of the local SDP and the individual publishing houses.[85]

In other areas, like notification of termination, the SDP leadership also claimed, in its own publication, to have won concessions from the union during these negotiations.[86] They "won" on three other major points. The SDP delegate was legally recognized as a necessary party to editorial decisions affecting journalists' earnings. In addition, it was established that journalists should be paid for all articles they wrote even if they were not published "through no fault of the journalists." This, though, did not include pay for censored articles. Given the cutbacks in allocations for the purchase of paper, this provision was particularly significant. Because of the piecework salary system for journalists, vacation pay was also a crucial issue on which journalists gained. Under the old "Work Code," journalists' vacation pay was equal to the average of their last three months earnings. In the new code, journalists' earnings for the entire year before their vacation were averaged.[87]

Prior to these 1964 negotiations, individual journalists, through unorganized actions and individual reactions to pressures, had pressed for changes. The visible results of these individual actions were then used by SDP leaders as evidence that changes had to be made. Not only did journalists complain but they also produced less. Many wrote only short articles certain to be published and, as a result, the quality and critical level of the press declined.[88] Leading journalists wrote articles about how their effectiveness in intervention and press criticism was decreasing because of the declining public image of journalists.[89] This they linked to their low socio-economic standing.[90] The SDP elite then made these spontaneous responses a basis for their demands. A study, commissioned and supported by the SDP, was done to buttress their case in negotiations. It claimed the quality of journalism was declining and that this led to poor quality propaganda. The SDP leaders then claimed this decline could only be halted with less pressure for quantity through payment for what was written and not only what was published.[91]

Both the situation and the rationale for journalists' demands changed between 1964 and 1967 when a new "Work Code" was negotiated. These three years were a time of declining opportunities for journalists at every level: paper allocations decreased, no new radio and television stations opened, the number of newspapers published in Poland declined, and virtually no new positions on old newspapers opened. Those who had entered after World War II were still far from retirement, they controlled the middle and upper level positions. As a result, younger journalists rapidly reached a plateau in their earnings. And, unlike their older colleagues, they did not have the personal connections to get freelance articles published in what was a shrinking market.

The SDP leadership demanded a role in decisions on paper allocation and investment in the media and were actually allowed to sit in on these discussions. But, as they voiced their demands directly to the Party and state elite, they found little credence was given to the profession and its needs, even when journalists' representatives tried to show the link between the professions's effective work and keeping people from using Radio Free Europe, Gomułka's great *bête noire*. To counter increasing membership dissatisfaction with their failure to make gains or to even hold the position of journalists steady, SDP leaders tried to aid journalists with their own resources. They talked publicly about the dangers of stagnation. They presented a large number of yearly financial awards to young journalists.[92] They also set up grants for journalists to study or do in-depth research for up to a year.[93] In addition, writing and research projects were not only paid for but often published by the association.

With its arguments that, with low earnings, journalists could not produce the needed effective propaganda, the leadership buttressed its case by referring to the bad health and high death rate of journalists.[94] The pressures of journalistic work made its practitioners, they argued, more likely than others to suffer "psychiatric and neurologically related illnesses." The claim was also that it led to a high rate of heart disease and heart attacks.[95]

In response to these problems, the SDP leadership continued to seek to raise salaries and abolish piecework; get longer vacations for journalists than for other professionals and workers; insure better working conditions for journalists by providing access to extra apartment space so that they could work at home; renovating journal offices; giving journalists special access to cars and reduced fares so that travel would be easier; and allowing journalists to retire earlier than other professionals.[96] The latter demand would also have eased the pressure for the professional mobility of young journalists. The actual demands the SDP presented in 1967, however, reflected their sense of what was achievable. They demanded only higher basic salaries, a wider pay range on each level, additional financial remuneration for good work or special talents, and a lengthened vacation period for journalists who had worked in the profession for twenty years. Even with these scaled-down demands, it again achieved only part of its goals.[97] As a result, the SDP leadership downplayed its position in drawing up the new "Work Code."[98]

The achievements of the SDP leadership in 1967 were much smaller than they had been in 1964. Other than salary increases, no other substantial gains were made. In the eyes of most of the membership, the results were disastrous and indicated that the SDP elite truly favored the "old guard." The compromises by which SDP negotiators tried to raise salaries for all were: paying "old guard" journalists enough for their foreign languages, and giving increases in monthly pay so that they would decrease the amount of piecework they did, leaving it for the young journalists.[99] These compromises were misperceived by most of the profession as saps for "old cronies" and those in the leadership.

After the upheavals of 1968, the new SDP leadership continued to demand better salaries and working conditions by stressing the poor health of the profession. This argument became part of the self-image of journalists and they spoke of it to each other.[100] Political elite criticism of the media was met by demands for more money. Association leaders felt that, under Gomułka, there was little possibility of any real change. The point of comparison came to be the situation of Katowice journalists under Gierek. Seen from a distance it looked ideal.

When Gierek took power in late December 1970, he immediately acknowledged the need for better propaganda and communication. He met with leaders of the SDP and seemed receptive to their demands. As early as 1971, investment in the media and paper allocations were significantly increased. Under these conditions, the SDP leadership felt that it could press for its unreached goals.

When a new "Work Code" appeared in 1972, the SDP leadership participated in the signing along with the union and publishers' representatives. It took credit for this agreement which met the demands SDP leaders had put forward before. Journalists were to be paid a high enough base salary that extra rewards would be needed only for high quality production. The piecework system was abolished except when journalists submitted articles to journals other than their own. Journalists' vacations were lengthened to a standard month with a six week vacation after twenty years in the profession. In addition, journalists were allowed to retire, with full benefits, earlier than any other professional group: at fifty-five for women and sixty for men.[101]

The significance of these reforms for the relationship of SDP leaders to their members was immense. Most journalists surveyed in 1976 cited the 1972 reform as *the* major accomplishment of the SDP and as evidence that the SDP played a significant role in professional life. For the rest of the seventies, these gains were maintained by periodic increases in salary scales for journalists. The only other groups who had such frequent increases were the police and the military.

By 1980, however, the economic crisis had hit home for journalists and these salary increases were hardly sufficient. As a result, pay and benefits were central issues in 1980. But, the involvement of SDP leaders in the battles over censorship and access to the media as well as the general economic crisis in Poland meant that no movement was made on journalists' salary demands. And, so, in spite of the fact that little real movement on salary issues could be made under these circumstances, the founders of the SDPRL used the lack of a salary accord as their prime evidence that the leadership elected after Solidarity's victories had abandoned the profession's real needs in its focus on championing the political challengers of the day.[102] The first visible "success" the new association's leadership claimed was a new work code passed in 1983 that raised salaries, lowered the retirement age, and increased vacations as well a specifying how journalists' flexible time should be measured.[103] This had an impact on low and middle-level professionals particularly. It allowed many prominent and not so prominent older journalists to retire with pay rather than become martyrs as boycotters of the press. And, it encouraged other less prominent journalists to retire and make way for new blood. Yet, it did not involve or affect those who boycotted the press or took jobs on tiny special interest journals. The importance of these gains was multiplied by the generally poor economic conditions in which people struggled to survive since price increases and the costs of black market purchases of scarce necessities made even the ample incomes of the seventies seem spartan.[104]

Public-oriented activities

As representatives of the profession, both associations have played the role of professional regulator holding the line in order to minimize the need for external interference. In addition, the SDP (and increasingly the SDPRL) sought to increase the public status of journalists by carrying on educational campaigns and protesting negative presentations of the profession.[105]

The most organizationally significant activities have been in regulating professional behavior. In 1957, a code of ethics was drawn up. It included provisions which required journalists and editors to protect their sources and to insure anonymity to authors when they requested it; provided sanctions against journalists who engaged in *ad hominem* attacks on other journalists; and set up a journalists' court, run by journalists elected at national conventions, to handle conflicts between members of the association and between members of the SDP and other citizens.[106] According to all the available data, the rulings of this Journalists' Court have been treated as public law by the state court system.[107]

Censorship problems have been brought to the national conventions most often by regional journalists since they do not have influential advocates to help them get the local censors' decisions reversed. This problem of censorship has been most explosive during periods of political unrest. In these periods, journalists have been openly criticized by the local populace for not providing sufficient information. The SDP, though, in times of relative quiet has also been expected to deal with censorship. But, between 1958 and 1980, it did not attempt to deal with censorship by attacking it as an institution. At most, it provided a forum where journalists could discuss the issue and get a sense of how widespread the opposition was to the way censorship was handled. The governing board and its executive officers discussed the problem in closed meetings and privately carried their grievances to the authorities. Their success or failure in getting some positive response was not in their hands. It was dependent on the receptivity of political leaders. Their demands in the 1960s, as a result, were focused on what seemed to be achievable: a general increase in the information made available to journalists and a rationalization of the regulations of the censors. In this area, journalists were unsuccessful in all but individual cases.

In the area of civil and criminal actions against journalists, the SDP has taken a more active and open role by providing journalists with lawyers and encouraging other journalists to write about and protect the accused (or to make it clear to the public that a guilty journalist does not represent the profession as a whole). Both the SDP and the SDPRL have stressed to the public that journalists have been unjustly attacked through the courts. They have often claimed that attacks on journalists were done to discourage journalists from writing critical articles.[108]

The SDP and individual newspapers pushed back the limits on them by trying to publicize instances of government officials' unwillingness to supply information. In doing this, they have both created public pressure for information to be made available and made it clear they could not be expected to work under these restraints. Both the SDP and individual journals were directly involved, for instance, in the drafting of the 1964 Administrative Code provisions requiring institutions to respond to press and private criticism within a stated period.[109] They continued privately and in print, to press for more effective sanctions to accompany the law. This has resulted in a number of Party statements on the responsibility of institutions to respond to the press criticism and queries. But, most of these have had little real impact on institutions' willingness to provide support and information for journalists.[101]

Finally, the associations (and the ousted leaders of the Solidarity era SDP) have made formal protests and had public discussions of cases in which the image of journalists was tarnished. They have been particularly active in trying to control books and film presentations of the profession and have also set up joint meetings between journalists and other professionals to discuss their conflicts and common problems.

Professional leadership

These various programs and policy moves are taken seriously enough by journalists for them to be quite concerned about who leads the organization. Groups of journalists from various regions and media bases want to see their interests represented on the governing board because it determines budgetary allocations and program activities for the entire organization. At the same time, membership of the governing board is not simply symbolic. It requires that individuals be willing to make this commitment. As with Western professional organizations,[111] not all professionals are interested or even willing to make such a commitment since it requires time and monetary sacrifice for successful professionals to give up some of their work time for an office that does not, except in small regional areas or in times of crisis, bring the community-wide status professional excellence does.[112] Therefore, as the profession became established, this organizational leadership has shifted from the true elite of the profession (established editors and "star-journalists") to middle-level professionals.

In reality, the governing board has been less representative of the periphery than of national and Warsaw journalists. Those who represent Warsaw or write from a national audience have had a longer tenure in the associations' offices than have regional representatives. They also know each other better than journalists based outside of Warsaw who have to take time off and travel to Warsaw for meetings.[113] They tend to control key committees of the governing board and,[114] because they are well connected in Warsaw and available, they also control the most active clubs.[115] Their greater prominence in national politics and a national readership also gives them status within the national organization. In addition, they are more readily available for meetings, consultations, and drop-in and informal gatherings, simply because they work in Warsaw. All of these factors tend to limit regional journalists to formally representing specific interests of their local areas and "pork-barrel" funding and activities for local units. This remains true even when their regions become major forces for change, as the tiny backwater Białystok group did in the fall of 1980, or when the regional press serves as a national role model, as *Gazeta Krakowska* did under its editor, Maciej Szumowski, himself a member of the Solidarity era executive committee who did not always have time to come to Warsaw for meetings.[116]

Shifting patterns of official leadership

When it formed after World War II, the Journalists' Union was led by highly respected interwar professionals, but, with the politicization of the organization in 1948, there was an immediate and forced shift to a leadership of Party propagandists – men who were either charged with running the press for the Party or who became editors because of their Party positions. All of the speakers at the 1951 convention were either Party representatives involved in supervising the press or journalists affiliated as Party members on Party papers. And, by 1954, the presidium of the governing board, proposed initially by the previous officers, included four Central Committee members or officials out of its nine members. The 1956 governing board had no representatives of the Party elite and apparatus, contrary to earlier patterns. Only 16.6 per cent were carry-overs from earlier boards. In open nominations and elections,[117] interwar journalists, previously excluded from the profession, were elected to the board, as were recent graduates from the school of journalism and student papers like *Po Prostu*.[118]

The period between 1958 and 1968 was marked by a sorting out and normalization of the association. The most radical participants in the 1956 convention were either barred from further political activities and journalism or were simply no longer relevant. Journalists became resigned to stabilization and focused on making practical gains for themselves and their profession. Those who dominated were working journalists trained and made cynical in Stalinist programs. Many of these, though, were moving into editorial positions, so, there was a shift to a leadership by editors.[119] Professional elders were elected. Only two Party officials were elected to the forty member board. In fact, formal ties between the Party and the SDP leadership appear to have been limited. Party officials no longer spoke at their meetings. Only journalists with close Party ties as well as established professional positions presented some of the Party "word" at meetings. In reality, though, there were only sporadic meetings, initiated by the SDP, between the leadership and the Party elite. None were successful from the point of view of the SDP. Much of the work of the leadership was handled instead through private contacts by journalistic elites, not necessarily officials in the professional organization, who had personal ties and friends in the Gomułka leadership.

The demands between 1956 and 1964 reflected the leadership's concerns. As editors and survivors of 1956, they made calls for greater freedom to criticize. At the same time, as editors and upwardly mobile journalists, they also focused on their own financial problems and those of the profession. The compromises they accepted were those which allowed editors to get young staff members and insured that middle to top level journalists in the major cities, from which most of the board came, made real gains.

Journalists who "cut their professional teeth" in 1956 and in the press developments which allowed Gomułka's takeover served as spokesmen until 1968. Some were highly respected as politicians and professionals. Others were known editors and noted local and national journalists with established reputations as good writers and journalists.[120] Because of dissatisfaction with the journalists' situation and with the work of the association in journalists' interests, as well as the Moczarist campaign to capture the media that fed on this disaffection, there was a major upheaval in 1968. That 1968 convention was marked by a return to national political concerns over strictly professional issues. It was also marked by the exclusion of the "professional elite" like Rakowski and Korotyński and their supporters. These former *prominente* suddenly found themselves unwelcome even in the convention halls.[121] A new leadership emerged that represented, in part, the strength of the Moczarist faction. Whatever their age, the delegates elected to the governing board were "young blood" who had taken up work in journalism in the sixties and generally were not yet in editorial positions. Instead, they claimed to have been blocked by the tenured but "unqualified hacks" who had come into the profession in the Stalinist political recruitment.[122]

The new governing board's work and impact were limited. The old professional elite, which had served as a liaison between the SDP and the political leadership, had been ousted and the increasing concern of the Gomułka regime with political control of the media meant that not much could be gained by those who attacked Gomułka and his supporters.

The stabilization which followed the Gierek takeover in December 1970, was matched by a stabilization and institutionalization in the professional leadership. The 1974 national convention voiced the Gierek ideal of a steady turnover of 50 percent of the governing board after every term. This had, on the surface, the potential of increasing the members' ability to pressure their delegates. But, in reality, no board had enough strong and well known leaders to really press the government.[123] Only a few of the top "professional elite" returned to be leaders in the association. Most of these, by their own admission, considered their roles largely honorific and did little work. According to observers, the new leadership was, on the whole, younger and more dependent on their position in the association than on their own journalistic work for professional status and salary gains. While regional journalists were not more represented than they had been at other conventions, the inactivity of "star" Warsaw journalists increased their role by default. These leaders, both in the administration and on the governing board, were not men who had ever challenged the system. On the whole, these were men whose power depended on their position and their ability to get along with the Gierek leadership. Their appointments and renewals were at the behest of the Gierek team. Therefore, loyalty to Gierek was a necessary if not sufficient requirement for their positions – made even more so because Gierek demanded a "loyal" press. For them, questions of criticism and censorship were not comfortable issues to deal with – they had seldom been critical enough in their writings to feel the sting of restraints. Besides, they were not "stars" with large incomes but middle and low level journalists and editors for whom money had long been a problem. So they focused on what the Gierek leadership was willing to hear and what they felt was important – material benefits. Achieving these aims, they knew, brought them the support of the rank and file which their predecessors had lost when they concerned themselves with criticism, and failed to deliver on mundane salary demands.

These leaders were rapidly overwhelmed by the winds of change that swept through the profession when journalists returned from the Gdańsk shipyard workers' strikes in August 1980, and called for the profession's house to be set in order. As administrators who had long fended off professional demands, they recognized the inevitability of change and quickly agreed to the "grassroots" call for a special congress.[124] At the congress, they had no role except as potential symbols of the profession's rejection of the old: many delegates had to be restrained from condemning their work.[125] Those who replaced them, like those who led in 1956, were "stars" – many also had been and remained role models for the profession – concerned with regaining their own and the profession's prestige and autonomy.[126] Many had known each other for years.[127] Yet, by choice, this was a leadership that represented not only liberals but conservatives, because it was felt that both sides should be represented and have links to the profession's leadership. It was also an active leadership that met often, represented the profession on various committees, and got very involved in its own publications.[128]

This built-in and deliberate division over ideology meant that, although the real professional elite was identified with the liberal wing of the SDP, there were members of the governing board who were willing to form a new association after martial law was in force.[129] These tended to be less prominent second-echelon leaders, many of whose personal connections with the journalists in the political elite, like Rakowski and Jerzy Urban, were minimal at best. This leadership, born out of that failed liberalization, was, once again, a typical professional association leadership whose merit and value were based on what they got for the association. They could not and did not claim to be part of the informal group of "star" professionals whose journalistic style and foci set the agenda for the profession. Most of the more respected writers had been active in pushing Solidarity changes and so were largely blocked from leadership in the new organization because they had rejected the new "normalization." However, the old leaders were able to remain as model journalists because they had been renowned for their work in Poland and abroad long before they took on leadership roles in 1980. So, although they rapidly disappeared from public view, they and their work remained powerful images for the profession. They used their contacts to organize everything, from relief shipments from abroad, and a code of ethics for all professional journalists, to informal seminars and statements on professional demands for Western journals. And, their writing styles remained honored models for young professionals, even as some of their names were forgotten.

Professional "stars" and leaders

Individuals who hold positions as role models and authorities for journalists do not necessarily participate in SDP activities. Editors-in-chief, who entered the profession as politicans, use the SDP merely to establish their professional credibility. Most of those identified as the "most influential and authoritative journalists in Poland" by their fellow professionals in 1976 had played some role in the SDP prior to 1968; but, by then, they had such strong commitments to writing and publication that they did not have time for the SDP when, as an organization, it was involved largely in financial and bureaucratic issues. The benefits of active membership – contacts, increased name recognition, aid for trips abroad, increased earnings – came to them from their own achievements without any help from the association. If

Table 2 *Ranking of Polish journalists as most influential, 1976*

(1) Karol Małcużyński	(7) Jerzy Urban
(2) Mieczysław Rakowski	(8) Edmund Osmańczyk
(3) Ryszard Kapuściński	(9) Bartosz Janiszewski
(4) Ryszard Wojna	(10) Daniel Passent
(5) Zygmunt Broniarek	(11) Krzysztof Kąkolewski
(6) Wiesław Górnicki	(12) Krzysztof Toeplitz

they were involved, it was normally as the heads of specialist clubs or as a part of the political responsibility involved in being an editor. Journalists' role models were political and civic activists who were also respected as writers. So, these men were often selected as delegates to Party committees and to the *Sejm* or other government bodies. Yet, no matter what, their professional position was clearly derived from their skill in writing rather than their politics.

Polish journalists surveyed in 1976 showed a remarkable consistency in their perceptions of the "most authoritative" members of the profession. Of the fifty journalists listed by journalists surveyed in 1976 as "the most influential journalists *vis-à-vis* the society and the elite," only twelve were listed more than ten times. Interestingly, they were also among the most respected journalists listed by readers in other surveys.[130] These journalists were "role models" and the "professional elite" for their fellows not only in the central press of Warsaw but in the regional media, even though all were from Warsaw.

This professional elite was composed of individuals with similar career patterns. All entered the profession in the immediate postwar period. A high percentage of them specialized in foreign affairs, although all have also written on domestic problems. Three of the top twelve journalists have been foreign correspondents (Ryszard Kapuściński in Latin America and Africa; and Wiesław Górnicki and Zygmunt Broniarek in the United States) and each of them has published popular volumes on his work abroad. Four others (Karol Małcużyński, Ryszard Wojna, Mieczysław Rakowski, and Edmund Osmańczyk) were specialists on the German question and wrote widely on the subject in the sixties. These four were all closely connected, both publicly in their writings and behind the scenes, with the establishment of Polish–West German relations in 1970 and all knew each other well from this and other policy projects. All had a large and regular following increased by the fact that they either published in several papers or appeared regularly as commentators on Polish television. All of them, as well as domestic specialists (Jerzy Urban, Daniel Passent, and Krzysztof Toeplitz), were nationally known for their literary style writing and their independent positions on issues. Their articles appeared in socio-political weeklies like *Polityka* (four of the twelve were long-time members), *Kultura* and *Literatura*. Other leading journalists (like Wojna and Górnicki) wrote for the prestigious daily *Życie Warszawy*. Some (Małcużyński, Osmańczyk, and Janiszewski) submitted articles to various journals and appeared on television regularly.

Achievement counted for more in gaining the respect of the profession than class background, political activities, and SDP membership. Some members of this "professional elite" were of working-class or peasant origin (Broniarek, Górnicki and Rakowski). But, although they were open about their background, they clearly had joined the intelligentsia in their behavior and connections. Others (Osmańczyk and Małcużyński) were from the prewar upper classes and had personal ties with the interwar profession. Osmańczyk, considered the "father of postwar journalism,"[131] was active in the interwar profession. Some of the journalists combined political activity (most visibly through membership in the *Sejm* or Central Committee) with their professional work (Rakowski, Wojna, and Osmańczyk). Others (like Górnicki and Urban) were under political attack at various points in their careers.[132] Few of the top twelve journalists had been active in the SDP activities and leadership. Małcużyński and Rakowski alone were closely associated with the SDP leadership for long periods of time. Others participated sporadically in the governing board. Some were active in 1956 and then ceased to participate. Some did not even hold membership in the SDP when the survey was done. But, as public representatives of "quality" journalism, they were seen to give the profession its social respect. They also set precedents by which journalists judged themselves.

Being professional "stars" and knowing each other and the other highly respected journalists well did not mean taking similar positions politically, although, in 1976, all but Broniarek, known as the correspondent from the United States, seemed to be critical of the regime. The movement of men like Rakowski, Urban, Górnicki, Wojna, Passent and Toeplitz into either official positions in the Jaruzelski government or public positions as supporters of what was rapidly perceived as an anti-journalism government left them "prominent" but drastically reduced their prestige.[133] At the same time, as many established journalists left the profession in 1982 and new, young journalists came in, these professional "elder stars" became historical heroes and not real professional leaders. For their successors, the legacy of the profession's old guard was hard to remember and capture.[134] This left those that worked in the media in the eighties with few "stars."

Informal interaction

The SDP, important as its role has been for its members and the profession, is not the only organization to which most journalists belong. A large percentage of the profession has always been active in the Polish United Workers Party or the other minor parties and has met in these groups at their workplaces. All journalists are required to belong to the trade union, although this is only a formality. Many also belong to intellectual and artistic organizations like the Writers' Association and Polish Authors' Association (*Zaiks*). In addition, they associate constantly in informal but very real groups of their peers. Within generational cohort groups, interaction is based on residence, journal affiliation, professional specialization, and political factions as well as common social circles and childhood ties. Most often, journalists as individuals use these ties before they use the SDP. They turn to the SDP when their political and professional ties and actions are ineffective.

On most Polish publications, working conditions and staff tenure have tended to encourage close personal relations at least among members of the same department. Most work in communal department offices. Contact with other staff members gives them information about the journal's relations with the censors' office and the political authorities. On most dailies, informal social contacts with journalists in one's own department are intense and those with journalists in other departments, minimal. Only at the level of the editorial staff are informal, cross-department social contacts made. On smaller journals, individuals know the personal and professional affairs of their colleagues and editors.[135] Small staff groups on politically significant journals often even invited their censors and other political figures to their "events" in order to "lobby with them." At all levels and in all offices, journal staffs hold social events for their staff members. For smaller journals, these are only one of an ongoing series of informal gatherings that old friendships and common interest spark. But, on large journals, these events provide an opportunity to "cross lines" and be known that is particularly important for young, unestablished staff.

Because of the comparatively long tenure of journalists on most papers, closely aligned generational groups exist alongside of departmental groups. The generation which entered the profession in the 1950s has dominated in editorial positions and in numbers. It remained very cohesive until 1980 when many took advantage of a national offer for early retirement and young entrants, emboldened by public criticism of journalists, challenged their elders. Young journalists normally have entered into the informal staff milieu by establishing a patronage relationship with an older member of the staff. They worked with him and he introduced them into already established social groups. Only in 1982, when new journals began, did young journalists "run their own show" on journals they "invented" like the consumer's weekly, *Veto*, and the weekly for feature journal, *Przegląd Tygodniowy*.

The cohort group that entered the profession in the 1960s has been less strong. In this period, limitations on hiring fragmented the group. Many have had close friends in other professional and social groups and their personal concerns were paramount. Informal group interaction and group pressure, then, are far less significant for this cohort group than for others.

The journalists who entered in the seventies came into the profession after years of education. They often spent time with each other socially. In these contexts, they often discussed work difficulties and experiences. On some journals, they articulated their concerns with youth and educational questions in series of joint articles. Their common professional and personal concerns were articulated to association representatives and editors on their individual journals as "group problems," and the SDP formed a group of "Young Journalists" to deal with their needs and encouraged clubs to concentrate on these problems – further enhancing their exclusive professionalism and group ties.

Two other lines of close interaction in the profession are those based on topical specializations and factional ties. Specialist club meetings are forums for informal discussions as well as occasions for policymakers and journalists to interact. Every club meeting observed in 1975–76 and 1983 broke informally into smaller groups to continue the discussion and exchange private information over coffee or lunch.

In periods of crisis, especially, factional ties brought individuals into close private contact with other journalists and politicans. Rumors of who was seen with whom spread widely throughout local circles. But, in the sixties and seventies, factional ties, unless they were used to hurt other professionals, did not split long-held friendships. Only in 1981 did martial law become such an issue that decisions about remaining in the profession or leaving it cut friendships. As a result, much of the informal communication between groups that had made most journalists, wherever they stood politically, be sensitive and protective of each other ended, although individuals continued, even in the most bitter days of martial law, to keep close tabs on each other's lives and, as martial law faded, came more and more to help each other, at least indirectly. Ultimately, they never forgot that all were journalists.[136]

Clearly journalists, then, live in a net of relationships based on the workplace, politics, professional specialization, and age. This serves as an information network independent of any outside control, supports individual professional allegiances, and reinforces loyalties through a system of individual favors and obligations. This also offers opportunities for the formation of common, if unspoken, professional platforms and prevents individual professionals from being isolated. Finally, while the complexity of the networks makes for cleavages, these informal ties help journalists develop some sense of the profession as a whole and their role in it as well as creating various personal shields to protect the ability of professionals to do their work.

The influence of political factors and forces on the SDP

The relationship of the SDP to the PUWP and national political events and crises is a complex one. The association is often closely tied to the Party and government through professionals who belong, with greater or lesser real commitment, to the Party; through Party influence over the financial base of the SDP; and through its specific responsibilities to the Party because of its self-proclaimed "leading role." Even its most autonomous bodies, the specialist clubs, depend on the willingness of Party and government officials to appear before them and speak candidly, if "off the record." The position of the profession itself is also closely related to elite policies, as was clear from the difference between the economic position of journalists in the Gomułka and Gierek eras.

On the other hand, leaders and members alike tend to see their association as more or less autonomous. The membership clearly expects leaders to champion their interests effectively with the political elite and judges them on this basis. The members normally focus on professional rather than political concerns. From 1956, Party positions and policies have not been presented or discussed at national conventions except in areas of direct professional concern. In fact, the journalists' association, even in times when political leaders were relatively disinterested in it, has advocated its own positions on professional issues.

In 1964, this political–professional relationship was a major issue. Mieczysław Rakowski, a leader of the association and editor of *Polityka*, suggested that planning be delayed until the Party Plenum had given its evaluation of the press so SDP policy discussions could be directly related to Party positions.[137] Other leaders of the SDP disagreed. They argued that they should do their own independent research and prepare their own material for the Central Committee Plenum on the role and responsibility of the press and its investment needs. In this way, they felt that journalists' views were presented and "society shown how journalists stand."[138]

> We, as journalists and as normal people, know that the theses of the Plenum do not come from nowhere. We, as journalists, should make our own presentation to the Party leaders before the development of their positions, of their speeches for the Party congress, and of the eventual decisions. We must present our position as to our perspective on the process of journalism in our own area . . . Policy is not simply based on hard economics . . . through the Press Bureau, we must see that the "White House" understands how we see the role of the press, how we want to inform the society in this way and not some other way. We want to influence the development of political thought of our society.[139]

On-going political–professional association interaction

National and local political events affect the openness of professional discussions, including those in the association journal, *Prasa Polska*.[140] In 1956, for example, the entire discussion of the national convention was reprinted. Subsequent conventions, until 1980, have been reported only in part, with the critical comments on censorship and broader regime policies omitted. External events also have affected the internal politics of the SDP.

Political turmoil involves individual journalists through Party meetings of staff members, journalists' personal contacts and conversations, and their reporting experiences. What they hear and do indirectly affects SDP politics and informal professional interaction through both the personal ties that are formed and the press-related proposals that are made. Professional ties, however, remain more significant than political conflicts. In crisis periods, when the political leadership has been least in control, journalists' discussions have tended to be the most critical. The National Conventions of 1956, 1958, 1968, and 1980 included heated debate about censorship, obstacles to press discussion and access to information, and the inability of the media to play an effective role in guiding society. (These discussions were then reported in more or less full form to the larger community through *Prasa Polska*.) However, professional association politics were never merely mirrors for external conflicts, even when the elite most wanted to control its own press.

Political–professional association relations in a time of crisis

The transformation of the profession from 1964 to 1968 serves as a demonstration of the influence of both internal professional pressures and external upheavals in the political world surrounding the profession. The other major test of professionalism among journalists was the more complex and all-encompassing events of 1980–84. Traditionally, Western analysts have treated the 1968 anti-semitic and nationalist Moczarist campaign as the cause of changes in the profession of journalism.[141] But, actually, professional turmoil was based on professional concerns that had developed for six years and would have led to change even without the definition and aid given it by the Moczarists. The accidental coincidence of the SDP Convention with the March student demonstrations merely provided a forum for the "new professional," who had established himself much earlier. The internal basis of the transformation is illustrated by the stability of the new elite throughout the Gierek period, even after the downfall of the Moczar faction.

The stagnation and stability in economic development and individual mobility that characterized the Gomułka years set the stage for the dissatisfaction expressed by journalists at the 1968 National Convention. The increasing division within the political elite was used by some professionals to achieve a high level of freedom in political discussion. By attaching themselves to patrons, journalists were able to air their professional frustrations. However, while fragmentation among the political elite, intellectual ferment, and the disaffection of low-level journalists climaxed simultaneously in March 1968, they were not all the same process. In the case of journalists, the cause of the upheaval within the SDP was stagnation and the desire of those recruited in the sixties to "make it." This had been the major professional issue since the early 1960s when new recruits suddenly found that the cutbacks in funding made it impossible for the media to expand and the stability of the profession left them virtually "unemployable." The issue itself developed into a generational conflict between older journalists, the "political" appointees of the immediate postwar years, and the more professionally trained young journalists who could neither find work in the profession nor advance within it if they did find work.

The bloodletting began in 1964, when there was the first review of members' affiliations and their payment of dues since 1957. A large number of members who had either not kept up with their dues or had left journalism for work in other areas were ousted.[142] This was, in effect, a move against the older generation of journalists who no longer took the association seriously and who had had the connections to get jobs outside the profession. The membership balance within the local units, if not the profession itself, thus shifted from older to newer journalists. This shift, in turn, influenced the election of delegates to the 1968 National Convention.

At the same time, the Moczarist faction, which "realized the importance of the press," began to "court" regional journalists, by offering them aid in getting articles published, obtaining passports, and making contacts with policy-makers in the Moczar group. These offers were phrased in terms of professional interests and perceptions. They stressed the importance of having people with training and skills, instead of untrained, political appointees, run the press,[143] and promised protection for actions against the "older generation." Moczarists, in veiled terms, likened the state of affairs in journalism to the situation in society as a whole. This had a real appeal since journalists were sympathetic to the view that society was ineffectively run and that individual administrators and politicians were not skilled. So, many journalists supported these views.

Journalists were also impressed by the statements of Moczar and his associates that there should be more freedom of information and aid for rapid reporting.[144] Moczar, who controlled the state security forces, and his cronies were actually able to provide specific information for critical stories they wanted to have appear. Journalists became braver as a result of these discussions and the precedents others were able to set. When editors told them that their articles were too critical and could not be published, the lower and middle level journalists perceived the editors and senior journalists as tied with the "incompetent local establishment." This put the generational rift on a political plane. But, most regional journalists claim not to have been aware between 1964 and early 1967 that they were involved directly and specifically with the Moczar faction. The willingness to write critically about local leaders was reinforced by the development of a national Moczarist press, far more vitriolic than the regional or even middle-level national journalists would ever have dared to be.[145] Attacks in this press suggested to regional journalists that this was a national trend.

In Warsaw, too, low and middle level journalists were courted by Moczar and his associates. Moczar made himself highly visible in the professional gathering places and held dinner parties for sympathetic journalists. Most editors and senior journalists, who were at first apathetic, were faced with increasing amounts of copy whose tone they did not sanction. There was little they could do.[146] In the end, they depended on the output of journalists to whom they did not traditionally give detailed directions. So, many became unwilling propagators of the Moczarist line.

The key exceptions were journals like *Trybuna Ludu* and *Polityka*. They were controlled by strong Gomułka loyalists and the fact that most of their journalists were well established in the profession and earned the highest salaries also helped keep the Moczarist appeal at a distance. *Polityka* was persecuted in 1968 for its refusal to join the campaign. It was even moved out of its centrally located offices and, for a period, did not have an office in Warsaw. Its phones were cut off and its building surrounded by police. The momentum for all of these pressures came from supporters of Moczar in the ministries and the Party. They were considered "shocking" by Warsaw journalists. One Moczarist (the only *Polityka* staff member to attend the national convention in 1968 as a delegate) was forced onto the staff of the journal. The staff then refused to hold meetings when he attended. Offers of other positions to *Polityka* journalists were not accepted and Rakowski ignored complaints against his staff. In addition, pressure was placed on Gomułka to appoint Rakowski as the ambassador to Germany or to the post of Assistant Minister of Culture. Kąkol, a Moczar "friend," editor, and dean of the School of Journalism, was to take his position. Rakowski is said to have refused all of these positions and threatened "if his journal was taken away from him" to retire and live on his wife's income. Most informants felt that Rakowski finally appealed to Gomułka personally to stop the persecution of his journal. By this point, it was easy to persuade Gomułka that *Polityka* was an ally that should be saved.[147]

Trybyba Ludu journalists, interviewed in the mid-seventies, claimed that they were approached by Moczarists; but, since they knew all of the details of the factionalism in the Party, they rebuffed these efforts.

According to those journalists, few left *Trybuna Ludu*, and those who did left of their own volition. In fact, *Trybuna Ludu* was criticized in a stereotypical Moczarist attack at the 1968 convention for being pro-Israeli.[148]

The national journals which were intentionally the organs of Moczar were those whose editors were, by personal predilection, a part of his camp. These were either journals which were house organs of the ministries Moczar had controlled for a long period – primarily the military journals and the Ministry of Justice journal, *Prawo i Życie*. Or, they were journals whose editors had personal interests and ambitions that set them against the Gomułka regime or some of its specific policies. Thus, often, involvement in the Moczar circles was a matter of the editors' personal ties and conversations. In fact, on two of the major journals *Kultura* and *Życie Literackie*, the editors were isolated from and disinterested in staff politics. They simply wrote their own pieces and published pieces by their cronies with little regard for the staff or its concerns.

The major institution on the periphery of the profession, other than the Institute of Journalism which was dominated by the Moczar camp, was the censorship bureaucracy. Since positions in the censors' office required clearance by the Ministry of Internal Security, Moczar was able to exert a great deal of control, in the absence of top Party interest in managing the press, over the selection of censors. This led to a gradual change in the attitudes of the censors' office. Editors only gradually became aware of the ties between the censors and Moczar once factional battles were in the open. What it meant was that those who toed the Moczar line or were active in his camp could publish much that had been inconceivable in earlier years simply because their copy had the *imprimatur* of having come from a Moczar man. Editors who had relationships with the Gomułka elite could sometimes appeal to their Party contacts to reverse censors' decisions but, when their supporters were losing out, these appeals sometimes fell on deaf ears. For many editors, though, the issue was less the censors' new leanings than it was unpredictability. In late 1964, the association's leadership had attempted to convince its members that it was trying to get better benefits, increased investment, and more positions within the profession by publishing a large number of articles on these problems. All clearly implied that the problems in the profession stemmed from the political leadership's low commitment to it, not from the profession itself or the SDP's weakness. The intent was to protect the professional leadership rather than support the Moczar faction. Its impact, though, was to make the SDP leaders look ineffective and to make change appear possible only through a change in the national political leadership. This gave inadvertent support to the Moczar faction's line.

The purge of the association in regional areas, beginning in early 1967, was accompanied by the "firing" of established journalists on many national journals. It was paralleled by the demise of editors' control. Journalists avoided editors they thought were too weak and went to factional leaders for story support. Editors, in turn, distanced themselves from their increasingly restless staff. With the outbreak of the 1967 Arab–Israeli War and Gomułka's trade union speech giving some credence to the anti-Semitism Moczarists had encouraged, staff hostility (encouraged by Moczar's courting) came into the open in Primary Party Organization sessions and staff meetings. Editors who were in conflict with lower-level journalists faced staff revolt. In general, it was editors who did not feel isolated from the Gomułka elite and had staff backing who could ignore occasional security reports on their staff and protect them. Others, particularly those who were faced with staff revolts, were in such weak positions that they had to give in. Most of the firings, however, occurred long before the March 1968 events and many were anticipated even before the summer of 1967 and the Arab–Israeli War.

The election of delegates to the 1968 national SDP Congress took place in late 1967 at regional meetings where local issues and personalities were paramount. The tenor of the convention reflected this shift in delegates as well as the general political tumult. The Convention met on 14–15 March 1968, after the Writers' Congress and during the student demonstration in Warsaw. Delegates entered the building through gatherings of demonstrators who were chanting, among other things, "the press lies." Therefore, while professional concerns were referred to even more consistently than they had been at the 1956 Convention, they were phrased in political terms. Delegates were critical both of the demonstrators and of the political controls that made journalists the subject of condemnation. But, none praised or criticized the nationalist Moczar faction explicitly.[149]

Three major speeches were given by well-known professional personalities, but only Zenon Kliszko spoke for the Party leadership.[150] The major speakers represented the central interests in the profession: Stanisław Mojkowski (the existing leadership of the SDP), Henryk Korotyński (the established journalists and editors), and Kazimierz Kąkol (the Moczar spokesman for the profession). Both Mojkowski and Korotyński clearly were on the defensive. Kąkol was on the attack.

Mojkowski termed the period since the last convention as "good years,"[151] noting that journalists had received pay raises [152] and that they were increasingly well trained and prepared for their work (something those in the younger generation had said was not true of their superiors).[153] He criticized the Gomułka leadership for failing to invest in the press[154] and allowing "the lowest organs to block texts and information" and, at the same time, "trying to force the press to paint them in a positive light."[155] Korotyński's more specific comments reflected his sense of being personally under attack. He blamed the demonstration on the fact that "the young are being used in an internal Party conflict."[156]

Kąkol set himself up as "an expert on public opinion"[157] and a leader in advocating specific policy changes.[158] The demonstrations, he claimed, were the product of the failure of the authorities to deal effectively with the tension in the population. This, he said, was also evidenced by their failure to allow full access to information.[159] He avoided blanket anti-semitism, so characteristc of many attacks, but attacked individuals in the profession by name as "vile" or "pro-Israeli Jews."[160] He justified censorship and external control in terms to which journalists could relate: that there was a need to be "not incidental but responsible" and "equal in treatment to all."[161]

Other delegates advocated increasing the specialization and qualifications for SDP members and,[162] also, criticized the SDP for not being activist enough[163] and not publishing the views of all factions within the profession.[164] The discussion ended without consensus on political or professional issues. But it also produced some striking resolutions:

(1) that the delegates should aid in calming the unrest by insuring full information availability;
(2) that the Main Office of Press Control be shifted to the Council of Ministers and statutorily limited; and
(3) that journalists' meetings be made public *in toto*.[165]

The only immediate and tangible result was a turnover in the executive body of the association (including the editorship of *Prasa Polska*). This lasted until 1971 when tenured executives returned to administering the SDP, although many governing board members who began in 1968 stayed on through the seventies, even as pro-Moczar individuals were pushed out by Gierek forces elsewhere.[166]

The Moczar faction, though, was stymied by opposition from established professionals working secretly and using their long trusted friends. Although many of these journalists and editors were being harassed and threatened, some provided funds or solace to their blacklisted friends to tide them over. And, they took direct action to stop the purges that were sweeping the profession and other intellectual and professional groups. One group of prominent journalists under attack worked secretly with individuals they knew and trusted, through personal contacts with other professionals, to collect the names of old Party loyalists who were being purged. These they compiled in a list and, then, had it presented to Gomułka by one of their number who was close to him. All of this was done in an effort to move him to stop the anti-Semitic attacks. Some claim it helped trigger his public denunciation of the purges.

Association realities and political science theories

The life and politics of the professional associations of journalists are perhaps the clearest indication that "transmission belts" must function like their freer Western counterparts. Professional realities often outweigh political forces. And, given the underlying Western assumption that these associations are "paper tigers" serving politicians' whims, they are also proof that, whatever the apparent role of the regime and the ideological pressure against group formation, individual and group politics have hardly been submerged. Instead, the decline in "star" journalists' leadership and the rise of bureaucratic leaders as well as the turmoil in the profession are more demonstrative of the coincidence of the natural dynamics of the profession and the position of political powers than of some supreme elite machinations. On basic questions of salary and benefit increases, journalists demanded their association take action and they got advocacy, admittedly scaled down to meet the tenor of the times, from their elected leaders. Finally, whatever their assigned role, it is clear that both leaders and members affect and direct each others options.

Given this, it is not surprising that, in dealing on the larger policy arena, journalists are committed and involved. They use many of the same methods that they and their association use in advocating specifically for their profession. Furthermore, it was only natural that the association – while criticized in 1980–81 as too weak and subservient – rapidly became the center of the story of the journalistic profession in the Solidarity and post-Solidarity period, a base of demands, action, and division for the profession and professionals in pushing for changes they wanted to make and issues they felt should be responded to.

5 Journalists as political actors

Politics and policy are for journalists the bread and butter of their professional lives. Their work consists of the stories they write extolling, reporting or criticizing policy. A part of their professional power stems from their ability to key into political life and get a handle on what can be said and where. And, their authority and ability to be viewed as competent and respected professionals doing their jobs is a product, at least in part, of their ability not only to write but also to publish critical articles on significant topics for their readers. Also, having their work result in some change or response is a key to professional status in the same way that doctors' professional authority comes from their ability to solve individuals' health problems or American lawyers' professional status is related to their ability to win cases and champion important issues. At the same time, given the thrust of the political world to see to it that journalists are their servants, journalists draw a line between professional and political life and work. Like Western sociologists defining "profession," they see professionalism as a measure of the autonomy and independence of their group.

Journalists' professional goals

Their definitions of their tasks as journalists are not the same as those of American journalists although both clearly value both their autonomy and their popularity and credibility with readers. (No conversation with a journalist passes without some story to demonstrate that he was recognized and respected by his readers.) Whatever the real convergence of professional journalists' and readers' values about the press, journalists perceive that being popular equals being skilled, seen as providing a necessary and unique service, identified as professional, and ethical – the very qualities that are common to all professionals. And, because of readers' dependence on them, as well as the ideology they have learned, they see themselves as "socially responsible," "a unique group with crucial social skills," and more knowledgeable and capable of making rational decisions in their own area of expertise than their clients.[1]

Given readers' needs, their experiences with bureaucrats, who are reluctant to give out information or accept criticism, and with politicians, who are out of touch with the realities around them, as well as a long-term tradition that journalism be a maker of society, Polish journalists feel that they should not simply report the news but lead in making changes. Most of them, in surveys on their reasons for entering the profession, included "the role of the press in society" as one of the main reasons they became journalists.[2] This role was not just one of "propagating government decisions" but having the right to supervise the making and administration of these decisions.[3]

Equally, journalists made it clear that they did not feel they should simply "reflect public opinion" but felt that they should create a press that played "its role openly as a directive channel of information and, when necessary, an alarm system."[4] This also meant, as one editor stated it, that readers are not fools but "the press is always a center of information about what people want and think. Sometimes we have to structure their desires for their own good."

Their sense of the Party and its leaders' credibility was no greater than their faith in their readers. So, without their professional aid and leadership, journalists stress the whole system would be weakened. They must be

> the tongue and eyes of the Party. Without a tongue the Party would be weak. Without eyes, the Party would be dependent only on the impulses of their own organism. I think it important to establish what we must do so the eyes of the Party will always be open.[5]

They also see themselves as the only honest and sensitive brokers in the local or national establishment. Also, given their reliance on laws and administrative regulations as the basis for their interventions and their battles to get laws passed, for journalists it is not the legal system but the bureaucracy and individual administrators that they have seen as the chief problem to be solved. Therefore, a number of leading journalists in 1976 characterized their expectations of themselves as those of a "loyal opposition party in the English sense." In this, even then, journalists felt that the press had a role.

The experience of journalists, both in seeing problems and failures more often and with more dimensions than average citizens or professionals, and in being forced to justify them to readers, has made them advocates of rationalization and modernization, involving, as it does, a limitation of bureaucratic power. From this perspective, journalists are not unlike the rest of the intelligentsia. At the same time, journalists do not equate this impetus for professionalization with full democratization or insulation from politics. "Reporter" is not a word of distinction for them. They are analysts and actors. In feeling paternalistic toward their readers, journalists tend to feel that they, as experts, should have the final say on issues in their field. And, yet, unlike other professional groups with a stake in modernization, journalists do not see the construction of an infrastructure and industrial base as key. They see a need to simultaneously develop education and institutional responsiveness as well as to shift power to professionals and experts.

Political involvement is required for journalists to do their work successfully. Presenting information, engaging in criticism, and mobilizing and aiding people are not simply journalism. By virtue of their impact, they are also political acts. Since the Party and state have a hand in every facet of life, then, no subject is beyond having political ramifications.

It follows then that journalists' involvement in politics is part and parcel of engaging in their profesion. In this then, publication is only part of their task. To have an impact on policy and to be an active mediator and director, be it in the press or behind the scenes, is a professional task and not an incidental and unprofessional activity.

Combining politics and professionalism

Like lawyers in the United States, journalists may move in and out of political life and professional work in order to enhance their professional options. Or, as individuals concerned about a given issue or simply personally attracted to politics, they may work as behind-the-scenes advisors, officials, or candidates in advocating policies or in formal or informal contests. However they are involved in politics, though, professionals carry their professionalism with them as they step out of their professional role into official political ones or as they doff their professional hats and combine them with political hats to fight for individual issues or to battle for broader changes. In all of their "political" work, journalists' professionalism provides avenues, pressures, and form for their political actions and their influence. Their involvement in their own world as well as their positions as journalists provide them with the ways and means of influencing policy. For political leaders at all levels, having media people directly involved in Party and government bodies is an important way to maintain contact with public opinion and ongoing media investigations as well as to insure that journalists and, therefore, the media are committed to leadership policies. Involving journalists as delegates or officials also gives Party and government organizations greater visibility since journalists have more name recognition than most other officials, a fact Polish officials and journalists discussed very explicitly in 1956 and 1980 when journalists deliberately sought to have "their own" to run for offices. This also means that, at least initially, fellow professionals tolerate journalists holding full-time government and Party posts while still holding positions as journalists or continuing to portray themselves as such. And even when control of the press was tight, in 1976, journalists and local leaders cited professional journalists' credibility and name recognition as their key virtues in politics.[6]

There are also, however, clear limits on this combination of professional and political life. Journalists judge each other on the basis of what they write and say – its impact and insight. So, to write about or publicly advocate something that is either not solvable or contrary to professional norms is considered counterproductive and dangerous for the profession. Journalists effectively impose an unspoken ethical code on their colleagues' political work. An important and relatively universal part of this code is that those working in the political arena must support and protect the profession's autonomy and its policy interests and also protect individual colleagues from harassment or censorship by giving them private counsel or by direct intervention. Ironically, though, while the profession has long prided itself on its protection of the rights of individual professionals to support whatever political position they wish, as long as they act as independent actors and not as "bought" servants, the movement of journalists into the political world means they are being judged on the basis of professionally related actions and stands taken in these political positions. For many, as a result, the desire to maintain credibility within their professional community is an important reason to elect to work behind the scenes and eschew work in official positions that put them in the public eye.

Journalists' basic involvement in policy-making is through the impact of what they publish or present as well as their individual political ties. It also entails deliberately engaging in criticism of existing policies and pushing for or creating new policies. This participation most often goes on simultaneously through behind-the-scenes pressure and connections and explicit public activities and leadership. In doing this, journalists work together as a group and also as individuals on policies. Some few step into official positions and leave journalism or combine professional roles with official Party, state, or organizational offices while others work informally when called on by the political leadership or when they have "windows of opportunity." This is often combined with press criticism, intervention work, or the organization of press actions. In all of this, journalists, girded with what they see as their professional role to be a loyal opposition, monitoring the government and forming public opinion, are involved in a complex net of relationships and initiatives that impact not only on specific policies but also on themselves as individuals and on their journal's or program's broader impact on an even wider range of policies.

Little of this activity is ever discussed explicitly and publicly. Only through interviews, like the ones on which this volume is based, is it possible to tell what the full spectrum of journalists' visible and invisible "political" or policy-related activities has been, what the intent and meaning of these activities are for those engaged in them, and how they impact on professional life in general. Based on what journalists reported they thought and did in times of quiet, the sudden appearance of journalists as leaders in 1956 and 1980 is not surprising nor does it disprove any contention that they are professionals. It is merely an unveiling of what have been normal patterns of action for journalists as professionals.

"Leadership" positions

In Poland journalism has been the profession with the highest percentage of Polish United Workers' Party members.[7] They are a presence in representative bodies ranging from parliament (see Table 3, p. 167) to local councils and the executive bodies for social associations. For most of them, though, this has involved only token participation,[8] or the advocacy of specific issues in governmental and organizational bodies. Most often, Party membership is an externally imposed requirement for editorial positions or specialization on important topics in prominent journals or it is a reflection of an individuals' longer term interest in playing a role or being heard. Party membership, as opposed to taking part in representative or official offices of Party, governmental, or social organizations, is then a formal necessity for professional mobility, not a way to have political power. Nor is it usually a particularly public activity.

Journalists play or hold leadership roles in the political establishment when, either because of their position or their personal inclinations, they function not only as organization members but also as officials. Some journalists or editors hold these posts because of their own stature as respected professionals and their personal desire to officially use that stature or increase it. For social organizations and for Party and state bodies, journalists are important because of their name recognition. With this recognition, journalists can generate public attention and support for their organization through what they write. Even in the Solidarity and martial law periods when working in the establishment press had lost much of its prestige, this pattern of journalists giving credibility to an organization with their name was mirrored in the staffing of the Solidarity press and advisory bodies as well as in the staffing decisions of many small social and economic organizations trying to gain recognition.[9]

The presence of editors or journalists (other than those who head Party organs) in politically prominent positions is, in fact, not only a product of their desires and the personal prestige they lend but also of the political elite's interest in the press. So, in the Gomułka years where there was little interest in popular involvement or change, few individuals, even those with close contacts to top political leaders, were made Central Committee members. In the early Gierek years, though, some prominent journalists who had made names for themselves in both the profession and the political arena, like Mieczysław Rakowski, Kazimierz Kąkol, and West German specialist Ryszard Wojna, were members or candidate members of the Central Committee. As independent figures appointed to these positions, they were more active as advocates than the political appointees who were editors of top Party organs as a part of their Party duties (see Table 3, p. 167).

Although there is little published information on Central Committee discussions, some of these actors were willing to talk in 1976 and 1979 about their positions and activities on the Central Committee. The editors who were relatively independent (and often their subordinates) reported that they used the work of their journalists to substantiate their own policy positions in the Central Committee and lower level Party bodies. They pictured themselves more as representatives of their journals than of the profession. As a result, they

Table 3 *Membership of professional journalists in the Sejm*

Year	Number of journalists	Total Sejm membership
1957	29	459
1961	19	460
1965	30	460
1969	27[a]	460
1972	27[b]	460
1977	25	460

Sources: George Mond, "La Presse, les Intellectuals, et le pouvoir en Union Sovetique et dans pays socialistes Europeens," Notes et Etudes Documentaires, La Documentation française, Secretariat General du Gouvernement, no. 3729–3720 (22 October 1970), p. 16 and Radio Free Europe, Polish Situation Report (2 April 1976).

Notes: [a]George Mond, in reporting these statistics, did not include Wincenty Krasko, Arthur Starewicz, and Włodzimierz Lechowicz in computing the number of journalists in the Polish parliament. This was in line with the listing done by *Trvbuna Ludu* which excluded these three in spite of the fact that they had been editors-in-chief or active journalists at some point in their professional careers. In 1969, they were no longer working as journalists and were not members of the Association of Polish Journalists.

[b]In the Radio Free Europe statistics which were used, writers, journalists, and columnists were listed together.

Table 4 *Membership of professional journalists in higher PUWP organs*

Year	Full CC member	Candidate CC member	Audit commission	Control commission
1959	6	7	0	1
1964	5	5	2	2
1969	7	8	4	(21)
1971	2	12	3	2
1975	3	11		

Sources: Mond, "La Presse . . .," p. 17 and Radio Free Europe, Polish Situation Report (19 December 1975), p. 2.

negotiated primarily for specific allowances for their own journals. They often spoke about the media and the profession at national Party meetings. But, in actual policy-making situations, they preferred to work as individuals using their reputations and the connections their Party posts gave them to force a reversal of a censor's decision or to get access to information. Often, they did not have to act; as they and their journalists knew, few censors wanted to risk opposing the editorial decision of a Central Committee member. Or, they had friends and cronies in the Central Committee on whom they could call for a favor if they thought an article or a statement was worth rescuing from censorship. Only in the late seventies did these shields weaken. Then, Party bureaucrats were often so strong that they called even Central Committee members who were editors and told them to stop their "black presentations" or refused even their requests to consider reversing censors' decisions. During this time, these editors felt frustrated and trapped into having to wait for some outside event to bring in new, more rational and sympathetic Party leadership.

As individuals, on the other hand, "journalism stars" closely tied to Party leaders, often have been candidates for the parliament (Sejm) or other governmental bodies. As candidates, they were popular figures in their own right and normally garnered more voter support than most other kinds of candidates. According to the available information, these journalists, when elected, tended to function in the Sejm, as they have in Party organs, not as representatives of their districts but as representatives of the profession and their papers or television programs. SDP organs referred to them as "our representatives in the Sejm" and pressured them to push the interests of the journalistic community.[10] So, journalists were particularly active in debates on budgetary allocations for paper; the technical needs of radio and television; Criminal and Civil Code discussions on provisions affecting journalists; discussions on cultural issues;[11] and, in 1980–81, all discussions of the censorship bill and the initial proposals for an overarching law on the press.[12]

Those tied to political factions or groups personally or through their papers advocated these views in the Sejm in championing "journalists' needs." Others brought their criticisms, growing out of their work in investigating and criticizing regional or national institutions, to the Sejm for action. For instance, one journalist reported that his editor-in-chief had been active in investigating the working conditions in a local porcelain factory and had, even before any of the investigations had been published, raised the issue in the Sejm: "Much was changed as a result of his presentations in the Sejm. The rest we journalists could do, with this public backing, through contacts with ministries and local officials. They knew that they had to respond because we were represented in the Sejm."

Except in unique cases of regional journalists, few advocate simply for their districts. Their ties with their electoral districts are limited to individual requests for intervention and aid. Journalist–delegates reported that they had used their positions as journalists to deal with constituents' problems at least as often as they had used their prerogatives as delegates. Because they were journalists and could turn to the press, they said they got better responses. From their perspective, 'the power of the press is clearly much greater than the power of any individual delegate."

This pattern continued into the eighties. When the censorship law was presented and introduced in the Sejm, for instance, it was the journalist Karol Małcużyński who took the lead. And, when there were clear moves against the profession and its gains from the Solidarity period, he spoke out as the journalists' representative and not as his constituents' representative.[13] Although he was often more articulate and critical than others from the profession, other journalist–delegates have taken similar if less visible actions.[14]

In the crisis of the early eighties, in fact, journalists who had been among the most respected professionals, both with readers and in the profession, were appointed to the posts of government press spokesman and also Deputy Prime Minister (Jerzy Urban and Mieczysław Rakowski, respectively). In each case, their initial appointments were intended to raise the prestige of the office and improve the public's respect for the government as a whole.[15] The significance of journalism to these men and the significance of their work as journalists to their prestige was clear from their reluctance to give up their professional posts. Both insisted on continuing in their professional positions for months after their political appointments and continued to claim to be journalists and to dabble in journalism even after they resigned their formal media positions. These resignations were, in fact, only a result of the discomfort of their staff and their own time pressures. Rakowski and Urban are not and were not, however, unique. In local level politics, in Solidarity work, and in various professional and social organizations that came to life in the Solidarity period, journalists appeared as officials, even as they held on to their journalistic posts (just as they had done in the sixties and seventies when some combined, for short periods, journalism and official Party or state posts).

Journalists basically, then, do not feel that a clear break is always necessary between their Party, government, or social organization roles and their professional roles and positions. But, they are no less professional in the full sense of the word. For the organizations they have helped lead, they are considered primarily as journalists, as links with public opinion. They see themselves in this same light, as professional journalists whose work is to use their professional expertise to present and interpret public issues and opinions. In their organizations and in their own minds, journalists who are officially involved are expected to report on topics raised by readers and other journalists. As a result of these reports, journalists in official positions feel they are "doing journalism" by stimulating action even without the publication of criticism. At the same time, solving readers' problems was and is a very important component of professional work for them. They have used these forums to present their interpretations of readers' letters and journalistic investigations in order to support their professional interests, particularly in areas of journalism in which they specialize.

For most, the ability to protect and even enlarge their professional autonomy and power is crucial. Most journalist-activists stated that, on some issues, in fact, they even had to "inflate public opinion a little" and that they were highly selective of the issues they raised and with whom they raised them. Again, their image of themselves has been as autonomous professional actors with personal, professional interests rather than as instruments of the party or organization they serve. Their ability to make judgments as to what is feasible professionally has been heightened, in turn, by what they learn from their political posts in the same way that their political positions are an outgrowth of their journalistic work.

The editors on Party executive committees who were interviewed, for instance, characterized themselves as representatives of their papers. In this, their role is a dual one. For their committee, they were a link to the press, reporting on the work of their journalists and the criticisms of the local situation brought to them by their readers. In these meetings, the others on the committee commented on the work of their journal. Editors responded with explanations of their goals and with demands for more access to information and more freedom. Editors, then, both communicated the criticisms and suggestions of the executive committee to the staff and, conversely, used their Party positions to protect the staff and the ability of their journal to take independent stands.

All the journalists interviewed took their dualism into consideration. They ranked editors according to the political power they wielded. "Good editors" were aware of Party discussions and communicated them to the staff. They also had enough political clout to protect the journal from daily intervention by the censors' office and Party functionaries. In doing this, they could see to it that journalists were able to solve the problems they took on and force changes. "Unprofessional editors" were those who did little more for the paper than take their delegated seat on a political body.

Chief editors of Party-affiliated journals do hold *nomenklatura* positions filled through the Party bureaucracy. Often, there is a carousel of journalists who enter the apparatus and leave it to serve as editors. Individuals then return to higher positions in the Party apparatus after serving as editors. None of those on the carousel, though, are leaders or particularly successful in journalism. A few, assigned to high status papers, have remained in journalism and built a personal power base for themselves as professional editors. Whatever the case, the editor with experience and connections in the Party apparatus almost never wants to sever them when he takes a journalistic position. At the same time, he is usually cautious about demeaning his editorship with reference to his Party role and power.

The interview data also reveal that these prominent politicians and journalists moving in and out of the apparatus are hardly the norm. Regional and central journalists with little or no popular following are most often the ones drafted into the Party apparatus. Because they do not have an independent professional base, these journalists frequently do not have the power or authority to take truly independent positions and be heard. Their inclination is, thus, to enhance their personal political position. In most instances, journalists become instructors on the Central Committee or hold camparable low to middle-level positions on regional bodies. Most work on special projects, on Party Leaders' speeches and public statements, or in areas unrelated to their former professional work. Few of these "grey men" are willing to work in positions where they are very visible to their colleagues. If they do become visible in the apparatus, they are then unwilling to return to the profession and the distrust of their colleagues unless they are rewarded with a chief editorship. Hence, most are the "grey eminences" of the Party apparatus and exert less direct influence on Party press relations than do higher level politicians who come in more temporarily and at higher levels. These *prominente* see their main loyalty in their professional ties in journalism. Their significance is basically in serving as links between Party needs and the journalists' mentality, so often incomprehensible to Party bureaucrats.

Most journalists in the Party bureaucracy have continued to submit articles to journals. This often was both a financial necessity, since journalists can earn more than Party bureaucrats, and an attempt to maintain profession status. In a few cases too, their articles served as voices for factions in the Party with the hope that their advocacy would be remembered if that faction won and they would have a leg up and move to some prominent editorial post.[16]

There is no hard evidence on the posture of any of these journalists toward the media, given that their work goes on inside the Party itself. Interviews with journalists suggest, though, that prominent Party officials who spent some period of their careers in media work were more likely to be supportive of the development of a media that appeals to readers and is critical. They also indicated that Party apparatus work builds neither a positive outlook toward the Party establishment nor a platform for individuals to increase their professional status.

The relations of journalists and editors working on minor Party, union, and association journals with their sponsoring organization have been much the same as those of the Party editor-activists. In these cases, journalism is often melded with political and organization leadership. As with PUWP journals, the whole staff does not necessarily belong to the minor Party or social organization. Even on the official Solidarity press, some individuals were originally hired as staff journalists simply because of their availability or writing ability. But, in most cases, the top editorial board consists of members of the sponsoring organization. The editor-in-chief of a minor party or association journal is customarily also on the executive committee of the organization.[17]

Journals sponsored by mass organizations such as trade unions (*Głos Pracy*) or youth organizations (*Sztandar Młodych* or *Walka Młodych*) often have editors who are political appointees with little experience in journalism. Their authority as political brakes on the journals, however, has been limited by the strength of staff traditions and the Party's need for the journal to be an effective link with readers.

Editors of minor party and social organization journals are aware of the restrictions placed on their sponsoring organization and their journal by the PUWP Press Department. It has instructors assigned to direct and review the work of all these organs. Therefore, until Solidarity shifted the balance of power, journalists and editors were unwilling to move politically without enough support from their organization's executive committee to protect them from the wrath of the PUWP officialdom. And, since pay scales on these "other party" journals have usually been low, so has been the status of an editorship. Editors, therefore, have been willing to move into or take on additional work in the administration of the sponsoring organization. This occurs especially since the leadership group in minor parties is so small that these former editors do not lose contact with "their" journals.

Catholic journals, generally, have had close communications with their sponsors. On the one hand, the pro-communist Catholic organization, PAX, was run so that the paper and the organization itself were the fiefdom of one man, Bolesław Piasecki, until his death in 1979. The editorial board of the PAX journal, *Słowo Powszechne*, tended to be made up of individuals closely connected with him. In explaining the position of *Słowo Powszechne* all interviewees said that Piasecki maintained daily supervision of articles as well as close personal ties with members of the staff and with the Party's Moczar faction, when it was active. In this group, his personal monopoly over the journal gave him a decisive role. This was particularly true because he had been allowed to develop a profitable publishing house and industry producing household goods and religious products.[18] His private "lobbying" in the factions and through his journal was, however, limited to periods of factional dispute within the PUWP. Then, Piasecki provided a forum for views which coincided with his own. Once he was out of the picture, there was a clear conflict in PAX over leadership of the organization.[19] The editor of the paper advocated his own line and candidacy against the head of the executive board. This led to a radicalization of both the paper and the PAX movement and, finally, the necessity for martial law authorities to restrain and reclaim PAX and its press.[20]

On the other hand, there has been a loose community in the Catholic intelligentsia groupings which, since the end of World War II, have struggled to communicate an alternative ideology to the communist one while restraining their opposition enough to be allowed to exist. *Tygodnik Powszechny* is formally an organ of the primary Catholic intelligentsia grouping, ZNAK, and its editor has been a member of the ZNAK parliamentary delegation.[21] This group, like the staff of the weekly, has been fairly stable since 1956. The organization itself is both small and very informal. The result has been that most consultations and decision-making occur on an informal basis with editors and journalists working as equals in the self-appointed leadership of the organization. For this reason, positions are easily shifted or combined in movements from organizational leaders to editors and back. Journalists' policy advocacy is assumed to be for the movement and not simply the opinion of journalists. For *Tygodnik Powszechny* and the monthlies and quarterlies ZNAK and other Catholic groups produce, financial support for the press and other activities come from the industries allocated them by the state as well as their earnings from circulation. Their censorship and circulation are strictly controlled by the state censors' office and RSW Prasa. This makes journalists and their editors very sensitive to the possibilities of further restrictions. Laying out public policy options is, then, less relevant. They are most often limited on their pages and in public forums to principled general criticism. In formulating policy, many Znak journalists serve as instigators for public forums and generate debates that are potentially, although not always, publishable. At these, experts and concerned critics are brought together before an audience of interested members of the Catholic Intelligentsia Clubs and the broader public.[22] These forums then are used as sources for the articles and some of the discussions published in the Catholic press. They have also served, sometimes, as the most open forum for journalists who wanted to come together with experts to discuss policy proposals they considered critical but which were strongly sanctioned by the political leadership and, therefore, even discussions of them were not easy to stage elsewhere. In the Solidarity period and in the era of martial law, these debates became one of the models and havens for intellectuals outside the Catholic circles.

This meant, in 1980, that journalists and editors could become involved with Solidarity or have close ties to dissident groups and still be harbored by ZNAK. It also meant, in the months after martial law and in 1968, that blacklisted journalists could be helped financially and allowed to write and publish by them as a humanitarian gesture and political statement since the boundary lines between employment and club membership were vague at best and Catholicism was hardly a qualifier.

Private contacts

Top journalists and professional officials have dealt with political leaders in a multitude of contexts. Some are formal meetings that are seldom mentioned or fully reported in the press. These have ranged from formal and publicly touted but not fully reported "news conferences" to confidential background sessions called by the Press Department or a ministry and also private meetings of select professionals with Party or state representatives. They have also made use of an entire spectrum of "private" channels ranging from conferences and consultations to speech writing and the circulation of private memos and "internal media," written for or, at least, given only to the political elite to read. How private communiction goes on and to what extent it is effective is a product of the interest of a political leadership in the problems and opinions of their societies as well as journalists' own energy. For the profession, this work, in spite of the fact that it is not published or public, is a critical element in their professional duties. It is one of the key ways journalists maintain their influence, engage in effective criticism and analysis, and circulate information. All of these, of course, are roles professionals in journalism consider key jobs of the profession.

Since the Stalinist period, journalists have been pictured to the public as meeting formally with political leaders and serving as questioners and advisors. Such formal meetings have been used by journalists to express concerns and to push for gains or policy changes. At the least, journalists have seen them as a chance to be seen and recognized. However, they have also never forgotten that these meetings are at the behest of and on the turf of the political leadership.

The Party leadership makes use of various forms of visible and ceremonial "consultation with journalists" to communicate with, inform and coopt journalists. In the Gierek era more than in Gomułka's time, well publicized press conferences and public meetings with Polish journalists were held. In these meetings, held at Ministries and Party headquarters or at the various SDP clubs, Party leaders responsible for the working of the press or Party or Ministry officials involved in a specific policy decision argued their case and attempted to buy the support of journalists. Journalists used the forums to make clear the problems and opposition to policies that were raised by people when they did their storygathering.

Journalists reported that, in many instances, they also met formally with groups or individuals as experts or as interviewers, either at their own initiative or on the invitation of other professionals. They then used those contacts to advocate specific policies censored out of the media. For instance, when journalists were concerned with the possibility that a psychiatric law allowing for involuntary commitment would be passed, they scheduled meetings with other concerned professionals and ministry spokesmen to reinforce their opposition, even though they could make only veiled illusions to the issue and its ramifications in the press.[23]

Expert testimony

Journalists with topical specialties, particularly in foreign affairs, are often called on to testify as experts before Party and government bodies. In the case of journalists who have worked abroad, they often have had more experience and exposure in a country or area than members of the Ministry of Foreign Affairs or the Central Committee's International Department. So, they are often the best independent experts available, especially given the limitations on foreign travel for Polish academics and the problems of making contacts for Polish diplomats. During crises abroad, the foreign correspondents sometimes write reports that they know cannot be published but were requested to write for private distribution to the Politburo or some limited group concerned with the issue. Correspondents are called in to discuss policy when they are on home leave or when there is a crisis in the area. One journalist who dealt with the Third World, characterized the consultations and his work in this way:

> They make no attempt to control what I write. In fact, they have no information on the situation other than what I give them or what the Soviets tell them. So I am able to tell them what to do. Or at least give them a report so they can anticipate Soviet policy. My censorship is my own, unless the situation becomes a major international incident. Then, I can remain quiet. The only time they call me to complain is if my articles offend some nation. That happens very seldom because I know better than they what I must write to keep my visa. They are always aware that they need me and my contacts.

Similar requests for advice and testimony are made of journalists known for their work and expertise on domestic issues. In these cases, journalists' expertise often extends to advice on what should be considered in policy decisions and who else should be called in for consultations. Particularly on domestic issues, journalists increase their impact by following up and focusing on these subjects in their writing.

In 1957 and 1980–81, Polish journalists served as experts not only to Polish officials but also to individuals and institutions outside Poland. Representatives of the SDP met with representatives of the Soviet Embassy in 1956 and 1980. They spoke about Soviet dissatisfaction with the behavior of Polish journalists and about "political issues which were agitating Poland."[24] Journalists argued the case for liberalization both for the society and the press. After their meeting in 1957, journalists, as representatives of the SDP, made careful notes and an analysis of the meetings and gave it to Central Committee members. In noncrisis periods journalist–politicians often have kept up these private contacts with officials so they can unofficially feel out policy alternatives and "communicate."

In 1980–81, this took on a greater urgency. Journalists felt an equal compulsion to protect themselves and Poland itself from attacks by the Soviet Union and other regimes in Eastern Europe. To this end, they often wined and dined individual Soviet and East European correspondents late into the night at the SDP dining room so that the reasoning would be heard. To convince them that SDP meetings were not revolutionary, they invited Soviet and East European correspondents to all their public meetings.

These efforts took on special urgency in the summer of 1981. In line with what they saw as their professional roles, even though they were snubbed at the meetings of the International Organization of Journalists held in Moscow during that summer, the SDP delegates continued to advocate what they saw as "their profession's interests." Lower level delegates attended panels in Moscow on problems and professional needs arguing their cases, where possible. They functioned like a professional group in need of material aid, unclear as to its full legal status, and concerned with insuring that its control and autonomy were broadened. In addition, since Soviet criticism had so often been thrown up to journalists as an indication of the real danger of invasion should the press be too critical, delegates, especially Bratkowski, took action to mobilize all their contacts to convince those Soviets they knew or could make contact with that the "Polish August" was not a threat. This involved heated formal and informal debates all over Moscow, where Bratkowski and his group tried to protect their profession's gains by communicating enough to discourage Soviet intervention. Thus, they used every formal and informal opportunity they had to sit as experts and information purveyors in order to avoid setting off a society-wide crackdown that would end media freedom.[25]

Personal contacts with the elite

Journalists and editors who have established personal ties with members of the political elite use them extensively to influence policy decisions and to protect their journals' interests and those of their colleagues. Many editors and journalists have family or childhood connections with political leaders. Other *prominente* spent the war together with men who were to become Party leaders. Some built personal links with members of the political hierarchy when they had temporary journalistic assignments or when they made contacts in the course of making reports. Finally, some politicians have courted journalists, especially when those politicians sought to build their own power base. Such ties have been part and parcel of journalism on the national level and on local levels.

Influential personal contacts with members of the national elite have been the almost exclusive domain of Warsaw journalists. Having these contacts and using them to enhance their writing and publishing ability have helped journalists get and keep themselves in high status professional positions. The primary exceptions to the Warsaw cabal were the journalists who had worked under Gierek in Katowice when he was head of the Silesian PUWP organization and who then moved with him to Warsaw when he became First Secretary.

Normally, journalists meet informally with their friends in the political leadership. Those in Warsaw meet with national officials and those in other areas with regional officials. Members of the leadership monitor closely what their "friends" say in the press and tend, journalists claim, to give it special consideration. Most members of the political leadership also tend to act on private and public criticism from journalists they know and see regularly. These journalists, in turn, use their "friends" or patrons as sources for information, both "off-the-record" and for publication. Through these personal contacts, leaders insure visibility for themselves and "their" positions and journalists enhance their access.

Most of this interchange goes on behind closed doors. Personal ties are rumored and "used" by journalists, they are not publicized. Nor is it acceptable for a politician or official to court journalists or for journalists to be "bought." Approaching professional journalists ostentatiously with private meetings, elaborate dinners, and the release of special information, as the Moczarists did in the mid-sixties, has not been the norm. From the reports of journalists, then, their contacts are ones they make, maintain, and use to further their interests, not contacts made to "use" them and their press.

These personal ties have also been used to protect individual journalists. For example, *Świat* (established in the early 1960s on the model of *Life* magazine) was closed down in 1968 on the grounds that it had been sympathetic to Israel in the 1967 war. Both its editors had had close personal contacts with Gomułka. When the decision was made to close the journal, Gomułka called the editors and assured them that comparable positions would be found for them and the staff. Together, the two top editors were put in charge of the foreign language publication of the Institute on International Relations.

And, although the dynamics of the post-Solidarity era made splits over politics far more bitter, editors with political power still helped colleagues and former colleagues get out of internment and also helped get them positions so they could survive. On a more day to day basis, journalists from the sixties on, both those remaining in the press and those who left it, reported calling their "friends" in the Central Committee or its apparatus to ask for assistance in publishing an article, or solving a problem raised by readers with which they, as individual journalists, had become personally identified.

Communiques and publications

The profession of journalism, as a whole, functions as one of the prime information gatherers for the elite. It does so in regular, if classified, publications and through private channels. In some instances, journal staffs also have produced policy proposals and distributed them to members of the political elite in the hope of influencing their positions. At times, these are simply individual letters or manuscripts they draft and distribute explicitly to draw attention to their concerns. At other times, this advocacy is more explicitly "journalism." Journals draw up yearly and quarterly plans. These are, sometimes, used as vague policy statements. Since these plans are often observed only in abeyance, journalists seldom treat them as anything more than limited advocacy. But, in periods of crisis, these have been the tools used by journalists to "seize the moment."

In 1970, in one of the most significant examples of this, a group of *Polityka* staff members used its yearly plan as a political platform. They drew up a plan with their editor, Rakowski, not only criticizing the general policies of Gomułka but also suggesting alternatives. Change in Poland was to be focused on the interests of the technical intelligentsia. This plan was then circulated to a limited number of Central Committee members and candidate members thought, by those who drafted the plan, to be potential supporters, including Edward Gierek. Its impact is clear: a comparison of the secret *Polityka* document shows that Gierek's early policy statements were taken almost directly from it. With this too, Rakowski and his journal earned a high position in the Gierek system until its (and their) economic program collapsed.

At a more mass advocacy level, readers are urged by journalists to contact newspapers with their comments on policy and to request intervention in specific problems. Collections of these comments or montages on issues journalists consider significant are made and sent to regional or central Party and, sometimes, state officials. When ministries' actions are questioned by readers, public press criticism is normally preceded by private contacts with the officials involved. Journalists report and ask the ministry to resolve a specific case or to act to limit general abuses. Normally, citizens' criticisms are published only when the cases are of general interest or when the ministry is not responsive to private intervention. If journalists' attempts at individual action are not effective, Party organs are then simultaneously notified of general abuses, alerted, and asked to help on individual cases.

Internal reports on readers' complaints and journalists' interventions as well as broad surveys of public opinion are produced by the staff. Journalists claim they sometimes could and did manipulate these reports on issues *they* as professionals considered crucial because their experience had been that crediting "the reader" was the most effective way to create pressure for policy change. For example, in the case of alimony law revision, journalists from the women's magazine, *Przyjaciółka*, sent regular collections of letters and tabulations of complaints on the problems of divorced women and their children as well as reports of individual tragedies to Party officials and relevant ministry officials. This, coupled with press discussion of the alternative solutions, led to a revised divorce and alimony law that made the state responsible for all unpaid alimony. In another case, journalists from regional papers collected and presented letters of complaint about the regionalization of schools. As a result of the problems of regionalization brought to light by journalists, the consolidation law was only loosely enforced and full regionalization was avoided. Journalists also customarily report any increases in the number of anonymous letters received by their journal. This they see as a sign of increased popular disaffection.

Journalists, even in non-public communications to the Party elite, maintain a professional ethical code. Any request for anonymity by readers in their letters or contacts with journalists was reported to be honored. Even without such a request, journalists tend to conceal the actual identity of their sources. Often, in the internal reports seen in the course of this research, readers' comments were identified only by sex, age, occupation, and general residence. This veiling of sources is, as one journalist noted, "not only ethical but necessary. Without it they [policy-makers and politicians] can destroy our links. With it, we control the information."

The censors' office, under the direction of the Press Department of the Central Committee, also published a confidential journal until the mid-seventies; then, elite tolerance for even unpublished criticism disappeared. *Signals* published articles blocked from publication by the censors' office that its directors felt would be of interest to the policy-makers but not safe for public consumption. For the political elite, this journal is a crucial "window on the real Poland." Although an organ of the censors, it also allowed for a limited monitoring of censors' work.

In the sixties and seventies, top leaders normally received only *Signals*, and *Polityka, Trybuna Ludu, Życie Gospodarcze*, and PAP Daily Internal Bulletins. Few read the regional or mass press unless an article was called to their attention by the Press Department or other leaders. So, an article censored and published in *Signals* by a regional or mass circulation writer got more "visibility" at the top than articles that went uncensored.

Therefore, journalists sometimes termed the censors' office and *Signals* as "liberating." It not only protected journalists from being punished for controversial articles but also brought their work to the attention of policy-makers. In interviews, journalists reported that they received personal notes and calls from top members of the Politburo in the sixties thanking them for the information and assuring them the problems they raised had or would be resolved. One even reported that he had been paid his standard rate for his article in *Signals*. All made clear that publication in *Signals* was a useful way to "make policy" and act politically as well as simply a regular part of professional work.

The ending of *Signals*, in the mid-seventies, broke down this channel of information. As a result, both journalists and the elite were made more dependent either on political leaders' assistants noticing articles and drawing them to the elite's attention or on using their personal contacts.

On other occasions, because journalists' writing and investigations made them known to Party and state leaders and bureaucrats, journalists often have been called on to draft speeches and internal Party reports for political figures. In doing this, journalists typically received only general instructions as to what they should write and how. They were expected to rely on their own well-developed sense of the political winds for direction. But, even on sensitive issues they have had leeway in these speeches particularly since the leaders seldom reviewed their speeches before they gave them and because speechwriters' identities were hidden. So, in doing these speeches and reports as well as informal and very personalized advising of individual leaders, journalists often made political points and support for their positions by setting up the leaders or by appearing to question or to provide objective advice.

Journalists and their publics

The media are not the only channels through which a journalist can distribute information and affect government opinion. In their own circle of friends, many of whom are other journalists or policymakers, journalists often discuss and disseminate information they cannot publish. They make it a point to let individual readers know their problems are not theirs alone and to suggest ways individuals can force administrative or policy changes. As a group, journalists are popular speakers at community gatherings. They are invited and paid by factory committees, local community groups, Book Clubs, and International Press and Book Clubs. National journalists with known specializations and connections are the most popular. Journalists interviewed stated that the listeners' demands for information were powerful and their questions so sharp and critical that "it makes one's blood run cold."

Most journalists reported, in interviews, speaking openly with these groups, divulging information that they could never have printed. They were often honest with listeners about what can and what cannot be published.[26] In some cases, meetings became so agitated that the most controversial of journalists were pressed by officials to take along a second, "safe journalist" to counteract their comments and to report on the meeting. For journalists, these forums were not so much money-making ventures as opportunities to make clear to their readers that they were more knowledgeable and independent than their articles showed. There was also a chance to "rally a public" and increase the pressure for policy changes or public action.

Journalists and alternate elites

Finally, journalists have tended to be a "loyal opposition party" not only in their constant monitoring, as members of the political "establishment," of the direction and reality of public policy but, also, in the linkage they provide between the "establishment" and those who question it. Even though Party and state elites have themselves frequently had friends who question the very system and its policies, it has been journalists who, as professionals, have consciously served as links and conduits of information between those who are in the leadership and administration and those who oppose it. In doing this, journalists often become very active not so much in declared opposition activities as in intellectual groups who question the working of the existing system.

Often journalists were the fulcrum of these networks and groupings. Throughout the postwar period, journal offices were meeting places for individual talks and informal, often spontaneous gatherings of like-minded intellectuals and policy advocates. In fact, *ad hoc* exchanges are daily events as journalists talk to readers, interview sources, and debate strategies. The association headquarters serve a similar function in Warsaw and other smaller media centers when clubs of specialists and their restaurants and cafes serve as both formal and impromptu forums for individuals to debate and build coalitions.[27]

The political landscape in which journalists work has, since the days of Stalinism, been peopled with informal groups of intellectuals concerned with the failings of the system or potential changes in it. On the whole, these groups have had no official sanction. They involve Party as well as non-Party members, Catholics and nonreligious, and individuals from various fields. Most are drawn together out of long-term friendship circles or from groups of individuals who had worked together on policy or programs. The bulk of these groups, particularly those with which journalists are most often connected, are not treated as opposition groups. Instead, they are minimally tolerated forms of internal dissent focused on encouraging specific changes through private discussions and contacts.

Journalists come into these groups naturally. They are "known commodities" because of their writings or productions and because they are seen questioning and reporting at all kinds of meetings and events. Beyond this, journalists are also seen as "informed informers" who can get and disseminate information. When journalists were asked why they thought they were contacted or when other professionals were asked why they brought journalists into discussions, their responses always dealt with the fact that they were "known" either because they had worked together as story writers or sources or because journalists were identifiable commodities with visible expertise.

These groups and journalists' involvement in them have varied dramatically. *Ad hoc* groups of specialists and concerned journalists have grown out of meetings called by various professional groupings to highlight the need for research to demonstrate a problem or for work to rethink proposed legislation, to issue information, or else, to provide information requested by a ministry. These groups have met either as professional forums to exchange ideas or, informally, to plan their attack on an issue or an existing policy and to share gossip. This they did during the seventies, for example, in opposition to a proposed "anti-parasite law" that would have allowed for the internment of people without work and a draft law that would have allowed for involuntary psychiatric commitment (both of which were considered potential ways for the government to repress dissidents).[28] Other groups have been formally organized to provide expertise on specific problems for the government or some social or economic organization. Journalists have been involved in these as specialists. In the course of their work, they have seen it as professional to give opinions and information. So, for instance, journalists on the historical monuments commission pressed for the saving of their favorite historic monuments and they also initiated discussions on the impact of pollution on the historic buildings in Kraków. This they did in concert with other professionals long before pollution was allowed to be discussed in the Polish media.[29]

Journalists and other intellectuals have come together to deal with broad political and social problems. In 1956, these groups included open discussion groups like the Club of the Crooked Circle, formed by those newly released from prison and others active in the movement of liberalization.[30] In these groups, taboos on information and criticism exploded. Journalists were their prime movers. Their meetings, often in rooms so packed with people that crowds stood outside hanging on every word, were journalists' initial "media" for presenting the information they had long resented having to hold back. The precedents, established by these group discussions, were stimulants for journalists to press to publish more information – the "vitamin I" they thought the society needed.

The experience and, often, some of the networks on which these groups were based continued after the Polish October. In the sixties, there were informal gatherings of concerned and often frustrated intellectuals and activists. But, since few explicit new policies were enacted, there were few triggers for real organization. In the seventies, Gierek policy changed this. By the mid seventies, these informal groups of establishment intellectuals were paralleled and eventually challenged by the emergence of declared opposition groups like the Committee to Protect Workers (KOR) organized after the repression against the strikes protesting the 1976 price increases.[31]

The most visible and formal of the "establishment" groups in which journalists served as key players, "Experience and the Future," began in 1978. Then, a number of journalists and scholars organized themselves to rethink Poland's policies. Initially, the organizers, including journalists like Stefan Bratkowski and some of the *Polityka* staff, arranged a meeting, about which they intended to report in the media. For this meeting, two of Gierek's advisors served as keynote speakers. Invitations were sent mostly to friends and known "idea people" in

Warsaw and the provinces. This group included a number of prominent journalists and editors. The gathering itself and the speeches were very critical. As a result, future meetings were banned. But a group, primarily of journalists from the 1956 generation, continued to work by circulating a questionnaire and compiling the responses they received. These they collected and collated, following their ethical code, as journalists, of not revealing their sources. Then, they circulated what had been collected to those within the "Experience and Future" group and among selected Party and state leaders. This process went on throughout the early and mid-eighties. In the heat of the Solidarity period, it sponsored many public forums – most of which were held at SDP headquarters since Bratkowski doubled as a leader of "Experience and the Future" and of the SDP. So, its leadership and focus came to be on Bratkowski and others from the new SDP leadership who had been using the group as an informal "media" since 1978.[32]

Through this as well as other professional organizations, Solidarity advisory councils, and some less formal and public groups, ranging from periodic gatherings of friends over tea or dinners where the conversation turned to politics, to small groups (like the "Red Couch" group of former communist intellectuals and their friends from all over the political spectrum), and Catholic Intellectual Club gatherings, journalists have carried out what they saw as their professional tasks of collecting and disseminating information, engaging in criticism, and pushing for policy changes. These groups also have generated information, created or maintained contact and communication networks, and established precedents for criticism and discussion that served as a basis from which journalists could try to write articles or do programs.

After all, journalists practiced "journalism" in these groups. They contacted political leaders, drew influential people together, exchanged information, and took policy positions. In doing this, even if nothing could be published, journalists assisted, as is their self-appointed role, in the monitoring, educating, and reformulating of policy. Their base in 1980–81, like that of the Solidarity groups who came to Warsaw, was the journalists' building where they met, "held court," and organized the Forum to bring influential leaders from all political positions together to hold public debates and, although martial law prevented the project from being completed, eventually to create a series of educational monographs to further widespread discussion of the crises facing Poland.

These informal groupings, in which journalists saw themselves not only as participants but also as communicators, were well enough developed to continue to function even after martial law forced journalists to make decisions about their commitments to the public roles they held. Informal groupings were engaged in the post-1981 period in exchanges of information and active discussions of policy. These spilled over into new and resurrected groups of intellectuals that engaged in private or only semi-official discussions about all the major issues in Poland's life. The difference in the post-martial law period was that politics had become a cause of division for these groups. Therefore, they lost their ability to link some of the establishment and some of those who disagreed with its policies together, as they had done in the sixties and seventies. Ironically, as conversations with members of these groups showed, it was journalists who felt most weakened by the seemingly unbridgeable gap between the establishment and those outside it, even as they had been the first and clearest in their willingness to draw lines between those who compromised themselves and those who openly opposed martial law. For them, more than for any of the other participants in these informal groupings, not to be able to function as sources and channels of information was to deny the very purpose of their profession.

Public communications channels

Political questions and policy questions about which journalists lobby and advocate in Party meetings, public organizations, and private contacts are central topics for journalists' writing as well. In fact, much of journalists' work "behind the scenes" is aimed at preparing issues for presentation in the media and enlarging the horizons for their publication. For journalists, the highest status professional work is not quick and unbiased information and the "scoop" of American journalistic tradition. What is "high status" work for journalists is the writing and publication of "press criticism" – critical analytical articles and presentations dealing either with specific problems or general trends.[33] For journalists, as well as the political elite, "press interventions" are also key aspects of professional work. These involve collecting information on what has gone wrong and then taking action to solve administrative problems. Finally, journalists also have had allocated to them and have allocated to themselves the responsibility for organizing readers to actively deal with and solve specific problems by using their own resources.[34]

These activities – "press criticism," "press intervention" and "press action" – are not only important elements of journalists' professional work but they are also important influences in determining journalists' sense of themselves, their work, and their society. Journalists rank each others' status and achievement in the profession by their success is having an impact on policy. They perceive, not incorrectly, that their ability to get readers and officials to give them interesting and accurate information on which to base their analyses and criticism is dependent not only on their contacts and private politiking but also on their reputation as active and published "criticizers." Furthermore, because they are deluged either with praise for their criticism or requests for help by individuals who deal with the bureaucracy or need to solve personal problems, they quickly learn to see themselves and their professional colleagues as popular leaders and as more competent problem solvers than the average citizen. They also are in the position to be prime targets for complaints about the system and its lower and middle-level administration. In their eyes, the system seems particularly flawed and the imperative for change and modernization – in industry and in the management of public particiption – is clear. Top politicians, on the other hand, they tend to see as weak, information deprived "pawns of the bureaucracy." Their conclusions are reflected in the direction and tactics of journalists' media work and in their moves to make problems known directly "at the top."

Press criticism, press intervention, and press actions are journalists' vehicles. Each has a different audience, status, and goal. But, all three are closely interrelated, and are sources of journalists' "behind the scenes" policy actions. Journalists gain authority with readers (who never know about most of their behind-the-scenes work) and with the political leadership through the skill they exhibit in research, writing, and criticism in public forums. That authority, then, often combines with or translates into a more powerful private lobbying position. In turn, "behind the scenes" contact with the elite allows individual journalists greater latitude in their criticism and insures a more immediate response by institutions to what they publish. Press actions, on the other hand, are often used by journalists as a way to demonstrate the need for some policy response or as a way to solve problems readers bring to them. Press interventions are piecemeal attempts to try to help individuals who have suffered through administrative and legal inadequacies or actions. In raising these issues through intervening and reporting on interventions, though, journalists make a deliberate and visible statement. They also serve the policy elite as a crucial link with and pacifier for the population. Often too, the sum of these interventions is the emergence of broad policy advocated by journalists both in their own publications and through their private contacts. To have personal contacts with whom they argue and work in order to have policy changes made is, for them, a mark of professional achievement and not a move from professional work to political advocacy.

Over time, patterns have been established. Criticism, intervention, and "press actions" have come to be used to solve different kinds of problems and address different audiences. Press criticism has occurred mainly in national journals with an elite readership and an elite staff. It deals with basic policy problems or the failures to effectively handle general problems. At times, it is a part of a policy drafting process, bringing various kinds of professional opinions together and then working to consolidate public opinion for or against a given government proposal or administrative policy. The multiple streams of debate in the Solidarity period, as well as in other, earlier periods of liberalization, have been the widest ranging kind of "press criticism" in postwar Poland. But, no period, no matter how active regime control was, has been without press criticism and discussion.

Intervention is basic to the work of journalists on regional and mass journals and, to a lesser extent, in the work of journalists on high status journals. There is normally a staff to handle letters from readers in all but scholarly and literary journals. The problems press intervention normally addresses range from requests for health and beauty information to questions of discrimination in housing or of harassment in the workplace. These come essentially from those who cannot solve their own problems. It is the job of journalists or, on some journals, of the staff members assigned to handle these letters to investigate claims and seek resolutions. Interventions appear in the press either as regular features of reports on complaints that have been made and resolved or as special articles pressing for an institution to respond (and, indirectly, warning others of the dangers of doing the same thing) or as features that are simply of interest to broader audiences.

Press criticism

The ability of journalists to carry out various kinds of press criticism has been largely determined by the political elite. In the Gomułka era, when the media was hardly a priority, press criticism often could be wide-ranging and sharp. It was restrained basically when the Party and state leaders stepped in to protect trusted lieutenants who had run afoul of the press. For journalists, the Gomułka elite's disinterest made press criticism a vehicle not to change policies but to be visible and respected as writers by the reading public. For, there was seldom if ever a response to what they wrote. The Gierek era, in contrast, was marked by the active attempts of Party leaders to control and mold the media to serve their goals. Broad criticism was blocked because it did not serve the Party elites' need to create a loyal population willing to make sacrifices for Gierek's policies. Journalists' old use of sharp press criticism to build their individual status with readers and colleagues was no longer tolerable. As one national journalist explained in 1976:

> my name and my views are well known to my readers. They see me as a significant political figure. Gierek doesn't like to share the limelight so he is working to establish a nameless press where the only thing readers read is about the glorious policies of the Gierek leadership. Not only are we accused of tearing down the system but we are suspected of displacing the leaders in popularity.

As a result, criticism and suggestions of alternative policies had to be limited to things of little interest to the elite. They also had to identify both the problems and those at fault in such veiled ways that they were virtually literary exercises. Or, they had to be orchestrated preludes to the Gierek leadership's own policies.

The explosion of press freedom and action in the Solidarity period brought press criticism back to the fore. For those well established and those new to the profession, criticism of reports on Polish history, the state of Poland's economy, the failings of the government and media, and reports on the popular movements that sprang up as well as policies that were suggested and the broad-ranging ideas, problems and goals that appeared were major parts of their work.[35] Professional journalists and their readers all focused on a great national debate waged through press criticism, traditional in form if untraditional in its scope and sharpness.

The advent of martial law and the new normalcy did not bring an end to criticism but its blunting. Criticism was considered necessary by the Jaruzelski regime. It was, for the Jaruzelski regime, a demonstration of the "tolerance" of the regime and also the hopelessness of Poland's situation. It seemed to serve them by demonstrating the impossibility of finding any agreeable solution. For journalists who continued to write for the "establishment" press, it was a way to claim credibility against attacks on their professionalism by those who had left work in the establishment press in protest over the repression of martial law. It was also, for younger journalists, a way simply to practice the journalism they had long admired and to, at least, make small changes. The forums and audience for this criticism shifted. Those who wrote for the "establishment" press shadow boxed with their colleagues and other intellectuals who had turned, as writers and readers, to the pages of underground journals. But, whatever the external conditions and limits, the impetus to engage in press criticism, the focus of criticism, and its style did not change. They continued to be determined by professional values and needs.

In all periods, press criticism has come from a number of stimuli. The political leaders in Poland have only occasionally been able to instigate "press criticism" by working through sympathetic journalists because "serving as a mouthpiece" is considered unprofessional by journalists. At the same time, press criticism often appears when broader government campaigns open the door for it. This occurred, for instance, with the drive for bureaucratic courtesy in 1973–74 when the Party elite called for more "communication" between the population and the Party and the press responded eagerly to this call for civility from bureaucrats. They did this with specific articles on officials who were either courteous or obstreperous and in general articles on the responsibility of government officials to please and serve the population.[36] Another example from the seventies of the parallel purpose of the press and the political elite was the campaign against alcoholism that was made possible by a broader Party campaign for greater work efficiency and less social waste.[37]

Journalists' opposition to legislative proposals has generated both specific attacks and veiled systemic criticism. In veiled discussions against the "anti-parasite law" of 1971, journalists made it clear that equating those not working with the Soviet notion of "social parasites sucking resources from the economy" would not increase the workforce but would allow the regime to fire and then jail its opponents. In this case, journalists concerned with legal reporting were alerted by sources in the Party and ministry that this issue was coming up and were alarmed by its potential. They then sought out specialists to speak against the law by using their positions and expertise in criminology, management or psychology.[38]

When, in 1975, the regime tried to put through a psychiatric law allowing for involuntary commitment, journalists were equally active. Journalists and those in the legal and medical professions, with whom many journalists had socialized and cooperated, joined forces in informally scheduled meetings, professional conferences, and commissioned articles to argue against the proposal for the law. Again, the issue was its potential and not the law itself and, again, journalists were leaders in a campaign molded in informal settings and then inserted in the media.[39]

The post-Gierek era was initially littered by similar discussions centered around government laws and proposals ranging from economic reform and censorship to curriculum changes. They also involved journalists in wider ranging topics undefined by any specific legislative act. These involved debates not only about the merits of change in Poland but also about issues like the legitimacy of working with the government. This was a specific concern to journalists criticized by those who, on principle, left the press after martial law or who were blacklisted for what they had done in the Solidarity period.[40]

Finally, journalists have initiated broad debates on national issues whenever they could. Most often, these have been crafted to take advantage of fissures in the elite. For instance, in 1964 prominent journalists in Warsaw used the question of press intervention and its viability to level a critique on the success of socialism in Poland.[41] Prior to 1968, nationalist journalists in the Moczarist faction initiated a critical debate on the current situation in Poland, veiled as historiographic discussions of the interwar and World War II period and the treatment of these periods by Party historiographers. Those involved in both sides of these debates claimed they were not explicitly controlled or orchestrated by any faction of the elite. Rather, they grew out of the growing personal allegiances of individual journalists and editors to political factions and journalists' own interest in airing these issues.[42]

Similarly, in the Solidarity period, journalists, speaking from almost all perspectives, acted not on orders from any faction or group but because they saw the opening as an opportunity and seized it. Even in the post-martial law period, those who were connected with the political leaders and even those who remained outside establishment circles were well atuned to the shifting balances of factional power and used this knowledge to place articles and argue their cases by linking themselves and their arguments to existing lines of argument in the political elite.

The value system and professional experiences common to journalists are reflected in the press criticism they undertake. Press criticism by Polish journalists usually takes one of two forms: *publicystyka* (the presentation of an argument supported by specific illustrations) and *felieuton* (a nonfiction essay on events in the society). Articles done as *publicystyka* are usually "calls to action" for policy-makers or the population in the tradition of French weekly journals of opinion. The opposition to psychiatric law drafts that appeared in the seventies and the arguments for an alimony law, as well as the discussions of economic reform in the eighties, are all examples of advocacy through *publicystyka*.

Felieutons more than *publicystyka*, are vehicles for veiled discussion of theoretical or political issues in which the author does not have to explicitly state the problem, his position, or recommendations.[43] The importance of these two writing styles to journalists is clear from the emphasis on them in professional education. Their continued use by journalists, when salary and production pressures make them unprofitable, is evidence of their importance as a key vehicle for professional action in policy as was their almost exclusive use by the journalistic elite even when rapid and much sought after information became publishable during the Solidarity era.

In interviews, journalists also saw these two styles as the most useful vehicles for bypassing censorship and affecting social policy. With these methods, press criticism often is artfully argued so that Party stands and statements integrate with criticism of these very stands. With these methods, subjects prohibited by censors are presented indirectly through more literary writing.

> [The author] becomes more skillful, tries to trick the censor, winks at the reader, uses dodges, allusions, plays on words. Some readers, aware of the situation, look for and appreciate such allusions. I flatter myself that, over the long years of journalistic struggle, I have educated a group of readers who can understand me. This is shown by the many letters I receive.

Two cases of journalistic use of the *felieuton* illustrate both the usefulness and the risk of this style for questioning the system. In 1970, immediately after censorship was ended on *Polityka*, a series of *felieutons* on the life of the remaining prewar aristocracy in Poland that had long been under preparation was published. The articles purportedly "pandered to public curiosity" about these individuals, but the underlying theme was the failure of socialist transformation to affect basic social values in Poland. This series appeared but resulted, almost immediately, in a return of censorship to *Polityka*.[44] Another *felieuton* series, censored from *Polityka* in 1974, was an account of daily life for a typical workers' family under Bierut, Gomułka, and Gierek. It discussed housing, consumption, and entertainment in each period, with the unstated intent of showing that, while some aspects of Polish life had improved since Stalin, the consumer situation under Gierek was more difficult than under Bierut. These articles were heavily cut as the parallels were not well enough veiled.[45]

Press criticism occurs in all journals in Poland but most extensively in the central dailies and socio-economic weeklies. Regional dailies are limited in space and staff resources and have a sense that they can have only a minimal impact on local policy or their local officials and no impact on national issues and leaders. Mass circulation monthlies and weeklies are basically designed to serve the specific needs of their sponsors or target readers. So, only in areas of specific interest to their readers do they engage in press criticism. Their journalists do, however, sometimes redefine what is of interest to their audience in order to expand the options for coverage. Central dailies and weeklies, on the other hand, can make it reasonably profitable to do the extensive and time consuming research required for press criticism or for outside writers to work on and submit articles. Because their staff members also tend to have closer connections to and are read by policy-makers, they know they can be heard and deliver on their proposals.

In all, socio-political weeklies engage in press criticism most intensively. Their journalist–politician editors use their own political importance and that of their journal to provide their staff with support for its research and battles with the censors.[46] Because they are able to provide political protection to their staff, they encourage more open criticism and attract leading writers[47] who have made their names by being critical and writing well. Both their tradition and the position of staff members and editors allow these socio-political weeklies to deal with issues on the edge of permissibility and take the risks of censorship. As a result, they are widely read and respected in the profession and seen as the proper initiators of national debates.[48]

All the leading campaigns of press criticism have been concentrated in the leading socio-political weeklies and in the central dailies, even with the proliferation of Solidarity media. Only occasionally are these campaigns echoed in national mass circulation journals or regional journals.[49] Problems brought out by one have reverberations throughout the rest of the central media and, sometimes, in the rest of the press. Seldom are issues addressed exclusively by one journal. In some cases, journalists or journals cooperate closely in promoting a single reform or policy stance. Journalists from lesser known papers also submit their articles to better journals sympathetic to their case. The focus on common topics reflects journalists' concern with following precedents for what can be published, as well as the existence of overarching problems. Journalists and censors, then, watch what appears elsewhere for indications of what is allowed and significant at the moment.

There are clear rules for these debates. When inter-journal conflict occurs, professional ethics demand that *ad hominum* criticism be avoided and that the debates themselves never be allowed to divide professionals from each other. For instance, the principals in a 1964 debate on whether journalists should do press criticism or intervention battled openly and took diametrically opposed views on the merit of intervention versus criticism (and the success or failure all this demonstrated for socialism). Yet, they continued to work together in the SDP and maintain close personal relationships with fellow professionals on both sides. Ironically, even when professional work became a question of political commitment and honor in the eighties, professionals responded to questions on each other – however acrimonious their personal relations had become over what they had done after martial law was declared – using journalistic standards and focusing on the substance and quality of what they wrote, as opposed to whether they wrote in the "establishment" or dissident media, as their point of evaluation. All of this grows out of a realization of professionalism. As a result, press debates and criticism come to be seen not as matters of professional conflict and personal relations but as the result of intellectual differences.

The interests and approaches advocated in press criticism have been, almost exclusively, those of the intelligentsia, even in the worker dominated Solidarity period. This reflects journalists' ties to other professionals and their sense of themselves as members of the intelligentsia or as intellectuals. In addition to the press campaigns for new legislation already discussed, journalists in the seventies engaged in criticism of the educational quality of high schools and universities in Poland, Polish historical treatment of the interwar and World War II period, and the managerial policies of state enterprises.[50] Only the wide ranging discussion of labor code revisions in the mid-seventies was of interest primarily to the working class. That campaign was also the only one reported to have been encouraged by the elite and to have been based outside of the elite's central dailies and weeklies. Even then, the discussion centered not on comments by workers but on specialists' opinions about the management of labor for greater productivity and the needs of individual citizens.

The impetus for professional journalists to advocate modernization and rationalization comes from their work experiences and intensive interaction within the profession. Journalists are constantly faced with the failings of the system. These cause difficulties both for them and, they believe, for the nation. Journalists also tend to interact with and value most highly the technical specialists in the society. They see their views as more significant than those of administrators and politicians. Finally, the drive for the professionalization of journalism has led to an emphasis on expertise. It is only logical, therefore, that, when they find policy-makers know less than they do, journalists are appalled.

The production of critical articles also creates a sense of authority for journalists. It requires a personal commitment to nurse an article through the necessarily long gestation period. Journalists must continually "court" their potential sources in ministries and the Party, among other professionals, and in the public. So, they keep up their personal ties. They act as experts who can be trusted in the exchange of ideas and of information. At times, too, journalists court other professionals and their sources through what they write. Whatever their personal ties and contacts, though, individuals who are favorably presented in the press are more willing to be sources later than those who are not well presented. At the same time, specialists prefer to work with journalists whose track record in an area is known to be good.

Because press criticism is valued in terms of its impact, journalists are further forced to play a role in the resolution of problems by becoming involved directly or indirectly in the policy process. Professional competence and status are measured by the impact of their work in the journalistic community and in policy circles, by a journalist's access to sources, and through the assessment of journalists by readers or clients. This then helps determine journalists' focus since it is in their professional interest to deal with issues on which they can be relatively sure to have an impact or, at least, can insure themselves that they will not simply be silenced.

Press intervention

For journalists and the various political elites that have controlled and used the postwar media, press interventions are the other major form of professional work. These interventions have real ramifications for the political sphere and on both individual journalists' and political leaders' assessments of "the public" as well as "the public's" evaluation of journalists. Not only are press interventions important to "establishment" journalists and political leaders but, in the Solidarity period, and, much less explicitly, in underground journalism work, readers' letters and requests as well as journalists' responses are important professional and political resources. This is true even if interventions are done informally.

Demand for and reports on press interventions are a way for the political elite to assess and control the work of administrative institutions. They also give journalists a measurement of public concerns and allow for direct responses to readers through journalists' interventions in specific cases or on specific issues. This allows at least limited action to be taken before issues mushroom and trigger discontent. In addition, because press intervention involves solving specific problems or responding to administrative failure directly, when journalists are effective it gives them and their readers a sense of journalists as powerful movers.

So it was that, as journalists' ability to pressure adminstrators and political leaders' willingness to deal with problems diminished in the seventies, both journalists and political leaders became more and more cut off from the public's concerns because the public lost faith in journalists and saw reporting problems to them as increasingly useless.[51] As a result, journalists felt readers came to see them as part of a great, unresponsive monolith of national government.

The number of letters sent to and processed by newspapers and Polish radio and television has always been significant. Even top journalists on intellectual socio-political weeklies writing on foreign affairs, the economy, or general political issues, reported in interviews that they received, on average, four to five letters a day. Others, in the mid-seventies, writing on topics of more public concern, reported receiving far more letters and being asked both in visits and in telephone calls to help readers with specific problems or to right wrongs done to them. Only when limits on press freedom cut down on media credibility do the numbers of these letters drop. But, even then, the media are the prime target of complaint and pleas for help.

Polish Radio and Television, in a study done in 1969, reported having received 100,000 letters yearly since 1949. In periods of "social change and unrest," that total had gone as high as 200,000.[52] In the pre-Solidarity days, in another case, *Przyjaciółka* received about 120,000 letters annually, and *Głos Pracy*, the trade union paper, received approximately 60,000 letters.[53] Other data indicate that regional journals also received a significant number of requests: in 1963, *Głos Koszaliński* received about 100 letters daily; in 1976, *Gazeta Krakowska* reported a similar number; and, in the late sixties, *Nasza Trybuna* (aimed at the areas around Warsaw), reported receiving approximately 10,000 letters annually.[54] In the Solidarity era, the use of establishment media channels for intervention declined as the union used other vehicles to press locally and nationally for better conditions. After the repression of Solidarity, citizens, once again, came to the media, however discredited, as a protector.

When a number of questions or problems appear, some departments of connections move to organize contests, campaigns, or meetings to deal with community desires or answer common questions. At these, journalists or outside experts are sometimes featured. These various non-media responses are said to be used in 70 per cent of the cases of press intervention in regional papers.[55]

These departments also collect letters they feel are of general enough interest to justify publication, either as a special feature on local concerns or as articles. To these, they may add their own commentary, often reporting their successes in solving problems. Most legal or administrative problems, questions of insurance and social welfare, and accusations of illegalities are handled in this way.[56] Municipal and work or administrative problems most often lend themselves both to individual intervention and to being the background data for critical articles in the press.

The letters that reach staff journalists asking them to intervene are either those which workers in the Department of Connections were unable to resolve through normal bureaucratic channels or those which are both eye-catching and symptomatic of broader problems.[57] Journalists know what the concerns of the Party elite are, what institutions are responsive to their interventions, and what ones are unassailable. They select issues and institutions where they know they can get a positive response and avoid issues for which there are no solutions – like housing or problems in institutions like industrial ministries or the military. They also are aware of the potential impact nonpublished communications forwarded to policy-makers by the Department of Connections can have. These internal communications they frequently couple with published articles in order to simulate the aggregation of demands or criticisms if the Party and state elite even indirectly indicate a willingness to police a bureaucracy or modify policy.

In cases where reforms have been implemented and citizens have difficulties adapting to them, journalists also use their published interventions to make citizens aware of the law or the possibility of modifications. This insures the multiplication of citizen complaints and, hence, pressure against the new policy. Finally, in connection with what they see as a faulty law, journalists seek public involvement in areas where there clearly are not enough state resources to solve the problems. One case of this was the problem created by regionalizing rural schools. This created the difficulty of transporting students to newly consolidated rural schools. Public buses on their normal routes and schedules did not work for many of these students. Since journalists knew that intervening with the Ministry of Transportation normally met with no response, they organized a campaign to have local factories use their buses to transport students. This had, according to journalists, a double impact. In the short run, it insured that students were able to get to their schools safely. In the long run, it also broadened community involvement in the problems of regional schools and made regionalization a problem that factory directors as well as parents had to deal with – all of this created a strong lobby for changing the policy.

This pattern of press intervention being used selectively to respond to the concerns of citizens, to provide journalists with professionally "useful" subjects (useful because they bring readers and political leaders to journalists for help), and to create the momentum for policy change continued during the upheavals of the eighties. The Solidarity press became a major recipient of readers' letters and processed large numbers of them. Solidarity journalists and their "establishment" peers relied on institutional channels to funnel and handle the bulk of these letters. They also used the most significant of the letters as bases for investigations and reports. In doing this journalists reinforced the image that they had power and authority. The plethora of these letters, though, also pushed journalists to concern themselves even more with time consuming, "behind the scenes" interventions as the population grew more and more demanding and unwilling to accept incompetence and administrative blocks.

The ability of the press to solve some individual problems has sustained a myth of the potential of press effectiveness. The large number of readers' letters that always come to the press and radio and television has been seen by journalists as an indication that they do have some impact and are taken seriously. It is, for most journalists, their major contact with average citizens and daily concerns. Even though research indicates that press intervention really is most successful in solving low level conflicts between individuals and single administrators and in getting modifications of the law for hardship cases, it continues to be seen by journalists as a critical "smoother" of crises and disaffection.

The actual political role of press intervention has been varied. It buffers citizens from misadministration and dissatisfaction. Citizens who are concerned enough to act have a legitimate channel through which to voice their demands without forming illegal groups. Intervention also provides a means of notifying citizens of changes in laws and of providing access to specialist advice. In addition, through it, the political elite is able to tap public opinion and analyze the effect of its policies.[58] Press intervention, also, is an ever present warning to administrators that their actions can be criticized.

Press actions

Press actions range from book fairs to community service projects such as sending poor children to camp, organizing buses to transport children to school or setting up displays showing Western conveniences and equipment for children to emphasize the fact that these goods are needed and not available in Poland.[59] Although actions are marginal to most journalists and their sense of themselves as professionals, these actions require a special commitment to time-consuming involvement in the policy process. They also were once great favorites of the political leadership. Most often, "press actions" consist of motivating the public to deal with a specific project through donating money or actually giving time and free labor. These are projects usually expected of and done by mass circulation journals and Party and readership dailies. They, after all, have the necessary administrative staff to manage the administration of most projects. Their staffs include journalists with few extra writing commitments who are free to commit themselves to organizing press action, and need to give themselves visibility as spokesmen on their journal's projects.

Only occasionally are press actions products of individual journalists' frustrations with a policy or their desire to circumvent policy-makers and dramatize a problem. In these cases, press actions ultimately depend on the visible interest and involvement of large numbers of people. Most often, these appear as special events that involve citizens in the policy process. Their goal is not to oppose elite decisions but, most often, to raise or solve marginal or local issues. Press actions may simply involve journalists meeting once with readers to provide them some special services. Or, they may necessitate long-term commitments, such as the organization of the program to send poor children to camp or to pay for the rebuilding of the Castle in Warsaw.[60]

No press action is an individual journalist's decision. The impetus for press action normally comes from one of three sources: a journalist's personal commitment; the Department of Connections on his paper; or the political elite.[61] It is brought up at a paper's long-term planning session and discussed by the editorial board. Everyone on the staff is then expected to participate.

One case much touted by journalists was the campaign for bureaucratic courtesy that took place in the seventies. It occurred in a number of journals and was the product of journalists' own concerns and the political leadership's willingness to admit these problems. Awards were given to bureaucrats nominated by readers for politeness. Then the information generated was used as the basis for press criticism of the bureaucracy. Finally, many journalists pressed privately for increased compensation for bureaucrats as an incentive for courtesy. In another case from the seventies, *Życie i Nowości*, a weekly supplement to the Warsaw daily *Życie Warszawy* that focused on encouraging economic modernization, initiated a campaign to point out that children had to be better provided for if population growth was to be encouraged. The staff arranged, on its own, to set up a number of exhibitions of Western children's clothing and products to stimulate citizen demands.[62] *Trybuna Ludu* in the seventies and eighties has even sponsored an annual fair and festival called "*Trybuna Ludu* days" where entertainers performed, crafts and scarce goods were sold, and the Department of Connections provided free advice. Finally, Departments of Connections on various journals have pushed for and received staff support for programs to provide summer camps for children, entertainment for the community, or special clinics with legal or other specialists to help readers resolve their problems. This was especially true in the Gierek era.

The fact that the normal mass journal in Poland runs approximately ten such action campaigns a year [63] is an indication of the commitment to this kind of community service. The real impact of these actions is hard to assess. In general, they are seen positively by readers, but they do not appear to increase any paper's overall credibility in any discernible way.[64] In some areas, they take pressure off the state budget by developing citizen-supported activities. To some degree too, some campaigns encourage the development of participation skills. Finally, a few campaigns have either supported existing policies or led to changes in the policy. This has occurred when campaigns have been tied to broader activities such as the compilation of statistics on citizens' concern and involvement, the stimulation of greater reader demands, the establishment of pseudo-programs and institutions which must eventually be taken over by the state, and published and unpublished comments by journalists to readers and the political leaders they contact.

Can political action be professional? The journalists' conundrum

Professionals in journalism in Poland clearly are political actors even as they carry out their professional tasks. Their professional attitudes, ethics, work patterns, and associational patterns have an impact on their roles in politics; and, their personal and professionally mandated roles in politics also impact on their abilities to do their professional work.

From interviews with journalists both before and after the rise of Solidarity, the reliance of both elites and the public on journalists to intervene and solve problems or sanction wrongdoers clearly also created a gulf between those who were expected to solve problems and those who turned to them for help. Journalists, although they have no specific qualifications for their work, came to see themselves as uniquely qualified to judge and deal with problems. In this way, they set themselves further apart from their clients just as Western professionals do. And, since journalists also find themselves battling with officials, they come to see themselves as separate from many of their peers. Ironically, not only did this professionalize them but it also led them to see and portray the administration as immutable and the population as weak and dependent on the press to protect it from the ever more isolated political elite.[65] One journalist on the trade union paper commented that "Workers' opinions are basically uneducated. We look to experts for good data." In the eighties, major press discussions reflected not so much the discussions in factories or in Solidarity but concerns long bottled up by intellectuals: the need for new more honest history in schools; the issues of economic reform and foreign debt but not the issue of working conditions; and the need for a censorship law, (sought by workers too), but not the question of increased internal access to statistics and specialized training for workers so they could effectively supervise factory management.[66]

Published press criticism has not only been biased toward the interests of the professional, white-collar class, but has also pushed the interests of the "modernizing intelligentsia" – managers, engineers, academics.[67] Journalists, publicly and in interviews, advocate social and economic modernization and the values accompanying it, as might be expected of those who are a part of any "professional class" bound by definitions of training and skills. As one journalist concluded in 1969, the posture of journalists has been that of professional and political personae. They assume that "highly skilled workers and the intelligentsia will make a difference in the future of Poland and the future development of the economy, not the workers and peasants."[68] This has remained true even though, by the end of the seventies, journalists saw workers as the only real battering ram for change. Pressure for a modern and rational policy has been the basic theme of press criticism since the 1950s. In interviews, journalists in the seventies and eighties did not criticize Gierek's commitment to move forward and industrialize, in effect, to create "news" and respond to their criticisms of the status quo. What they criticized was the "deformations and incompetence" with which it was carried out.

In the same vein, journalists from all ideological sides in the 1968 press discussion maintained that anti-semitism had been a by-product of a campaign intended to point out the irrationality and status quo orientation of decisions made by policy-makers without professional training, most of whom had taken up their positions when they came to Poland with the Red Army after the war. When questioned about "the reasoning behind an anti-semitic campaign in the press in 1968," journalists involved with the Moczar group explained it by claiming that the primary reason behind the attacks on these individuals was their inefficient and "primitive" decision-making. One journalist who led the 1968 press attacks stated, in retrospect, that

> Of course having Jewish targets helped us. Nationalism can stimulate public opinion. Modernization can't. We talked about their ridiculous decisions . . . made from uneducated technical ignorance. The population only picked up on their Jewish names. We knew that they would react that way. Historically, the Jews in the PUWP have always been seen as Russian agents. But, really our only concern was with modernization.

Even a strong opponent of the "anti-semitic" debate supported this conception: "Yes, anti-semitism was morally repugnant. But all journalists also shared the common goal of getting our profession and national policy rationalized and getting Poland out of stagnation – making it a country run by professionals again." In other broad social critiques such as the 1964 debate over intervention *versus* criticism (as a veiled critique of socialism's failures to solve basic problems), economic discussions,[69] and historical discussions, journalists have also advocated the establishment of rational, modern planning and administrative mechanisms. They have pressed for legal codes to make social processes predictable. They have also presented research on the most "modern" legislation in the West and advocated the use of social science in making legislative decisions. In addition, they have been active in attempts to "liquidate ineffective laws"[70] and to make citizens aware of their rights so that they could press for laws to be enforced.[71] With this went an increased commitment by journalists to their roles and work as one of the last, and threatened, bastions of honest and competent thinking. With it too went a sense that their destiny was to lead. This pushed them into informal, behind-the-scenes "politics" as a part of their professional life and, into leading the population to "take action" to resolve problems the leadership avoided dealing with by organizing the public in what, in normal periods, are called press actions.

Whatever journalists do – be it hold political positions; engage in "behind the scenes" reporting, information exchange, and advocacy; focus on various policy issues in preparing press criticism or interventions; or work, as members of staff, on various press actions – they feel they are doing professional work. In doing this work, they play by journalists' rules of the game and see themselves as professionals whose work goes on inside and outside the actual media. After all, gatekeeping, issue definition, and guidance are all a part of their self-defined and socially defined role. They and their public judge professional journalists by what they are able to say and accomplish. All of this depends on their ability to communicate and to get information as well as to be heard. For those who labor in a controlled press, even as they push back the boundaries of control, they cannot simply write and publish. Journalism must go on in less public forums.

This examination of journalists' roles in policy-making, based as it is largely on interviews with journalists, answers the question of how the inside of that "black box" of policy-making looks from the perspective of one of its most active elements. It provides us with models of how journalism is carried into the policy-making sphere and how journalists in their professional work, are able to influence policy. More importantly, the presence of journalists who see themselves as professionals, maintain their professional work and associational patterns, and are aligned first as professionals and, only to better their professional options, as political actors (public or private) made the eruption of the profession in 1980 less than surprising. Journalists were acting as they had always acted. The policies they were advocating simply moved from being advocated in the backrooms to being argued on the front pages of the press. Old private connections became links for groups of advocates to work together in dealing with the crisis that was Poland. The definition of journalists' work did not change, only the opportunities and priorities.

What remains is the question of whether a group that is so clearly involved in politics can be considered a professional group. The question, itself, is an ethnocentric one for Polish journalists. "Journalism" in Poland is simply not the same as journalism in the United States or even Western Europe, the chief sources of our image of media professionals. Given their own self-definition of the profession, Polish journalists need to distribute and broker information and opinions. They need to lead the population. But, to do this, they must protect their boundaries as a group. They form a community, and they hold to professional rules and leadership that are far different from that outside their group. In all, they are not professional politicians but professionals whose lives and work continually intersect with politics and political life. When politics change, unlike "politicians", they do not change their attitudes or the rules of their games. Instead, they merely respond to the constriction or expansion of the space the system allows them for their professional journalistic work. Changes in political policies, then, dictate how far they will go as professionals and not where they will go. Journalism merely moves from opposition groups to elite groups, from secret journals and internal memoranda to published or broadcast reports, and from one-on-one conversations to public discussions in the press and on journalists' forums.

6 Solidarity and beyond: the critical test of professionals and professionality

In August, 1980, strikes in the shipyards and later in the coal mines of Poland marked the beginning of what, for many journalists, was both their moment of glory and their Waterloo. As they were drawn in and swept along by the tides of political reform and demands for more and more change, the professionalism of Polish journalists was tested at all levels. Political restraints were lifted so that the professional powers journalists had long sought suddenly became a reality. New papers were formed and editors brought in who were committed to supporting the profession and its rights. At the same time, journalists were challenged by "grassroots writers" who sought, sometimes successfully, to displace them and the media they produced. Journalists' reactions, as individuals and as a group, were a test, then, of their professionalism as well as their powers.

With the imposition of martial law, journalists initially had to face more political intervention than at any time since the Stalinism of the fifties. This intervention, in turn, forced them to reconsider the level of their professional commitment, and their willingness to tolerate public political intervention in their work. For some, the promise of upward mobility within their profession was an important consideration. For others, the primary issue was their self-definition as professionals. With this, they could no longer tolerate working under visible political controls and being seen as political henchmen for the regime. Many left the profession, at least for a time, or redrew their personal hierarchies and definitions of what was appropriate professional work.

Unexpected as the political demands of the strikers and their ability to force the government to concede to them were, these successes both challenged and liberated the profession. Demand three of the Gdańsk Accords (for the media to be open to a variety of viewpoints) brought a sudden change in the level of censorship with which journalists had to contend. At least initially, though, the old cynicism of readers toward their media did not change.[1] This was an issue that journalists had to, and openly did, struggle with. At the same time, the flourishing of "independent" papers and leaflets produced by workers and other "nonjournalists" challenged the control of the profession over its own boundaries and field of expertise. No longer was the media simply what journalists produced and the profession simply those who did traditional full-time professional work. The new press was begun by those who neither valued nor listened to established professional journalists. The political world moved from one dominated by Party and state leaders, openly challenged only by the small but determined dissident groups, to one in which large groups formed, argued, lobbied, and shifted and in which material gains and political gains were interlocked. Journalists were caught in an arena that required them, at least in their minds, to separate professional from political; personal political commitment from institutional press roles; and professional and personal needs from decisions on overall social policy.

Journalists' reactions to the events and options of the Solidarity sixteen months and the repression of martial law that followed it are a colorful and complicated story in themselves. They are also a test of the extent to which journalists act primarily as professionals. In the fifteen months of liberalization triggered by Solidarity, journalists were freer of political constraints for longer than ever before in postwar history. They were also very much a part of the swirl of "political" activities and freedoms. As professionals, they could have been expected to, and did, remain true to their past professional values and objectives, and set out professional demands. These professional demands were consistent whether they were loyal to the Party elite or turned to Solidarity and other highly critical groups. Journalists coming from formal work in the media all held out for the same "rights" and privileges because they were "journalists." As professionals, they also could have been expected to, and did, hold on to the boundaries of their professional world and react against intervention and displacement not only by the Party and state elite but also by young workers, students, and intellectuals who took on work in journalism. Even as Solidarity provided muscle for journalists' demands, the profession did not follow Solidarity. Individual journalists and the profession as a group, through the SDP, took the position that, as professionals, they knew better than anyone else what information should be provided and under what conditions.

The repression of martial law – addressed as it was to controlling the flow of information and restraining journalists – forced journalists to define their professionalism even further. Whether they stayed in the profession, left it, or left leading roles in it, journalists took positions with clear reference to their definition of their profession and the prerequisites they felt it required. The gains journalists had made as professionals were formally and publicly lost early in the martial law period. This challenged them as a group. In addition, martial law further politicized the situation and led to attempts by all sides to involve journalists in their cause. Journalists had to make decisions as to what the limits and constraints were within which they could tolerably work. They also had to make decisions on what the tolerable boundary was between professional work and politics.

The professional life and expectations of the early eighties were not, though, qualitatively different from what had evolved since the fifties. Journalists' work patterns, definitions of their professional roles, associational patterns, and relations with the world outside changed little. Journalism remained hemmed in by the political environment and its realities. Their work undeniably had a political impact, wherever it was published and whatever the subject matter. And, the boundaries of journalism, long more fluid than those of any other profession in the West or the East, became even less clear – in spite of journalists' efforts – as new spaces opened up and individuals from all walks of life began, on their own initiative, to "do journalism."

Professional values for all times

Polish journalists developed and retained, under this pressure, the characteristics of true professionals. In this, the major irony, given Western theorists' emphasis on professionalism occurring because of professionals' total dominance and control over their world, is that their professionalism is a product not of their autonomy but of the unpleasant push and pull of political forces. In response to these pressures in the years of "normalcy" and control, beginning under Stalin and rising and falling throughout the sixties and seventies and momentarily climaxing in the eighties, government and Party authorities at all levels have attempted to influence journalists, to get them to write what they wanted to see published, and to avoid sensitive and negative subjects when they come upon them. The result of their intervention has, on the surface, been a politicized press that does the bidding of the rulers. But, compared to the press elsewhere in Eastern Europe, the Polish press is the most critical and independent. And, as the behavior of Polish journalists – public and behind the scenes –

shows, journalists have developed a code of ethics, barriers allowing them to put limits on who can be a "journalist," and patterns of work and interaction that allow them to regulate and protect themselves from outside manipulation. All of this occurred while journalists were subjected to heavy political pressure and involved, publicly or "behind the lines," in policy-making and political actions. In fact, the impact of political pressures and the inconsistencies between the demands on journalists and the realities they see have made journalists retreat from politics and look at themselves as professionals who are more competent to make decisions about information and serve as policy advocates than those around them, and, who must guard against irrational outside interference.

As individuals and as a formal and informal group, their behavior reflects an imperative of achieving and maintaining: (1) a coherent philosophy; (2) public authority; (3) professional control; (4) ethical codes; and (5) a unique group culture. In doing this, the norm has been for them, as for other professions, to be moved by and also to seek: (1) common values on professional issues; (2) control over entrance and membership in the profession; (3) isolation from the influence of non-professionals; (4) the establishment of an informal, if not formal, association or series of associational patterns that are stable; and (5) the regulation of links between the professional and his environment. Like Western groups that do these things, they are potentially strong but not necessarily visible actors in the policy realm. They pursue the imperatives and interests of their group explicitly and implicitly; studies show interest groups in the Soviet Union and Eastern Europe have done the same.

This was clearly true even in the Stalinist period when journalists left schools of journalism, having been told that socialism brought peace and satisfaction to Poland, and found that the peasants and officials they contacted neither lived by the "wonders of socialism" nor saw journalists and their press as reputable. This has certainly been no less the experience for journalists elsewhere in the Soviet bloc, although the greater resistance to Stalinism in Poland perhaps made these objections more open.

In the post-Stalin period, the countervailing pressures and conflicts were no less. They gave journalists a sense of themselves as a group, unjustifiably harassed by non-experts in getting information and trying to get it published, and of the need to take independent professional positions to better their situations and "do their jobs," as they perceived them. The shifts in demands on and possibilities for journalists in the years after Stalin's death, first under Gomułka and then under Gierek; the upheavals and openings for the press in 1956, 1968, and 1970; and the growing challenge from the "uncensored press' after 1976 further encouraged Polish journalists to see themselves as a group with unique knowledge and skills, separate and under siege from all others. It was these experiences, in all likelihood, that heightened journalists' sense of their professional role and mission to a far greater extent than has been experienced by journalists in the more stable worlds of journalism elsewhere in the Soviet Union and Eastern Europe. Given this, Polish journalists, particularly, have felt that they had to insure their own autonomy in order to protect their interests and those of the society they served, have worked for independence and have taken active roles as "a loyal opposition party," monitoring policy and chiding policy-makers in periods of stability and of upheaval.

Journalists' evaluations of their roles, their professional satisfaction and the problems that they face are clearly those of traditional professionals troubled by this outside interference. Most journalists interviewed or surveyed in relatively comparable studies done in 1958, 1972, and 1976 maintained that they were happy in their profession and did not want to leave it. They also clearly expressed dissatisfaction with the limits on their work and their status in society. Even when they found themselves in a difficult work situation, however, they still reported happiness in their profession. The problem, to their minds, was that the outside world did not treat them as professionals.[2]

In explaining what made them happy in their careers, although "freedom in work" was valued by journalists surveyed in 1965 (and, in different terms in earlier surveys)[3] because it allowed journalists to manage both their personal and their professional lives, they ranked their impact on the society far higher than their ability to get "social status" or "influence personal concerns." They also showed a clear drive to perform a service role that characterizes the values of typical professional groups. So, they gave high ranking to their ability to "influence public concerns." Their service values were also reflected in the high ranking they gave to the way professional work facilitates their contact with people as leaders and ombudsmen,[4] even though leading Polish journalists, in interviews, stressed their "influence" and "information access" far more than did the middle ranking journalists surveyed. At the same time, journalists were critical of their ability to achieve this goal. As one regional journalist put it in an interview: "At this [regional level] it is hardly worth trying, no one up there cares and our readers sense this. We try to solve their little problems and hope that what we say will be heard somehow."

In ranking the negative characteristics of the profession, journalists made it clear that interference from the outside was an unwelcome hindrance. They almost universally indicated that they considered their work demanding and difficult because of externally imposed problems. This perception, when held by any profession, heightens the sense of professional mission and the necessary powers journalists should have in the society.[5] In the case of journalists, it is also a sign of the extent to which they see politics as outside their professional realm. The greatest problem for the profession in 1976 was that it was "politically risky." Interviews repeated in the eighties indicated that this impatience with political pressures is clear not only from the complaint that journalism is "politically risky" but also from the incidence in 1976 of criticisms such as "there are too many difficulties in getting and publishing information" (55 listings), "not enough chance to influence decisions" (33 listings), and "too many chances to make enemies" (66 listings). The next major problem identified by journalists was that the work occurred at too fast and high pressured a pace. Coupled with this was the third ranking problem of "poor salary and working conditions" – both of which were considered below the norm that was acceptable for the profession.[6]

In a survey done in 1972, journalists were asked to rank the degree to which elements such as (1) sense of self respect; (2) sense of security; (3) the possibility of independent action and thought; (4) the possibility of individual development; and (5) the possibility to use one's full capabilities, existed in journalism, were important to the individual journalist, and should exist. The responses indicated that there was a large disparity between the externally imposed possibilities of journalists and the ideals held for the profession by its practitioners. Furthermore, individuals' differentiation between their individual professional needs and their image of what is correct for the profession as a whole was also clear.[7] The ranking of possibilities for independence (independent action, individual development, and the full use of one's capabilities) was the lowest of any of the variables. While in their own professional life, 71.6 percent of journalists wished for more independence of action, only 49.2 percent felt that it was necessary for the profession. This reflects some acceptance of the political nature of the profession (96.5 percent of those surveyed considered journalism a political profession in 1976). Journalists also had a high sense of their personal capacities (68.4 percent felt that the possibility to use those capacities fully should exist) and felt stifled in their professional work (only 5.4 percent felt they could fully use their capabilities). Finally, individual and professional development, journalists clearly felt, were not encouraged or facilitated by the system. They were also considered both personally and professionally necessary (68.8 percent felt that it should exist and 75.8 percent felt that it was important for them as individuals).[8] Furthermore, the extent to which journalists want to have full control of the media is clear not only from their public statements and proposals in the Solidarity era and in interviews before that but also from the results of the survey done in 1958 (during the first period of independence for the media in post-World War II Poland). One-quarter of the journalists who had come into the profession under Stalinism felt even this liberalized system did not offer them sufficient opportunities to "write the whole truth."[9]

Leading journalists from both eras have tended to see the limits on their writing both as a challenge and a major drawback. Journalists talk of the enforced need for creativity in getting information and in veiling articles on politically questionable subjects. They perceive their role as to "question and challenge" in spite of attempts by the elite to control them and, in fact, see these attempts as an indication that they need to question the system. Since the articles they write require a major time commitment and since they have access to more information than they can publish, censors' unexpected limits on what they can publish are the most personally, economically, and professionally trying for them.[10] The demands of the profession have always been major sources of concern for professionals especially since 91.9 percent think journalism requires special qualifications and think that journalists receive too little money and status for their work. In 1958, "journalists most frequently cited the physical and psychological exhaustion of the profession" as a negative characteristic.[11] In 1976, 26.2 percent of the total responses involved journalism having "too fast a work pace." Furthermore, 10 percent of journalists in 1958 said that their salaries were too low[12] and 7 percent of journalists in 1976 felt that their salaries and working conditions were not adequate, in spite of the major improvements in salary and working conditions which had occurred in 1972. This concern with salary and benefits, a major cause of concern in 1958, was reinforced and stressed by the leadership of the professional association in the sixties until it became a standard part of the image of journalists that they portrayed. Professional publications presented a number of sociological studies of the profession which revealed its early death rate and the comparatively low pay scale for journalists.

This issue was championed publicly by the officials of the SDP and became engrained in journalists' sense of themselves and their profession. At the same time, journalists are realists. They do not confuse what their roles should be with what they actually are. So, when asked in 1976 "in your view, on whom does the press have influence?," no journalist said it had influence on public opinion, something journalists often termed either immeasurable or insignificant in the communist system. Sixteen journalists said the press had no influence at all while most considered affecting administration through intervention as the prime area of press influence. The evaluation of the potential influence of the press on government and Sejm decisions is lower than journalists' stated sense of what their role should be. This reflects journalists' difficulties in working directly in policy-making and also the fact that the sample was concentrated heavily on regional journals and comparatively less prominent Warsaw papers where policy influence is limited to monitoring the administration.

In interviews done in 1976 and in the early eighties, however, prominent national journalists[13] stressed these more global roles – impact on government and legal decisions – in discussing their roles. They expressed this directly by saying they should "act as a loyal opposition party in the English sense." A court reporter said that "The press is a major form of control of the judiciary procedure. It is the journalist's social duty to sound the alarm of illegality." Journalists clearly see their professional activity as significant to the politics and development of the Polish state and as a special service and responsibility which only they can perform. They do not, however, feel responsible to any institutional authority for the specifics of what they write. Instead, they feel that control should rest in the professional group and its ethical code. In response to a question in the 1976 survey, 5.2 percent said that they felt responsible to the courts, 4.6 percent to the PUWP, 1.1 percent to the journalism court (seen rather as an arbitrator in professional conflicts and violations of professional ethics), and 17.8 percent to their editorial offices. Furthermore, journalists feel that the professional ethics codified in an extra-legal professional code should be recognized by state courts and, in areas such as the journalists' right not to reveal their sources, they most often are.[14]

Journalists and the challenges of the eighties

The events of the eighties in Poland brought all of these disaffections, pressures and professionalizing forces to the fore in a far more explicit way than before. Journalists were challenged and their positions contested both by the Party and state elite and by workers and others who were so critical of the media that they produced their own *ad hoc* or regular news sheets and journals. New journals and positions opened up. Informal patterns had to be extended or preserved and the boundary lines of the profession reconsidered. Politicians from both the regime and its challengers sought journalists as members of their elite circles because they were established experts.

After forty years of censorship and government-press regulation without any legal base, Solidarity's demand for limited and legally controlled censorship opened the door for professional action in developing legal protections that had come to be seen as increasingly important when journalists found their old informal channels blocked by an impenetrable bureaucracy. The development of unions and the breakdown of the rulers' control over social organizations and associations meant that the SDP could be what journalists wanted it to be and could negotiate for work conditions and the recompense journalists felt they deserved. In comparison with earlier periods, this fifteen months offers the ideal "control" to test journalists' professionalism – a time when journalists' actions could be judged as professional and not the product of political limits and, yet, also a time when the profession was so challenged to be politically involved that it had to consciously fight to distinguish its professional interests from political concerns even more strongly than it had done before.

Furthermore, the response to these openings by journalists who felt paralyzed by the Party and state apparatus in the waning years of the Gierek era and who were seen as "political men" serving the leadership as "mouthpieces" is neither predictable nor explicable on the basis of traditional theories of socialization in communist societies or the models of "red-experts." Their response was immediate, coordinated, and consistent. They focused on informal professional groupings and leaders as well as behaviors that long predated the emergence of Solidarity and that went far beyond those of "institutional or social groups" discussed in the Western interest group literature. Finally, the ideas, actions, and reactions of journalists in the Solidarity and martial law periods were consistent with those they had expressed earlier in surveys, published and unpublished statements, and interviews. They were not completely consistent with those of the Solidarity trade union or the rest of the intelligentsia.

Their responses and postures were those that would logically have been the outgrowth of the model of professionalism set out in Western sociological research. From these models, not only are Polish journalists' "normal actions" and "Solidarity era" responses understandable but it is also possible to understand the dramatic response of Polish journalists to the imposition of martial law and their ability to survive the destruction of their formal professional association and attacks on their rights and gains. Whatever their political leanings, journalists expected colleagues to remain loyal to "professional interests"; maintained strong professional relations even when their formal organization was disbanded and a quisling organization established in its stead; and preserved some degree of professional autonomy either by refusing to work under new restraints or by using old patterns of protecting their autonomy.

At the same time, whatever their specific professional goals, journalists were not atypical in their clear ability to be heard as experts. As a group, they demanded material benefits, autonomy, and work rules just as doctors, lawyers, managers, and others have done in the West.

The strikes that spread through Poland as food prices were increased region by region shocked the entire Polish intelligentsia. Journalists' information on the strikes outside their areas in July and early August 1980, was limited at best. Internal reports were few. Media coverage was virtually non-existent, even when the strikes were right in newspaper towns. After all, "strike" was not a word that censors would allow to slip through their nets. Many journalists had heard that two Politburo officials had gone to Party committees and warned local leaders that they would have to negotiate with their workers rather than use police force against the strikes that were expected to follow the price increases. So, the drama seemed to be going as planned.[15] Nationally, the press was not only strictly controlled but also in its summer doldrums. Many journalists were on vacation. Papers had fewer pages. Major issues were delayed until the fall. Only Mieczysław Rakowski, of all the editors and journalists on major papers, was raising issues and criticizing Gierek's policies when the strikes took hold.[16]

In mid-August when strikers in the Gdańsk shipyards refused promises of salary increases and locked themselves in the yards to demand real political rights that would guarantee the concessions they had just been promised, a new era began. News spread rapidly to Poland's main cities through dissident channels, already established with the shipyard worker dissidents and through networks of friends and acquaintances. Journalists were instantly drawn to the story. Coming from all over – on their own vacation time, as reporters with their editors' permission, and as part of delegations of intellectuals coming, initially, to warn that moderation was needed and, eventually, to help workers and government officials negotiate – journalists converged on Gdańsk and the shipyards. Once there, since the telephone lines were all cut off between the shipyard towns and the rest of Poland, they were totally involved in the story.[17]

As they came to the shipyards, they had to come to grips with their past and their public image. Some, especially those from television, found themselves barred from the yards by worker-guards. Some went to Party headquarters to "observe" the strikes and use Party lines to report back to Warsaw. Others who had visibly supported government policies were questioned on the streets and in the yards about what they had done in the past and why. For many, this was difficult to explain at best. Still others were welcomed to the shipyards and found themselves listening and watching conversations and events that they had never imagined could happen openly in People's Poland. According to one journalist,

> This was not only a professional trip. Important too were the changes that occurred in our sense of things, in our evaluation of the country in which we live, in our image of Poland. Most of us did not work while we were in Gdańsk. As is known, during a strike there is nothing special to do, you sit around, listen, stand in groups of people, talk, sit, smoke cigarettes, and wait and wait. It was not done to write. Writing was purposeless. Nothing could appear. It was a matter of sharing a common fate.[18]

The drama for the forty or so journalists from dailies and weeklies who settled into the shipyards was further heightened by the foreign journalists who were making headlines with their reports about the strikes – reports Polish journalists, often the Westerners' sources or translators, could never hope to present in their own media. For, until 20 August (seven days after the workers of Gdańsk had banded together to make joint demands for political guarantees and six weeks after the first strikes over the 1 July price increases had occurred), no matter how momentous the events seemed, journalists were unable to publish articles about the strikes. This left them so frustrated professionally that many signed petitions while they were in the shipyards decrying the falsehoods they had had to publish.[19]

Journalists' and workers' fates were all the more entwined since workers made the press and its lack of information a prime issue. Point three in the Gdańsk Accords dealt explicitly with the demand that the government "respect freedom of expression and publication, as upheld by the constitution of People's Poland, and to take no measures against independent publications, as well as to grant access to the mass media to representatives of all religions."[20] and, although journalists were not the initiators of this point, it symbolized for them both the importance of their professional role and their failure to perform it. They were also aware, from the past experiences of Czechoslovakia and Hungary, that press freedom was a risky business and would mean their expertise would be cast aside. They knew it could be a trigger for a Soviet invasion. This they made clear, as did prominent intellectuals and some Solidarity leaders, to all who would listen when radical activists demanded that there simply be an abolition of censorship.[21] To journalists, the optimal solution was for them alone, as the rightful makers of the media, to design the censorship law as they saw fit.

The signing of the accords, thus, made the nature of the media a major political issue and, to journalists, a key issue in their professional work, a key issue for the very independence of Poland. Journalists' personal involvement with the strikers and with government negotiators affected the accords signed in Gdańsk.[22] New issues crucial and beneficial to journalists alone were inserted into the accords near the end of the debate, as a compromise between radicalized workers and cautious intellectual advisors.[23] As a result, the issue of legal protection and of an appeals process for censors' decisions – processes that were shrouded from readers' view even as they were daily concerns for journalists – were key points in the final accords even though they had never appeared in the initial workers' demands. So, the accords stipulated that

> The government will bring before the Sejm within three months a proposal for a law on the control of the press, of publications, and of other public manifestations . . . The proposals will include the right to make a complaint against press control and similar institutions to a higher administrative tribunal . . . Radio and television as well as the press and publishing houses must offer expression of different points of view. They must be under the control of the society. The press, as well as citizens and their organizations, must have access to public documents, and above all to administrative instructions and socio-economic plans, in the form in which they are published by the government and by the administrative bodies that draw them up . . .[24]

When journalists returned to work during the strikes, which lasted nearly a month, and talks on the Baltic coast, they were eagerly questioned by their colleagues. Even editors who were reluctant to publish what journalists wrote wanted them to give private reports on the strikes. At the same time, government and Party officials' meetings with journalists presented ever changing and hardly believable stories. These attempts to give even the most loyal journalists and editors an official line were openly challenged as never before. For those who attended official briefings, it was clear that the Party was on the defensive and its leaders increasingly powerless or out of touch.[25]

To fill the void in information, returning reporters spoke to hastily arranged gatherings of friends and at meetings in their offices and local journalism associations. These talks, in rooms packed with journalists and others, who had simply come to hear, rapidly led to calls for the SDP to do something to clear its name and salvage the credibility of the media. Many demanded that a special congress be held to "take a position on the events in the country, as well as to define the rules of journalism work and the functioning of the mass media."[26] These calls came from journalists in backwaters like Białystok and in major journalistic centers of Warsaw, Kraków, and Gdańsk.[27]

In Warsaw, at an explosive meeting for journalists to report what they had seen in Gdańsk, Szczecin and other centres, the SDP officials dared the audience to vote them out if they did not support what had been done in the seventies. Almost instantly, they were voted down and, having lost, they agreed, as leaders of the profession to call an Extraordinary Congress.[28]

From the initial call for that Extraordinary Congress until the Congress was actually held 29–30 October, journalists worked to strengthen their professional prerogatives by organizing the most effective Congress possible. The old officials, whose actions were being attacked, championed the basic demands of the profession for changes in both SDP positions and the general media situation. They claimed that "never has our professional community had such significant problems and decisions before it as it does now."[29] Forthcoming articles, prepared and advertised for the next issues of *Prasa Polska*, were shelved so that the October issue could carry calls for the Congress, current and past statements from the SDP and its leaders, and lists of issues up for discussion at the Extraordinary Congress. (Even its publication became an event as printers were asked to and did work overtime so this issue could come out not in months but in days after it was drawn up.)[30]

Finally, from the Warsaw group which ultimately called the Congress, an informal working group formed to coordinate the drafting of study documents and the selection of lists of officers for the Extraordinary Congress.[31] At their suggestion, delegates elected by various staffs to be representatives at the upcoming congress were not the only ones eligible for SDP posts. Men like Stefan Bratkowski, who had been blacklisted from journalism in the later half of the seventies, were included as candidates because journalists felt "they would have been [eligible] as full-time journalists but for the interference of politics."[33] Under the umbrella of the past association leadership, five committees were organized to draw up propositions and prepare information for delegates on the long-standing and professionally key issues of: (1) information and propaganda; (2) internal regulation of the profession itself; (3) a law on press control and access to information; (4) the character and work of the professional association, and (5) the social and professional conditions of journalism.[33]

Selection of the candidate lists and program planning was equally professionalized and consciously depoliticized. There was a deliberate attempt to convince respected professionals, in and out of the seventies' professional establishment and from all sides of the political spectrum, to run for office. The only concern was that these individuals be committed primarily to *professional* issues. They tried to insure that the Congress was not a forum for politicians even as they recognized many of their gains had to come from the outside. So, they included in their roster of speakers: Józef Klasa, head of the Central Committee Press Department; Ryszard Bugajski, a representative of Solidarity; and leaders from other artists' and professional unions, many of which had been far more active and critical in the seventies than the SDP. In effect, though, they tried to limit those from outside the SDP to statements on issues relevant to journalists and journalism.[34] Even then, there were complaints from the floor that outsiders had been let in at all.[35]

Delegates turned their fury on past officers of the association. One of the most contested issues was whether to give the traditional, token affirmation to the past governing board or to publicly attack their work. The discussion was a tactical and a professional one. The questions involved were not questions of the old board's failure. Even they themselves agreed that they had failed to work as they should have for the profession. But, they maintained, political pressures had made it impossible.[36] The questions that were raised on this issue were: could a single leadership be repudiated because it had failed to stand up to an entire system, would this absolve the profession as a whole of its failings of personal courage, and should those leaders get some credit for gains in the working conditions and earnings of journalists?[37] The final compromise on what became a symbol of journalists' failed autonomy was the conditional affirmation of the executive which left it to those past officers to decide how to credit themselves.[38] This was put in the context of sharp criticism of these leaders for failing to protect the autonomy of the profession and represent its interests to the outside.[39]

The priorities of the 367 delegates were clear. The decisions on what the demands would be for salary and benefit scales were left to the executive committee. And, although laws on censorship and access to information were discussed, only an impression of the Congress was given. But, on issues of the SDP, delegates insisted on voting on all the proposals for membership rules and structural changes. When proposals on these issues were not ready, delegates voted to oust the committee chairman and call on a new chairman to draw up final proposals overnight so that they could vote while they were still gathered as a Congress.[40]

The proposals that were made and the delegates' votes demonstrated both continuity of professional goals and rejection of the old politically imposed ways. Membership rules were kept the same even though they would exclude many of those writers rapidly gaining visibility in the post-August "uncensored" press. Therefore, a three-year candidacy was retained. This decision knowingly and explicitly excluded those "using the media in the wake of political passions."[41] Also retained was the notion of the SDP as a "professional–creative" organization. What was added were the rights and responsibilities of "protecting the well-being of its members."[42] This, *de facto*, had been a key, if unofficial, element of professional actions since the fifties. This time, however, the SDP officially took on not only the rights and responsibilities of "a creative association to improve the profession and develop its options" but also of a union to "negotiate and sign salary agreements as well as to be involved in work inspections, and so on."[43]

Little else remained as it had either *de facto* or *de jure*. Moribund institutions like the Qualifications Board and the Collegial Court were invigorated as demands poured in for them to adjudicate cases and regulate professional behavior using the existing codes.[44] Mechanisms were added to insure closer on-going control over SDP officials' decisions and to make better and more autonomous links between the profession's representatives and the outside in the form of the Association Conference Group and an Intervention Commission.

The Conference Group was an elected body of seventy delegates from the Congress who were selected by secret ballot to serve as "the highest authority of the SDP" between Congresses.[45] They were charged with: "electing from its own membership the Governing Board; selecting a General Secretary, Secretary of the Board, and treasurer; approving the budget; reviewing the report of the Governing Board and ratifying yearly, by secret ballot, the head of the Governing Board, his assistant, the General Secretary, and the rest of the Governing Board. . ."[46] To further insure responsive and collegial leadership, the Chairman of the Governing Board for each session was to be elected at the preceding quarterly session.[47]

The two links for work with the outside were the Intervention Commission and the head of the SDP. The Commission was responsible for mediating disputes between journalists and their employers,[48] thus, giving journalists, as professionals, the power to determine solutions to work conflicts within the bureaucratic hierarchies of the newsrooms rather than making them dependent on "bosses" from outside the profession. The head of the association was formally empowered "to represent the profession on the outside with all authorities with whom our organization has contact."[49] This formalized the separation and the links between the profession and other professional groups as well as Party and government groups that journalists had long sought, and often achieved, informally in the past.

The SDP, in this Congress, seized the opportunity afforded by the concessions Solidarity had won to formalize and strengthen a number of "professional" standards. They also clearly acted as professionals in:

(1) that, whatever their political leanings and ties, journalists (or at least their representatives) had a common professional agenda and could agree on most basic issues relevant to their professional lives, as evidenced by the relative unanimity of votes on even the most criticial issues[50] and by the fact that, on a number of major issues related to professional powers and roles, there was enough sense of a shared agenda for delegates to trust their elected representatives to deal with these issues;

(2) that the profession made it clear that individual professionals were responsible for their own behavior and could not, as professionals, claim that the political rulers and their constraints were responsible for their behavior;

(3) that, in spite of the public outcry against the establishment press and the blossoming of new uncensored "media" within the Solidarity movement, it was not in the profession's interest to allow any group to move in on its territory. Membership in the pro-

fession and access to its benefits were not allowed to be publicly defined but were defined and regulated by established professionals without regard for the tides of public opinion. The requirements for a three-year candidacy, thus, remained. This consciously put most new entrants out of the bounds of the professional organization and the benefits it ensured;

(4) that most respected professionals, as measured in 1976, were reflected in the list selected to lead the SDP in 1980;

(5) that the Association was actively to regulate its own members in order to maintain the profession's standing and to insure fair competition among professionals;

(6) that, in professionals' disputes with the bureaucracies in which they worked or with whom they had working relationships, it was professional journalistic authorities who had the ultimate authority;

(7) that there were boundaries between the profession and the outside so the professional organization was not a "transmission belt" for the political authorities but had the right to be a spokesman and authority in all areas of professional life. It legislated for itself the right to insure autonomy for special interest clubs and the SDP itself; to represent the profession in all negotiations for material and welfare benefits, legislation, and disputes between members of the profession and nonprofessionals in areas of common concern; and to speak as a single voice with all outside groups – Party, government, unions, foreign journalists' organizations, and other professional associations;

(8) And, finally, that, as intellectuals and service oriented professionals, it established that journalists' prime concerns were their profession's public status and the insurance of their autonomy and control over the association. Thus, although material concerns were significant and would become more so as economic conditions worsened, the Congress record makes clear that the priorities were "professional interests and power."

The crosscurrents of the Solidarity era

The path of this pure professionalism, however, was not so clear. Journalists could deny professional protection and benefits to those who were not eligible to be "members" by SDP's definition. But, they could not prevent them from acting as journalists and producing a media that was read and compared to the media produced by establishment journalists. Instead, as events and conflicts escalated in the months of Solidarity, journalists were forced to go beyond what they, as professionals, regarded as safe limits in order to compete with stories coming from the "uncensored" press. Nor, as new union sponsored journals were legalized, could the profession control staffing. In fact, journalists found themselves welcomed more as facilitators than as leaders. Furthermore, media issues were no longer their purview alone, the presence of a media control provision in the Accords made "the media" an issue for public discussion: censorship was a matter not simply for journalists to act on but also something printers and the broader public considered their own problem.

Beyond this, the personalities of those who rose to leadership positions made the lines between "professional" and "political" difficult to maintain. In the organization of the Extraordinary Congress, two groups of delegates had been elected: delegates well respected and established as "role model" journalists, many of whom had not been able to publish for much of the seventies, and delegates who had been less visible as professionals but who had distinguished themselves as activists in professional causes both informally and in formal associational duties. Because they were known to all, professionally established and prominent journalists were elected as top leaders for the association. They were well known, because of their writing, not only to other professional journalists but also to workers and government and Party officials. Since there was a dearth of alternative leaders, advisors, and spokespeople who were known but not implicated as spokespeople for the Gierek regime, those who became association leaders were often sought after to lead political circles as well – even though, from the start, the dangers of combining personal political involvement with professional leadership were clear to all. Stefan Bratkowski, the newly elected Chairman, recognized this the moment he accepted his election:

> The function of Chairman is quite difficult for a person of my personality and inclinations. I have always very much valued privacy and the right to speak in my own name. From this time on, I will not have this kind of freedom . . . I hope that it will be possible for us with our Association to enliven this Foksal [the SDP headquarters] building to a point of prominence in the next years and bring this down to the regions and newsrooms. Naturally, if we all take part in various events, this will be useful for journalists and the rest of society.[51]

He is and his deputies' acceptance of this conundrum and the relationship between the association's activities and the rest of the society did not simplify the maintenance of the line between professional and public politics. As an individual, he was unwilling to resign from his professional roles to administer the association. He remained deeply involved in critical intellectual groups like "Experience and the Future" (DiP) and in the weekly newspaper supplement he edited, *Życie i Nowoczesność*. This editorship gave him a platform for highly critical discussions of economic and political failures. These commitments, plus his involvement as an advisor to workers' groups (begun during the Gdańsk strike), made him very much a part of the flow of political events. It also, by virtue of the fact that the SDP was his primary commitment and the place where he spent most of his time, made the SDP building a meeting place for far more than pure gatherings of journalists. The leaders of "Experience and the Future" met in the restaurant (which remained one of the best in Warsaw). Workers who had ties to Bratkowski negotiated with the government. At times, they came to use SDP wires to contact their home groups and, even, occasionally to sleep in its halls. Others came for advice or mediation.[52] After all, Bratkowski and those around him were men both known and respected by workers and Party and state elites.

His two vice-presidents as well as much of the membership of the Executive Committee and Advisory Council were also active and successful journalists. They earned their salaries primarily from journalism not association work. Even the new full-time association officials were prominent journalists who, although they were on the payroll of the SDP, continued to do side work with their old papers and to be identified as active journalists.[53]

The same patterns were played out outside of Warsaw. Those who were elected as leaders of the SDP were prominent journalists long critical of local governance but with personal ties to many of the new local political leaders. And, in their positions, they tried to expand their personal contacts to include the emerging leaders of Solidarity and other groups that appeared. So, men like the editor of *Gazeta Krakowska* Maciej Szumowski,[54] found themselves playing a variety of roles. He, for instance, was on the national SDP board; editor of a daily that took independent enough stands to make a single issue of the paper worth in Warsaw one hundred times its news-stand price and even more elsewhere in the country; a link and sounding board to one-time Kraków Party boss Józef Klasa (the Central Committee Press Department head in the initial months of the Solidarity era), and a popular spokesman and behind-the-scenes advisor for a range of political groupings. Yet, according to those involved, he, like other regional leaders, perceived journalism as his profession and his other "political tasks" as outgrowths or costs of his professional work.[55]

More important, however, was the fact that – for non-journalists – journalism and journalists were by definition political, whatever their claims to the contrary. And that, of all the professional and occupational groups activated under Solidarity, journalists and their work had the most name recognition and visibility. This meant that actions normally deemed "professional" were visible and were reacted to both by Solidarity and by Party and government elites. Furthermore, at least as important, those who lead the SDP had been friends and colleagues of other leading professionals who had tied themselves to the rulers, taken government posts, and still retained their positions, at least initially, as journalists or editors. For these men, their old colleagues' criticism of their pro-regime political activities or positions was difficult to take since it challenged their cherished positions as journalists.[56]

Finally, in continuing their old tradition of a journalism that involved far more than what could be printed, journalists, individually and through the SDP, intervened personally on specific issues. In doing this, they played the role of "loyal opposition" that they had long allocated for themselves. They monitored areas they had specialized in as writers. They used their writing to argue cases, participated in critical discussions in and out of the media, and used non-media forums to spread information. The difference in the Solidarity period was that they acted more loudly and more visibly before a public that lined up at dawn to get their papers and crowded in meetings to hear them speak.[57]

Journalists further attempted to institutionalize their role as information mediators and links by establishing a series of open discussions on sensitive and controversial topics like pre-war Polish history, popular relations with the government, economic reform options, and Polish–Soviet relations. To these, they brought prominent spokesmen of opposing views to debate the issues.[58] In doing this, they were playing out their tradition of generating discussion and molding public consciousness. After all, the organizers planned to print transcripts of the "most socially valuable" meetings in Warsaw to be used as educational tools for enlivening public discussions.[59] (This later project was never realized because of martial law.)

As a professional group, the SDP, in tandem with its individual members' and leaders' personal postures, stood independent of all sides. The SDP leadership was unwilling to have other groups decide how the media "should be" or dictate to them. Instead, in conflicts between the rulers and the ruled, they attempted to act as mediators,[60] as they had done earlier in more veiled ways through their writing and their nonpublished "journalism" activities. They made reference to their significance to other groups in the society or the general state of the society. They also refused to back down in the face of regime threats and challenges. At all times, they tried to protect their professional prerogatives. Two key challenges tested this resolve: (1) the counterveiling moves on the part of some elements of Solidarity and on the part of Party and state officials to deal with censorship and control of the media and; (2) institutional challenges designed to displace the SDP and its leaders.

The challenge for control over censorship

The problem of censorship was, for journalists, a painful one. The censorship law was repeatedly delayed. Work was done slowly by government drafters. And, over the most basic provisions, journalists (who basically were given *carte blanche* by Solidarity to design the best law) and government negotiators disagreed at every step. And, given the flow of events, they rapidly found out that censorship was far from Solidarity's first priority. So, journalists were the ones who had to generate pressure for the government to concede to them.

At the same time, journalists were faced with the reality of an ever expanding "independent," unlicensed press that printed much they could not get past the censors. In this context, though, readers assumed that the established media and the journalists that produced it deliberately lied and avoided sensitive issues.[61] This impression deepened during the winter of 1981 when censorship interventions increased dramatically. For instance, one SDP memorandum reported that:

> *Życie Warszawy* in December, 1980, and January, 1981, had removed from it information on the decision of the Supreme Court on the registration of Peasant Solidarity, information from the Polish Press Agency on the naming of the film "Workers 1980" for the award of the Film Critics Club, sections from reports on Lech Wałęsa's visit to Rome quoting the Pope's reasoned statement on the proper role of trade unions . . . This decision was upheld in spite of the Chief Editor's protests to the Main Office of Control. Similarly, the calendar of the events of December, 1970, which was to appear the day the statue in honor of those slain in these disturbances was to be unveiled, was completely removed even though much of its information was contained elsewhere [in the Polish press] . . . After battles with the censors, one-third of the material was allowed to appear . . . [62]

Journalists responded in a number of ways. The SDP leadership used reports made by its own commission to document the censorship and false information that was appearing in the media. These reports they sent to government press spokesman and journalist, Jerzy Urban, used for discussion among themselves, and circulated widely to other groups and leaders.[63] Prominent journalists linked censorship with the broader issue of the unwillingness of officials to set aside their old, insular ways.[64] SDP leaders made official and private complaints about censorship.[65] Individuals actively fought the censors. Some journals began using blank space and elipses – with the encouragement of the SDP leaders – to denote portions of texts that had been censored.[66] And, as they had in the past, journalists turned to private contacts and speaking engagements to exchange information with their readers and push back the limits.

In spite of this, when printers threatened to strike on 13 February 1981, to force action on censorship, journalists did not welcome their "advocacy." Instead, the SDP leadership and other leading journalists, even most of those who combined SDP and Solidarity membership, opposed the strike. They held that: "The state of the mass media was scandalous but, at the same time, other pressures should be used instead of 'A Day without the Press.' Channels of communication for the society should be kept open."[67] The SDP leaders mediated to end the strike threat. They brought government and printers' representatives together in the SDP building; ran messages back and forth when government negotiators refused to sit in the same room with a Solidarity advisor who had been a founder of the Committee to Protect the Workers (KOR); and pressed Solidarity representatives to accept government promises.[68]

In the months that followed, SDP officials' ongoing attempts to advocate as specialists for improved media policy were treated by Party and state officials as betrayals.[69] Censorship and false reporting as well as the appearance of conservative papers staffed by professional unknowns marked a steadily worsening situation. The pressures for a freer press and counter-pressures by the Soviet Union and the Polish Party and state officials for the media to be respectful and restrained were accompanied by a turnover in the Central Committee Press Department. Józef Klasa, a Party advocate for a freer press was replaced and the media put under the thumb of Stefan Olszowski, a long-time opponent of a "free press," after the Extraordinary Party Congress of July 1981. The media then came to be a battleground, ruled by conservative Party and state officials, run by increasingly activated journalists and editors who saw little good being done by the rulers' policies, and challenged by informal information channels and Solidarity media.

The SDP, on local and national disputes, tried to focus on common professional concerns. Its court acted against professional journalists who made ideological battles into personal battles or who falsified reports to serve any faction.[70] Professional leaders from all sides went to talk to Party and state officials whenever they could.[71] At the same time, they continually documented the false and limited information appearing in some of the media.[72] Their argument was made a clearly professional one – that a wise and independent media was a social necessity and a continuation of the tradition of journalists as gatekeepers in the society:

> The statuatory obligation of the SDP is to insure the multi-sided and factual information for all citizens by the mass media . . . The SDP council turns to the heads of all the mass media, government, and the unions, to observe the Sejm decision of April 10, 1981, calling for the presentation of correct propaganda sought by the population. We are turning to journalists to carry out all that will build respect, moderate conflicts, and integrate the society in order for us to be able to move away from the crisis. From the Extraordinary SDP Congress on, we have carried out a number of mediation initiatives during periods of sharp conflict such as . . . the February strike of Warsaw printers and the LOT conflict. We want to continue in this tradition and, at the same time, signal public opinion about any attempts to violate the line of public understanding and dialogue without regard for who is violating the agreements.
>
> The SDP Council is convinced that the journalism community has no right to differentiate either for the Party, the government of General Jaruzielski, or the union movement . . . We feel that without an information policy in line with the society's interests, getting out of the crisis will be impossible.[73]

By the beginning of the summer of 1981 and in spite of the enactment of the censorship law in July 1981, to become effective in November of that year, there was increasing repression of the media. Cutbacks were proposed in media resources. Also, there were ongoing delays and debate on the draft law on censorship. These problems highlighted the challenges to journalists' positions as the Party Congress, Solidarity's Congress, and the return of Solidarity's strike action calling for "Days Without Press" rocked the summer doldrums.

In response to these challenges, journalists acted as authorities "advising" their clients. They presented the Party Congress with an official statement on the current state and needs of the mass media.[74] They responded to plans to cut back paper supplies by calling on newspaper staffs to insure that methods, other than cutting the size and circulation of the press, were used to save paper resources.[75] Going further, they proposed a total revision of the press system, breaking the monopoly of Party publishing and distribution so the media would actually be run by competitive publishing houses.[76] Those who went to the Solidarity National Congress as elected delegates or as editors or advisors for official and unofficial Solidarity press worked to bring union positions in line with the need they felt for a decentralized, professionally controlled media.[77] They also opposed Solidarity's refusal to let Polish television into its Congress sessions. This they saw as an illegitimate imposition of control by non-professionals even though they were highly critical of radio and television reporting.[78]

All this came to a head publicly 7 August when Solidarity announced a two day printers' strike for 19 and 20 August. The five leaders of the SDP who were in Warsaw at the time put out a letter documenting the false reporting ordered in Polish Press Agency and Polish Radio and Television in an attempt to respond to complaints by Solidarity about misrepresentation. The letter made it clear that journalists on radio and television did not want to have any connection with the falsehoods that had appeared. The letter criticized professional journalists who were involved in this false reporting and slander. It emphasized that "credibility is a critical element of our work – it must be protected over all, no matter what one's sympathies or views."[79] This letter was sent to various government officials, editorial offices, and the Polish Press Agency.[80] In the end, though, most journals were blocked from publishing the letter and relegated to publishing official attacks on it.[81]

The response of the SDP leadership and membership to the attack and the independent Solidarity order for a two-day printers' strike was to demonstrate their solidarity with the letter's authors and, while being clear that the printers' evaluation of the increasing falseness of some parts of the media was correct, to work to avoid a printers' strike. Letters with hundreds of signatures were circulated in defense of the "letter of five".[82] Regional SDP bodies also put out official letters of support. Journalists blamed government information policy and opposition to the SDP for their inability to prevent the printers' strike. They also made clear that the profession was not divided and that they were determined to "be professional":

> the current campaign against us has [from our perspective] as its goals disintegrating our professional community, making it impossible for the SDP to play its role of mediation, and eliminating the common ground between opponents. We continue to stand for unity and will do all we can to preserve it. We will do all, but we will not do everything: among other things we will not give up the principles set out in the Extraordinary SDP Congress. . .
>
> Never on the altar of compromise will we sacrifice our own existence and our belief that our truthfulness, factualness, and honesty are, today, the one road to social understanding.[83]

The two day printers' strike was formally opposed by the SDP. But, this time, journalists could not stop it. They reported and observed. As individuals, they continued to champion the position that no one – government or union – had the right to block information and, in doing so, tell them as journalists how to do their jobs. So, many worked to produce archival skeletons of the dailies that could not be printed.[84] On the other hand, most avoided any open involvement with Party and military papers printed during the strike in military facilities.[85] It was Solidarity and government officials who claimed victories. Journalists, instead, argued that their professional rights and options were limited and all they could do was hope that these "Days Without Press," unfortunate as this action was, would force the kind of changes they had been unable to achieve through expert advice and negotiations.[86]

Paralleling the increases in censorship, the condemnation of misreporting, and Party and government officials' intervention were a series of negotiations on a draft law on censorship. These were carried on with Ministry of Justice specialists and with legal specialists who had long done work in this once esoteric area. SDP representatives took the lead. The other active force working with journalists was the Committee of Intellectual Associations. Together they pressed for explicit regulations on what could and could not appear in the media, an appeals procedure that was expeditious and independent of the censors themselves, and a way for authors to signal readers that their text had been censored.[87] On this, Solidarity, artists' representatives, and academic colleagues added provisions exempting their own work (including union papers, university publications, and artists' exhibits or performances) from prior censorship.[88] None of these were acceptable to Ministry negotiators. As a result, while the public battles over media control raged on, the discussions on the censorship law proceeded.

By June 1981, it was clear to journalists that there was no solution but to pass a law. For both Party officials and Solidarity, the failure to resolve this issue left an at least symbolic aspect of the Gdańsk Accords embarrassingly unresolved as both went into their Congress sessions. SDP representatives got the support of journalists who were delegates to the Sejm. They insisted that the law be introduced.[89] To resolve the deadlock between the Ministry and the draft supported by journalists, the Committee of Intellectual Associations, and Solidarity, both drafts were taken before the Sejm's Cultural Affairs Committee, chaired by Karol Małcużyński, the most respected journalist in Poland. This was the first time two alternate drafts had been presented to the Sejm for it to draft a compromise. Journalists came to argue their case as did those who were delegates to the Sejm.[90] The result was the 31 July 1981 law granting precise limits on censorship and the right, that journalists had sought, to mark where passages had been removed. It also provided the explicit exemptions of "internal" association or union publications, scholarly books, and artistic events Solidarity and the intellectual associations sought. But, it left ultimate control of the censors not with the Sejm, as these groups had wanted, but with the administrative court. Accompanying that law was a commitment on the part of the Sejm for there to be follow-up laws on the press and the right of confidentiality.[91]

The battle to represent

The SDP, historically rooted though it was in the very beginnings of communist rule in Poland, faced institutional challenges both to its leaders and to its position as a professional organization. None of these challenges came from any significant group in the journalistic community. But, they did challenge both the ability of the SDP to negotiate for benefits and its singular position as "the representative of journalists," something which concerned it as it concerns professional associations in the West.

These challenges reflected, from journalists' perspective, on the prominence of the profession, its organization, and its leadership. They also reflected and threatened its autonomy and its ability to negotiate effectively. Journalists' responses to these threats demonstrated both their desire to preserve the autonomy of the professional organization (and the profession itself) and also their sense of a special professional mission.

The focus of the challenge to the SDP was the Congress of the

International Organization of Journalists which was held in Moscow, in October 1981. By statute, the head of the SDP automatically would have been the vice president of the IOJ. For officials in Moscow, having activist journalist Stefan Bratkowski in this role was intolerable. Polish officials, therefore, used their personal and professional ties to privately request that Bratkowski not head the delegation.[92] The SDP leadership felt it was their professional right and obligation to keep their group as it had been elected.[93] Given the SDP officials' insistence and refusal to bend, the authorities could do little in Poland.

Polish Party leaders did move to oust Bratkowski from the Party days before the Congress was to start, drawing sharp public retorts from him and his SDP colleagues.[94] But, while this made SDP delegates fearful, it was not sufficient to stop them from going to Moscow.[95] Instead, to circumvent them, the Soviets invited another group of delegates from Poland. This they did with the private encouragement of the Polish authorities. These delegates were unknowns in the journalistic community. They had declared themselves a union in the spring. Initially, they claimed to want to work with the SDP in supplementing the efforts of the SDP in the area of social welfare. But, for the SDP leaders, this group seemed, at the time, to be simply a "meaningless attempt to get attention."[96] In Moscow, though, the SDP leaders found themselves displaced by what they came to see as a "Judas union."[97]

This displacement was an issue worth fighting about for them even though the IOJ, as a Soviet based organization, offered little concrete gain and no real prestige in Poland itself or in the West. Why then did they engage in this battle? From their own explanations, it is clear that the defiance was a reflection of their desire to play their professional roles of communication and representation. Bratkowski and others went to the planning meeting in Prague and the final meeting in Moscow to demonstrate that "Polish journalists and journalism are not devils but reasoned and reasoning communists concerned with the same things as their colleagues and not what the Soviet bloc press said they were."[98]

They were, in this way, playing their self-appointed professional role and claiming their organizational rights in an atypical framework. To do this, individuals from the SDP met with former acquaintances and colleagues, as well as Soviet officials, to report their story directly and defend their professionality just as they sought out and courted Soviet embassy officials in Warsaw "to get the true story to Moscow."[99] They were attempting to court Soviet and East European colleagues as a "media" through which they could get to Poland's international audience and, in doing this, protect their profession from repression that would be caused by misunderstandings. They made a point of ignoring the Union of Journalists in Poland. They held themselves to be, whatever their international position, the representatives of the profession, and jealously guarded this ground as Western professional associations have guarded their ground against interlopers and alternative organizations.

Journalists in a new professional world

The rise of Solidarity brought with it new opportunities and a world of greater conflicts than journalists had ever faced before. It also brought very real battles over professional "ground." Just as Solidarity had been a movement that demanded freedom of information and open discussion, it was also a movement that spawned its own media. This left journalists on "established" journals challenged as never before and without the control government censors and publishing houses had provided for them before.

Because the regular Polish media could report nothing about the strikes that swept across Poland in the summer of 1980, the strikers initially developed their own "media". These included factory bulletins (some based on already functioning factory newspapers), public address system announcements, and even messages scribbled inside freight cars going from one strike centre to another. As the movement spread, so too did the new media: "If an office had a mimeograph machine or a xerox machine, it had a press. That was it, everyone wrote about everything."[100]

For journalists, this new "media" was a challenge. Since it was uncensored, it dealt with things journalists had long had to avoid or veil. At the same time, journalists feared that, without their professional expertise, the new media would go too far and bring on full-scale repression. In all but a few cases, like the Kraków based Solidarity weekly, *Wiadomości Krakowskie*, those who had worked as journalists did not write for or edit these "papers" – partly because they were not asked to and partly because this was not, to them, "real journalism." This media was used as a yardstick by establishment journalists but, at the same time, they and their Party and government bosses felt pressed to compete in what they covered. This competition was possible because the censors were told to see to it that "negative information" was presented.[101] But, as both the economic and political situation worsened, more and more restrictions were put on the press, even as journalists were more and more prepared to fight for their right to publish.

The limits on and distortions of the coverage of Solidarity and its activities were too much for the new unions. As a part of the negotiations in March 1981, to end a strike threat caused by the Bydgoszcz beatings and the general deterioration of conditions, Solidarity was given the right to publish a weekly paper. It was not, however, given the right to produce its own radio and television programs, although some allowances were made for Solidarity representatives to appear with government spokesmen on discussion programs. Later, Solidarity refused Polish television access to its national convention, forcing television to buy Western coverage.

Here, as on the issue of the "Days Without Press," journalists viewed Solidarity's demands with some mixed feelings. They documented, at their own initiative, the misrepresentations and falsehoods that had appeared on radio and television.[102] Radio and television journalists made complaints to the SDP about their professional rights being ignored.[103] But, for the government to grant Solidarity control over its own programs went against their professional grain; to do this was, for them the equivalent of, "letting the source write his own news."[104] This denied them what they saw as their most central right and role, the control over presentation and interpretation. So, neither the concept of separately controlled programming nor the Solidarity compromise proposal for the union to have the right to approve any reporting on its affairs was supported by the SDP, even when it was clear to them that the government totally disregarded journalists as well.[105] Nor was the refusal of Solidarity to let Polish Television and Radio cover its convention given SDP support. The irony was clear. Polish Television and Radio staff were delegates, they helped produce the foreign language editions of the Solidarity Congress bulletins, and they worked with foreign correspondents. In all, they supported the position of Solidarity against the government while they openly criticized Solidarity for putting itself above the profession and not giving them the opportunity to report to their own public.[106]

The Solidarity weekly was also taken as a challenge to professional journalists' roles. For the Solidarity leadership, staffing its legal weekly was a union issue, and an important one, as spontaneous Solidarity "journals" sprang up all over Poland. Lech Wałęsa himself had the deciding voice in selecting the editors for the new weekly. After a number of alternate proposals, Tadeusz Mazowiecki, the former editor of the Catholic intellectual journal *Więź*, was selected as the chief editor.[107] He then attempted to bring together a staff that balanced the various contending forces in Solidarity. Three groups were in competition for positions on the Solidarity weekly even before it began publication: dissident writers from the KOR press of the late seventies, Solidarity activists with no writing experience, and established journalism professionals.[108] Mazowiecki's own preference was to fill the staff with men from his own community of liberal journalists who had worked in the press since the fifties or sixties. This was rejected out of hand by Solidarity officials. Instead, only a few experienced journalists were recruited. Moves to bring in the KOR writers were equally problematic since most refused to join unless they were hired as a total group. The young Solidarity activists came, from the journalists' perspective, "with no background and no way to be checked out. To say nothing of the fact that they had no experience at writing or the mechanics of making a paper."[109]

In the end, the staff was an incongruous amalgam of young workers, KOR activists, and established journalists who were known for having battled the system before. According to the original managing editor (a professional journalist who had been in journalism since the late forties), "two-thirds had never seen a typewriter before."[110] Other professionals – all of whom were active in the SDP – served as assistant editors and heads of important departments. Their powers, however, were limited.[111] On most issues, they found they were treated as resource people to train others in the "rules of the game."[112]

The established journalists on the staff were also discouraged by the strictures imposed on them by Solidarity. On the one hand, *Tygodnik Solidarność* published much that previously could not even have been considered for publication: the SDP letter on the state of the media, an interview with a censor on his work, articles on official corruption, and, in its last issue before martial law, an article on the legal process for declaring a "state of emergency."[113] On the other hand, in dealing with Solidarity issues and policies about which Solidarity was negotiating, professional journalists felt unjustly hamstrung by the Solidarity rules that its paper should only publish documents and report events, not argue cases or engage in any criticism of the union movement. They were blocked, in effect, from raising and debating many policy issues because Solidarity was involved in virtually everything and was so factionalized that any discussion was a potential trigger for internal union conflicts. This was, for them, particularly problematic when they covered the Solidarity congress under instructions not to do anything but record what went on.[114] It was this cramping of their traditional roles as a "loyal opposition" and "educator" for the community, far more than the untrained staff with whom they worked or their publication difficulties that pushed them, in spite of their opposition to the old system, almost to a man to resign their editorial positions and shift back to simply writing advocacy articles. Indeed, by the fall of 1981, the professional journalists who had initially served as editors dropped out of those positions and stayed on merely as mentors or were writers while working elsewhere.[115]

In their work and professional worlds, then, journalists were trapped. They shared Solidarity's fury over the limits on what they and their media could present. On the one hand, they rejected Gierek era interference in the media and its messages. They bridled at the new attempts by the government and the censors to control. Government officials even had to use American officials' predictions of an imminent Soviet invasion to convince journalists that they could not publish an article or line of criticism. And, journalists vociferously criticized falsehoods produced by those in the profession or claiming to be part of it.

On the other hand, although where controls were very restrictive and deformed the news, Solidarity units were often formed to supplement the SDP, journalists were no more receptive to Solidarity's demands and restrictions than they were to those from the government. They felt that they themselves, not "mere" workers or readers, should control the flow of information, its availability, and content. They also felt that no organization's internal needs should deny them the right to "educate, criticize, and confront." They resisted attempts to control them by pushing the limits and maintaining clear lines between themselves and "nonjournalists." As a result, although the SDP worked with Solidarity on censorship and other issues, journalists tended to focus their political and policy hopes and loyalties on the SDP and not on Solidarity.

The one area of conjunction for journalists and Solidarity was the need for wage and benefit increases. The difference was that journalists were not willing to negotiate as individual staffs. They wanted the issue to be a professional issue with the SDP as their negotiating agent. Improving journalists' earnings was clearly specified as one of the leadership's tasks by the Extraordinary Congress. A commission was set up to negotiate with the government. The commission's progress was closely monitored by the governing council. Criticism of SDP leaders and challenges to their authority were made on the grounds of their inability, given their treatment as opposition by government officials and the economic disaster all around them, to get benefits for the profession. The worsening of relations between the profession or its leaders and the political elite was signaled by the stalling of the negotiations on material benefits. In the end, only after much delay and discussion, a salary scale was established which raised the base salaries but still allowed for substantial earnings from piecework.[116] Its gains were diminished not only by its lateness – at the end of 1981 – but also by the virtual collapse of the economy and by the almost immediate imposition of martial law.

The state of war

If journalists had demonstrated their professionalism in the cross-pressures and opportunities of the Solidarity period,their independence from both Solidarity and the Party and government had not made them seem apolitical to any of the other actors in the "Polish drama." Instead, when martial law was declared, the black cars of the security police rolled up to the houses of the leaders of the SDP and its Warsaw branch, to those of some journalists who were active in Solidarity organizations or who were staff members on *Tygodnik Solidarność*, to others who were active in professional and intellectual organizations, and even to the apartments of the entire crew of Wrocław television (including one woman who had also been a delegate at the Ninth Party Congress). In interning those they could find (a number on the internment lists went into hiding until the orders for their internment were rescinded), journalists contend, and the evidence seems to indicate, the police interned a larger proportion of journalists than of members of any other professional group.[117]

The SDP was one of the few organizations explicitly attacked for "threatening the interest of the security of the state."[118] While, in other areas of life, the key was for business to go on as usual, only three national newspapers and a militarized radio and television, its doors closed to all but those temporarily drafted into the military, were open. All other media and their staffs – even those that had separated themselves from Solidarity – were suspended. And, ultimately, long before any other creative or professional union was dealt with, the SDP was disbanded and a new regime-supported association opened in its place. Journalists were the only profession forced to undergo "political verification" to prove their political reliability. At the same time, the authorities claimed legitimacy for the regime based on the "openness" they allowed in their press and in their public discussions.

According to journalists' own accounts of the days after the "state of war" was declared, it was fellow journalists they sought. Many reported that, since all telephone lines had been cut, they walked from one colleague's home to another to see who had been interned, what others knew and thought, and what needed to be done. A number went to the SDP building to try and protect it and its contents. Their hold was short; the building was quickly put under military guard. Others tried to go to their offices only to find them locked and guarded. That Sunday evening, 13 December, journalists gathered at "their" church, atheists and believers alike from all over the city of Warsaw. There they spoke their minds and organized relief for interned colleagues and their families. Here too they tried to account for their profession and identify those who had disappeared. Those who had evaded the officials who came to intern them found havens with colleagues.

Even for those who were not threatened with internment, the shock of hearing General Jaruzelski's announcement of the "state of war," finding soldiers guarding the streets, having all communications within Poland and between Poles and the outside world cut after the heady months of freedom and knowing that established, long-time professionals were being interned created in them both fear and fury. This was not a repression that had either been expected or experienced before. It seemed "to betray all the rules and harken back to the worst years of Stalinism."[119]

Ironically, even those who were involved with the Jaruzelski regime and the decision to declare "the state of war" as well as later acts against media freedom were loyal to their journalistic community. While Mieczysław Rakowski and his colleagues defended martial law and the internments, they also intervened in individual cases to free or lift the internment orders from colleagues and fellow staff members (even for those who had attacked them and gone their separate ways earlier). They spent time on professional concerns. Rakowski met with the *Polityka* staff 28 December 1981, in a private gathering to discuss the fate of the paper. He heard their condemnations of martial law and their arguments for and against reestablishing the journal. In the end, he made his case for the importance of their professional work on the journal continuing as an independent, if loyal, bastion and said the paper would, eventually, be reconstituted with whichever staff members wished to continue. He then even gave rides home to some staff members who were hiding and arranged for those on the internment lists to be dropped from them.

These individual acts, although special both because of Rakowski's position as Deputy Prime Minister and the prominence of a large number of the *Polityka* staff as journalists and as association activists, were not unique. Journalists saw their professional choices – to stay as journalists with limited professional autonomy or leave the profession – as moral and political choices so basic that lifelong friendships were severed because of differences over the individuals' decisions. However, a sense of the larger professional community remained. Even when the choice was between making a token statement of affiliation to the political authorities or losing years of professional gain, for journalists the power of the community's support and their loyalty to the autonomy and respect they felt was their right as professional journalists was strong. A Code of Ethics was set out for professional journalists that regulated intraprofessional interaction and professional behavior.[120] Later, many refused to submit to verification as they considered it an explicit insult to their professionalism.[121] However, even as journalists left the profession and condemned those who did not,[122] they knew what was happening in the larger professional community. And, whether or not they maintained contact, they felt that their actions reflected on the profession as a whole. These personal threads, although cut and frayed by bitter splits over what was the right decision to make as professionals, kept, among the pre-Solidarity journalists, a sense of a professional world even if they no longer formally worked in journalism.

For young professionals, the professionalizing pressures were different but equally as strong. The self-exile of their mentors and senior journalists gave them unthinkable opportunities to hold prestigious positions and to establish themselves. New journals were opened offering, at least in their initial presentations, opportunities for prestigious writing. Even the "rebels" in the profession had the opportunity to write on the various marginal journals that suddenly became havens. Although many refused, as a sign of solidarity with the profession's elders, to join the SDPRL when it was opened, the option of leaving the profession was not as real for them as it was for senior journalists. They simply did not have the financial wherewithal to support themselves outside the profession. The options of private industry were not appealing to many because that was not "professional work" and did not offer either the contacts or the challenges that journalism did. Those who left formally often continued to remain in journalism by working in the underground press either while they did establishment journalism or under cover of their other, new work.[123]

The dramatic shifts in personnel in the media, the disbanding of the Association of Polish Journalists, and the temporary closing and then the restaffing of the Polish media did not mark an end of journalism or of all the attitudes and patterns that had long marked Polish journalism. In the months that followed the declaration of martial law, the press began to reappear. Some journals like *Kultura* disappeared as their staff members to a man did not want to concede to martial law by returning. Others returned in form but with dramatically different staffs. Others, still, especially the regional and less prestigious central press, returned to their old status quo. Still other journals emerged from nowhere. Some were tiny publications that had long been the purview of "two old ladies working half a day a week" whose sponsors befriended the activists blacklisted from jobs connected with the main publishing houses in the hope that they could make a name and money for their organization. The presence of prominent journalists on these journals made them a new "elite publication." Others were new journals that had been opened or planned before the advent of martial law and brought together only after martial law. These tended to represent the spectrum of political views from the very right wing, *Rzeczywistość*, to the liberal journals such as *Zdanie* and the consumers' unions' *Veto*. All of these journals offered jobs and, giving the initial exodus from the profession, went searching for staff – trading off journalists' expertise for concessions on what and how freely they could write. At the same time, the underground press emerged more actively than ever. Journalists who had worked in the establishment press became, to a greater extent than they had been in the seventies, users and producers of this press. And, ultimately, the pressures and restrictions of martial law meant that the kinds of informal communication and exchance that had been the meat of journalists' work were even more important and consuming than they had been before.

Formally or informally, the journalistic community continued to exist, even as its members were split into angry groups by disagreements over what the right posture was toward "the new Poland" of Jaruzelski's martial law. Those who rose in the profession lived by the models of their predecessors. They expressed the same professional goals as those who had gone before them and, in spite of the fact that they had elected to work with the martial law regime and its restrictions, they worried and expressed the same fury over political involvement in their work as had their predecessors. So, even as it was seen as an organization of collaborators and "Judases," the SDPRL fought, in the revisions of the censorship law and the drafting of the press law, for the very same professional autonomy the SDP had fought for in its thirty years.

Even as its members changed or turned from one job to another, the torch was passed on. Professionalization of new generations and the realities of doing a job in the face of political pressures left journalism very much a profession troubled within itself but working as it had before to protect what it saw as a special calling.

Conclusion

Did journalists, once they were "freed" by Solidarity and "trapped" by martial law, react to the new options and worlds they faced as professionals or as politicos? In this whipsawing world in which they found themselves during the fifteen months of Solidarity and the months of repression that followed, were they creating new agendas, merely responding to the options they had as individuals – not as professionals – or were they acting out agendas that had long been set and pushed for by them as individuals and as a professional group? Can one be a professional without real autonomy?

There is no ultimate test of professionalism but, what does seem clear is that journalists responded as individuals and as a group with agendas they had long advocated through all their professional activities. They advocated those agendas, as they had before, in whatever ways they could. So, instead of doing one to one combat with the censors, they took the lead in preparing and advocating a new press law. Instead of battling privately over the problems they faced in providing the coverage they felt they should provide, they collected data and distributed it to show what inaccuracies had been forced into the media. And, instead of internal and often informal actions to better journalists' conditions, the SDP fought for a change in the press system and the entire system of pay for journalists.

Even as they relished the professional gains they were able to make as a result of Solidarity, journalists kept their professional boundaries as clean as they could. For them, Solidarity's incursions into their work were no more welcome than those of the Party leadership. As they had done before with their "political mentors," journalists pressed for the right to lead Solidarity. When they could not control, they tried to teach. So, the Association made no moves to open itself up to the flood of self-styled journalists. Nor were they willing to have printers and Solidarity unions stop the publication of the press even as it made the very point that they had been trying to make – that the media's falseness was not right. Journalists pressed government and Party officials for the right to act without censorship and to determine for themselves what should be printed. In this, they battled both sides. Their political activities, even as they overlay their professional ones, were products of the roles they played as professionals and the values they cherished in their professional work. So, as Stefan Bratkowski catapulted himself into a frenzy of political mediation, he acted as a journalist in mediating and facilitating communication. And, even as the SDP delegation insisted on going to Moscow, they were, in their own mind, on a desperate mission of communicating and explaining the realities of Poland to this their foreign audience.

And, the departure of many from their cherished professional positions was not a sign of a lack of commitment to the profession but, given the fact that most continued to live in the world of journalists and to do self-styled journalistic work, a sign of the level of their commitment to the profession's public image and autonomy. At the same time, the movement of newcomers and beginners into positions that had been left vacant was not, as it was often claimed, a sign of non-professional careerism. For those men and women who took new posts, these openings offered them a chance to practice journalism as their mentors and professional models had done for thirty years. Ultimately, then, as only a professional group could, values, ways of work, and a professional community have allowed journalists to become an autonomous unit and live on even as the political world with which they were tied by the very nature of their work was transformed.

In the end, then, the story of the profession of journalism in the era of Solidarity and martial law is colorful and intricate but it is not a special story. Journalists did not change, they worked in the open as they had worked behind the scenes before. They were not chameleons. Their demands and needs changed not at all from those they had expressed in surveys and interviews in the years when the freedoms and questions of the Solidarity era could only have been a dream. What the story of journalists in this period ultimately demonstrates is the value of using professionalization theory to explain and penetrate the behavior of groups of professionals, however drawn into bureaucratic and political milieus they are, in times of normalcy and in times of crisis. For, ultimately, created as they are by their work experiences and the professional community in which they live and in which they work, journalists are professionals in the fullest sense of the definition given for the professionals of the West.

Appendix
Research methodology: Unwritten answers

This research is intended to present the story of Polish journalism. It is a story that, in spite of journalists' control of the press, does not appear in that press. Journalists, as a matter of professional pride, have not "hung their dirty linen in public" and, furthermore, like the word "censorship" in the seventies, much of what they had to say about themselves could not have been published. In this, they are not unique as a profession. Furthermore, like other professionals' they have never been involved in continually reflecting on what and why they are acting.

To tell this story then, I could rely only in part on the published materials that were available in the Polish press and the professional press that journalists published – even in the Solidarity period when there was a sudden flood of discussion of long taboo subjects. And, even with the access I was able to have to internal documents of press research institutes, the SDP and SDPRL, and various groups and individuals, these documents alone could never have made the story complete. So, I used research techniques that had long been assumed to be impossible to use to any major degree in the Soviet bloc: the interview and survey research. In asking questions of my subjects, however, I was able to deal with issues of professionalization and of professional activity and attitudes in ways that would not have been conceivable at all with only written documentation. Such research methodology raises two basic questions:

(1) What was the likelihood of accuracy in the presentations and representativeness in the sample that I generated? (How could I insure that the responses were not geared for my American ears or for whoever a journalist might assume would be listening?)
(2) Is this a methodology that is applicable only to this literate and explicity verbal population of professional newspeople?

(1) The accuracy of the information

Although this is not nor could it have been a sample in which size and distribution were controlled for all variables, the results have proven both credible and reliable. Controls were built into my use of the material. I assured my subjects that I would follow the practice of making all interview material anonymous, noted only with the year in which the interview was done. Beyond this, I have avoided using any specific information that was not spontaneously corroborated by two other sources. (In the case of both the pre- and post-Solidarity interviews, this was further validated by the fact that the information I was given in Poland was frequently given to me in no greater detail when I interviewed *emigrés* or Polish journalists living in the United States and in Western Europe – individuals with presumably less to hide or fear.) In addition, wherever possible, I have sought written corroboration by checking what was said to have been published or written.

The interviews themselves were done with some 249 journalists in Poland and outside of Poland. In some cases, repeat interviews were done during successive phases of this research. Two types of journalists were interviewed:[1] editors and others on regional papers where my survey was done and[2] elite journalists – often complete staffs – on nationally prominent papers or radio and television. Contacts were made both directly with specific staffs and through recommendations of prominent journalists to other colleagues who would be valuable to interview. (Given the sense of professional community, this served in fact to open many doors and ease the credibility problem, to become established in the milieu.) In the interviews outside of Poland, journalists and media officials were interviewed in relation to their availability and the information they could provide. Significantly, as I became known for this research in Poland, I found journalists more and more willing to give me archival data and specific information that would normally not be made available to a Western researcher (censors' documents, internal SDP or journal papers, and unpublished commentaries and studies).

In the end, I interviewed, some for a number of times and in a number of settings, all of the prominent journalists, as listed by their professional peers, in Poland during the seventies and in the pre- and post-Solidarity period. Those who were less represented in this study, foreign correspondents and agency journalists, are also the least professionally involved segment of the profession.

Paralleling these open-ended interviews, aimed at getting journalists to explain their positions and work as well as to tap their attitudes and their experiences in their professional world and their work, a survey of Polish journalists was done in 1976. This survey was designed by this researcher and translated with the help of faculty of the University of Warsaw School of Journalism. It was distributed through the SDP as a survey done by a Polish researcher, to a sample of ten journals selected as representatives of "average" dailies in Poland in terms of readership population, regional issues, and staff size. Those who received the survey were on Party, national, economic, social and connections with readers departments. They were asked to fill out the survey and return it to the SDP. The return rate was slightly under 50 percent. The questions included political questions as well as questions used in 1956 and 1958. After the survey was administered, I then went into the field and interviewed the editors and representative department heads, those too prominent to receive and be expected to fill out a mail questionnaire.

This methodology proved to be one that was foreign to Polish journalists' experiences at the time. They were not accustomed to survey research in general or to mail questionnaires – hence, the low return rate and the often unexpected comments in the margins. It was also one fraught with risks since the political pressure on journalists, mounting as it was in 1976, and the fact that these were distributed by newsroom officials, might be assumed to lead to biased results. In fact, as can be seen in the data reported here, the responses that journalists gave were far from veiled criticism or positive comments on the regime and its media policy. They were, on the whole, extremely critical of political interference and pressures as well as journalists' own job situation and the work of their Association. The responses they gave corroborated with the responses given in open-ended interviews.

As a final check, sections and the manuscript as a whole were given to Polish journalists. Their comments were taken into consideration in terms of substance as opposed to analysis. The validity of the research seems to have been testified to by the fact that information in it has been referred to explicitly as the expert source on Polish journalism in both the anti-establishment underground press and the establishment press. Those living outside Poland have also been asked to comment in areas of their expertize, as have those in fields adjacent to journalism. Again, where they seemed valid, substantive, but not analytical, criticisms were taken into consideration.

(2) A methodology for journalists

The question for similar research in a larger context is whether one could expect to do such interviews only with journalists, men and women of words involved in periods of professional stress. The evidence indicates that this is not necessarily the case. Similar interviews have been done by Western journalists stationed in Eastern Europe and the Soviet Union as the mainstay of the very news reports we have used as evidence for thirty years now. In addition, comparable research has been done on other professionals, including that on medical doctors and engineers, by Michael Kennedy in 1983–84 with equally fruitful results. Also, I have used a similar technique in a smaller study of professional and specialist influence with equally valuable results. Ultimately, then, it appears that journalists' way with words does not make them specially competent reporters of their own life or their own professional world.

What this research methodology would indicate is that there is much to be learned by trying to ask questions of our subjects, especially in countries like Poland where much that is discussed and that occurs appears in print only in limited circulation documents, accessible only through personal contacts based on respect and trust, and where the bulk of policy relevant activities occur only on a person to person, unrecorded level. It is these events that we have missed in all but our various interview projects with *émigrés* and that we need to understand to be able to explain the moments of action and forthright speech that occur when the lid of control is lifted on these systems.

Notes

1 Introduction: journalists as professionals in theory and reality

1 Talcott Parsons, "Professions", in the *International Encyclopedia of Social Sciences*, XII (New York: Macmillan Company and the Free Press, 1968), pp. 536–45.
2 Terrance Johnson, *Professions and Power* (London: Macmillan, 1972).
3 Parsons, "Professions," pp. 536–45; David H. Weaver and G. Cleveland Wilhoit, *The American Journalist* (Bloomington: Indiana University Press, 1986), pp. 104–5.
4 Joseph Ben-David, "Professions in the Class System of Present Day Society," *Current Sociology*, XII (1963/64), pp. 247–330.
5 Elliot Friedson, *Professional Dominance: The Social Structure of Medical Care* (New York: Atherton Press, 1970), p. 99.
6 Among the seminal works focused on professional inputs are: H. Gordon Skilling, "Groups in Soviet Politics: Some Hypotheses," in *Interest Groups in Soviet Politics*, in H. Gordon Skilling and Franklyn Griffiths, eds. (Princeton: Princeton University Press, 1971); Donald D. Barry, "The Specialist in Soviet Policy-Making: The Adoption of a Law," *Soviet Studies*, XVI, no. 2 (October, 1964), pp. 152–65; Harold Berman, "The Struggle of Soviet Jurists Against a Return to Stalinist Terror," *Slavic Review*, XXII (June, 1963), pp. 314–20; Andreas Bilinsky, "The Lawyer in Soviet Society," *Problems of Communism*, XII–XIV (March–April, 1965), pp. 62–71; Zbigniew Brzeziński, *Political Power: USA–USSR* (New York: Random House, 1964); Theodore Friedgut, "Interests and Groups in Soviet Policy Making: The MTS Reforms," *Soviet Studies*, XXVIII, no. 4 (October, 1976), pp. 524–47; Linda Greenberg, "Soviet Science Policy and the Scientific Establishment," *Survey*, XIX, no. 81 (Autumn, 1971), pp. 51–63; Andrzej Korboński, "Bureaucracy and Interest Groups in Communist Societies: The Case of Czechoslovakia," *Studies in Comparative Communism*, IV, no. 1 (January, 1971); David Lane and George Kolankiewicz, *Social Groups in Polish Society* (New York: Columbia University Press, 1973); Joel J. Schwartz and William R. Keech, "Group Influence and the Policy Process in the Soviet Union," *American Political Science Review*, LXIII, no. 3 (September, 1968), pp. 840–51; H. Gordon Skilling and Franklyn Griffiths, *Interest Groups in Soviet Politics* (Princeton: Princeton University

Press, 1971); and Phillip Stewart, "Soviet Interest Groups and the Policy Process: The Repeal of Production Education," *World Politics*, xx (October, 1969), pp. 29–50; Thomas A. Baylis, *The Technical Intelligentsia and the East German Elite* (Berkeley: University of California Press, 1974).

In two major studies of groups in Eastern Europe, Western researchers have used opinion polls: Joseph R. Fiszman, *Revolution and Tradition in People's Poland* (Princeton: Princeton University Press, 1972), and Allan A. Barton, Bodgan Denitch and Charles Kadusin, *Opinion-Making Elite in Yugoslavia* (New York: Praeger, 1973).

7 The basic works on communication and development have been: Daniel Lerner, *The Passing of Traditional Society* (Glencoe, Illinois: Free Press, 1958); Lucien Pye, ed., *Communications and Political Development* (Princeton: Princeton University Press, 1963); Everett M. Rogers, *Modernization Among Peasants* (New York: Holt, Rinehart and Winston, 1969); and Wilbur Schramm, *Mass Media and National Development* (Stanford: Stanford University Press, 1964).

Initial studies such as Paul Lazarsfeld, Bernard Berelson, and Mazie Gaudet, *The People's Choice* (New York: Columbia University Press, 1944), actually showed that on all issues where there was an alternative, more immediate source of information, the media was not significant. But, in more recent studies since the advent of television campaigns, such as that of John P. Robinson, "The Press as King Maker," *Journalism Quarterly*, LI (Winter, 1974), pp. 87–94, it has been shown that the media has a greater impact than previously thought, but that the conflicting messages put out by radio, television, and the press limit the impact of any one medium.

In addition, basic psychological and sociological research on communication and attitude formation demonstrates both the impact and the multitude of constraints on communications: Raymond A. Bauer, "The Communicator and the Audience" in *People, Society and Mass Communications*, Lewis Dexter, ed. (New York: Free Press of Glencoe, 1964), pp. 126–38; Carle J. Hovland, Irving L. Janis, and Harold H. Kelley, *Communications and Persuasion* (New Haven: Yale University Press, 1953); Daniel Katz, ed., *Attitude Change, Public Opinion Quarterly*, Special Edition, XXIV (1960); and Joseph T. Klapper, *The Effects of Mass Communication* (Glencoe, Illinois: Free Press, 1960).

8 John W. C. Johnstone, Edward J. Sławski, William W. Bowman, *The News People* (Urbana, Illinois: University of Illinois Press, 1976), provides a full discussion of the American journalistic profession with some reference to other more traditional professions as do Weaver and Wilhoit, *The American Journalist*. Broad sociological discussions of professionals frequently include some passing reference to journalists as a unique group which does not fit in any one category. Penn Kimball's rather journalistic account of journalism as a profession, "Journalism: Art, Craft, or Profession?" in *The Professions in America*, Kenneth S. Lynn, ed. (Boston: Beacon Press, 1963), pp. 242–60, makes rather clear the special nature of journalism. Recent scholarly studies include: John W. C. Johnston, "Organizational Constraints on News Work," *Journalism Quarterly* (Spring, 1976), pp. 5–12; David R. Bowers, "A Report on

Activity by Publishers in Directing Newsroom Decisions," *Journalism Quarterly*, 44 (Spring, 1967), pp. 43–50; Leo Mann, "Counting the Crowd: Effects of Editorial Policy on Estimates," *Journalism Quarterly*, 51 (Summer, 1974), pp. 278–85; David L. Grey, "Decision Making by a Reporter under Deadline Pressure," *Journalism Quarterly*, 42 (Autumn, 1966); and Benn H. Bagdikan, "Shaping Media Content: Professional Personnel and Organizational Structure," *Public Opinion Quarterly*, 36, no. 4 (Winter, 1973–74), pp. 569–79.

In addition, there have been a number of journalistic accounts of professional work by American journalists such as: Timothy Crouse, *The Boys on the Bus* (New York: Random House, 1973); Robert Cirino, *Don't Blame the People* (Los Angeles: Diversity Press, 1971); Edward J. Epstein, *News From Nowhere* (New York: Random House, 1973), and *Between Fact and Fiction* (New York: Viking, 1978). Clearly, all of this research has been done in the American context. Comparable research has been done to a more limited degree on other press systems, e.g., Jeremy Turnstall, *Journalists at Work*, (London: Constable, 1971).

In the Soviet area, Mark Hopkins, *Mass Media in the Soviet Union* (New York: Praeger, 1970) focuses largely on the press system with little discussion of the story process. The Rand Corporation study, *The Media and Intra-Elite Communication in the USSR*, by Lilita Dzirkals, Thane Gustafson, and A. Ross Johnson (Rand Report no. R–2869, Santa Monica, California, September, 1982) focuses largely on the structures and pressures involved in the production of articles and media controversies with a focus on finding the links which would help to explain the significance of what appears in the press to understanding elite conflict. Gertrude J. Robinson, *Tito's Maverick Media* (Champaign, Illinois: University of Illinois Press, 1977), makes some references to story process but does not analyze the factors influencing it. More recently, Thomas Remington has done a number of studies of newspaper journalists in the Soviet Union such as "Politics and Professionalism in Soviet Journalism", *Slavic Review*, XLIV, no. 3 (Fall, 1985) pp. 488–503. Ellen Mickiewicz has looked at the media officials in the Soviet establishment and the processes through which stories are produced: Ellen Mickiewicz, "Policy Issues in the Soviet Media System" in Erik P. Hoffman, ed., *The Soviet Union in the 1980s* (New York: Proceedings of the Academy of Political Science, 1984), and "The Functions of Communications Officials in the USSR: A Biographical Study," *Slavic Review*, XVIII, no. 4 (Winter, 1984), pp. 641–56. In addition, see the contemporary studies of the media, its production and output, in Owen Johnson, *The Media in Eastern Europe*, forthcoming.

9 Fred S. Siebert, *et al.*, *Four Theories of the Press* (Urbana, Illinois: University of Illinois Press, 1956), chs. 2 and 3.

10 For a full discussion of the role of the Polish press during the partitions, see Jane L. Curry, "The Partitions and the Polish Press" (paper presented at Indiana University conference on the Mass Media in Eastern Europe, 1981). See also, University of Warsaw Institute of Journalism, *Polish Mass Media and National Culture* (Warsaw, 1978).

11 Hopkins, *Mass Media*, p. 40.

12 Ibid., p. 57.
13 Discussion in this section will be limited to the political ideology presented to Polish journalists. It is not intended to be a comprehensive discussion of Marxist–Leninist theory of the press. For a fuller discussion, see Hopkins, *Mass Media*, p. 55.
14 Ibid.
15 V. I. Lenin, "What Is To Be Done?" in *Collected Works*, Vol. 1 (Moscow: Progress Publishers, 1967), p. 234.
16 Ibid., p. 233.
17 Ibid., p. 227
18 Hopkins, *Mass Media*, p. 20.
19 See discussion in Bernard A. Ramundo, "They Answer to *Pravda*," *The University of Illinois Law Forum* (Spring, 1964).
20 Hopkins, *Mass Media*, p. 104.
21 Evidence for this comes from intensive interviews of Polish journalists done in 1976, 1979, and 1983. One study of Western lawyers' special role in politics is Heinz Eulau and John Sprague, *Lawyers in Politics* (Indianapolis: Bobbs-Merrill, 1964), pp. 11–30.
22 Skilling, "Groups: Some Hypotheses," p. 34.
23 Schwartz and Keech, "Group Interest," p. 850.
24 Almost exclusively, this may be typed as bureaucratic behavior. It is an area the East Europeans and Soviets have long seen as problematical both to their achievement of a Marxist–Leninist state and to finding successful solutions to systemic problems. Dissidents and political leaders alike have dealt with these problems from the inception of communist rule. See, for example, Paul Cocks, "Rationalization of Party Control" in Chalmers Johnson, ed., *Change in Communist Systems* (Stanford: Stanford University Press, 1970) and Andias Hegedus, *Socialism and Bureaucracy* (New York: St. Martins, 1976).

However, this class and the workings of the bureaucracies have remained particularly elusive to Western observers. Even defining "bureaucrat" as opposed to "intelligentsia" has proved difficult (David Lane, *The Socialist Industrial State,* London: George Allen and Unwin, 1976). Furthermore, in dealing with bureaucrats and bureaucracies' role in the policy process – a role that is not very often described in professional periodicals – the focus has been almost exclusively on industrial settings and/or on Party–state bureaucratic relations. For example, see Joseph S. Berliner, *The Innovation Decision in Soviet Industry* (Cambridge, Massachusetts, 1976); Leslie Holmes, *The Policy Process in Communist States* (Beverly Hills: Sage Library of Social Research, 1981); Jerry Hough, *The Local Party Organs In Industrial Decision Making* (Cambridge: Harvard, 1969); Bruce Parrott, *Politics and Technology in the Soviet Union* (Cambridge: MIT Press, 1985), and Gordon B. Smith, *Public Policy and Administration in the Soviet Union* (New York: Praeger, 1980).

Exceptions to these foci or our concern with scholars as subjects have been Andrzej Korboński's article "Bureaucracy and Interest Groups in

Communist Societies: The Case of Czechoslovakia," and his book *Politics of Socialist Agriculture in Poland: 1945–1960* (New York: Columbia University Press, 1965) as well as Thane Gustafson, *Reform in Soviet Politics* (New York: Cambridge University Press, 1981).

25 Schwartz and Keech, "Group Interest and Policy," p. 850.

26 Ibid.

27 Skilling, "Groups: Some Hypotheses," p. 34.

28 For two documented case studies of this, see Jeremy Azrael, *Managerial Power in Soviet Politics* (Cambridge: Harvard University Press, 1966) and Stewart, "Soviet Interest Groups," pp. 30–31.

29 H. Gordon Skilling, "Group Conflict and Political Change" in *Change in Communist Systems*, Chalmers Johnson, ed. (Stanford: Stanford University Press, 1970), pp. 215–34.

30 See, for example, Erik P. Hoffman, "Changing Soviet Perspectives on Leadership and Administration" in *The Soviet Union Since Stalin*, Stephen P. Cohen, Alexander Rabinowitch, and Robert Sharlet, eds. (Bloomington, Indiana: Indiana University Press, 1980), pp. 71–92, and Radovan Richta, *Civilization at the Crossroads* (Prague: International Arts and Sciences Press, 1969).

31 Kenneth Jowitt, "Inclusion and Mobilization in European Leninist Regimes," *World Politics*, XXVIII, no. 1 (October, 1975), pp. 69–97.

32 In Gabriel Almond and Bingham Powell, *Comparative Politics: A Development Approach* (the summary work applying structural functionalism and the British and American initial studies on interest groups internationally), there is no mention of the Soviet Union or Soviet model societies having any interest groups or interest articulation.

33 See Berman, "Soviet Jurists;" Bilinsky, "The Lawyer"; Brzezinski, *Power: USA–USSR*; and, Friedgut, "The MTS Reforms."

34 Phillip D. Stewart, "Soviet Interest Groups," XXII, pp. 30–31.

35 Two of the strongest theoretical critiques of the assumption in interest group theory that groups do exist are made by Franklyn Griffiths, "Tendency Analysis in Soviet Policy-Making," in Skilling and Griffiths, *Interest Groups*, p. 365 and William Odom, "A Dissenting View on the Group Approach to Soviet Politics," *World Politics*, XXIX (July, 1976), pp. 546–67.

36 Skilling, *Interest Groups*.

37 See standard studies on the impact of specialists as well as Peter M. Solomon, "Specialists in Soviet Policy Making: Criminal Policy, 1938–70," in Richard B. Remnek, *Social Scientists and Policy Making in the USSR* (New York: Praeger Publishers, 1977), p. 19 and Hough, "The Problem of the Measurement of Power."

38 Skilling, *Interest Groups in Communist Societies*, is the most complete collection of such studies. See also Milton C. Lodge, *Soviet Elite Attitudes Since Stalin* (Columbia, Ohio: Charles E. Merrill, 1969), and Josef R. Fiszman, *Revolution and Tradition in People's Poland: Education and Socialization* (Princeton: Princeton University Press, 1972).

39 One of the standard measurements used in Western studies of communist "groups" is the percentage of their members in the Party.
40 Peter Bachrach and Morton S. Baratz, *Power and Poverty* (New York: Oxford University Press, 1970), p. 16.
41 Włodzimierz Wesołowski and Kazimierz M. Słomczyński, *Investigations on Class Structure and Social Stratification in Poland, 1945–75* (Warsaw: The Polish Academy of Sciences, 1977), pp. 61 and 75–77.
42 Ibid., p. 61.
43 See data on social stratification including David Lane, *The End of Inequality?* (London: Penguin, 1971).
44 Friedson, *Professional Dominance*, p. 96.
45 Mancur Olson, *The Logic of Collective Action* (New York: Schocken Books, 1968), p. 11.
46 Corine Gilb, *Hidden Hierarchies* (New York: Harper and Row, 1966), p. 109.
47 Studies of the social backgrounds of Party officials, such as those of T. H. Rigby, "The Soviet Politburo: A Comparative Profile 1951–1971," *Soviet Studies*, XXVI, no. 1 (February, 1972), pp. 134–52; Robert E. Blackwell, Jr., "Career Development in the Soviet Obkom Elite: A Conservative Trend," *Soviet Studies*, XXIV, no. 1 (July, 1972), pp. 24–41; Frederic J. Fleron, Jr., ed., *Communist Studies and the Social Sciences* (Chicago: Rand McNally, 1969); Carl Beck *et al.*, *Comparative Communist Political Leadership* (New York: David McKay, 1973); and R. Barry Farrell, ed., *Political Leadership in Eastern Europe and the Soviet Union* (Chicago: Aldine, 1970); and Jerry F. Hough, *Soviet Leadership in Transition* (Washington, D.C.: Brookings 1980), also frequently discussed the extent to which the training and experiences of members of the Party apparatus have enabled them to use and interpret scientific evidence and their connections with each other.
48 With the exception of the work of Jerry Hough, "The Party *Apparatchiki*," in Skilling and Griffiths, *Interest Groups in Soviet Politics*, and sociological studies of the character of various social groups, Lane and George, *Social Groups*, little has been done on the internal qualities of groups or on group dynamics. The focus of most studies has been at the point of elite decision-making. The concern has been with measuring the extent of groups' ability to modify policy in their own, externally perceived interests.
49 Skilling, "Political Change," pp. 222–28; and Skilling "Group Conflict," pp. 403–5; Lodge, "Soviet Elite," p. 839; Stewart, "Policy Process," and Barry, "Specialist," pp. 152–65.
50 See Jane L. Curry and Sharon L. Wolchik, "Specialists and Professionals in Policy-Making in Czechoslovakia and Poland" (unpublished manuscript, 1984).
51 Ibid.
52 On the other hand, Western interest in professionals and politics has been primarily on the fact that they "render obsolete the primacy of the old issues of political authority and capitalist exploitation" (Parson, "Professions," p. 545) and "engender modes of life, habits of thought and standards of judgement which render them centers of resistance to crude

forces which threaten steady and peaceful evolution" (A. M. Carr Saunders and P. A. Wilson, *The Professions*, Oxford: The Clarendon Press, 1933). Others of like mind include Heinz Eulau, "The Skill Revolution and Consultative Commonwealth," *American Political Science Review*, LXVII, no. 1 (March, 1973), p. 189 who sees professions as forcing an end to individual control of governance.

53 Huntington and Brzezinski, *Political Power*; Jerry Hough, *How the Soviet Union is Governed* (Cambridge: Harvard University Press, 1979), chapter 6; and Alfred Meyer, *The Soviet Political System* (New York: Random House, 1965), chapter 22; Roman Kolankiewiez, *The Soviet Military and the Communist Party* (Princeton: Princeton University Press, 1967), p. 12; Jeremy R. Azrael, *Managerial Power and Soviet Politics* (Cambridge: Harvard University Press, 1966), p. 173; Richard C. Gripp, *The Political System of Communism* (New York: Dodd, Mead and Company, 1973), p. 137.

54 Michael Crozier, *The Bureaucratic Phenomenon* (Chicago; University of Chicago Press, 1964) and Max Weber *The Theory of Social and Economic Organization* (New York, Free Press, 1964).

55 Johnson, *Professions and Power*, pp. 68–82.

56 Gilb, *Hidden Hierarchies*, p. 109.

57 William Goode, "Community within a Community," *American Sociological Review*, XXII, no. 2 (April, 1957), p. 194 and Ben-David, "Professions".

58 Friedson, *Professional Dominance*, p. 99.

59 From the *Sociology of Work* by Caplow and Wilensky (1964), as presented in Johnson, *Professions and Power*, p. 28 and Parsons, "Professions," p. 538.

60 H. Wilensky, "The Professionalization of Everyone?", *American Journal of Sociology*, LXX (September, 1964), pp. 142–44.

61 Ibid., pp. 146–50.

62 Gilb, *Hidden Hierarchies*, p. 134.

63 For a comparative policy-making study using these rubrics, see Curry and Wolchik manuscript, 1983.

64 Gilb, *Hidden Hierarchies*, p. 134.

65 Ibid., p. 110.

66 Ibid., p. 134.

67 Ibid., pp. 110–11.

68 Ibid.

69 Ibid., p. 149.

70 See Bilinsky, "The Lawyer"; Gustafson *Reform in Soviet Politics*; Schwartz and Keech, "Group Influence"; and Solomon, "Specialists," for examples of this.

71 Gilb, *Hidden Hierarchies*, p. 111.

72 Ibid., p. 110.

73 Ibid., p. 115.

74 A parallel can be found in the work of Congressional Committees in the United States and the use by Congressmen of letters by constituents as well as expert testimony in their presentations.

75 Ramundo, "They Answer to *Pravda*," pp. 103–27.

76 Elite studies of Soviet policy-making use the career history of individuals to indicate their policy leanings.
77 William Glaser, "Doctors and Politics," *American Journal of Sociology*, LXVI, no. 3 (November, 1960), p. 230.
78 Stefania Dzięcielska, *Sytuacja Społeczna Dziennikarzy Polskich* (Wrocław: Ossolineum, 1962) and Tadeusz Kupis, *Zawód Dziennikarza w Polsce Ludowej* (Warsaw: Książka i Wiedza, 1966).
79 The 1976 survey of Polish journalists and interviews in 1975–76 were done under the auspices of the International Research and Exchanges Board. Later interviews were done privately as part of a research project on *The Media and Intra-Elite Discussions* by the Rand Corporation and with funding from the Ralf Kauntenborne Foundation.
80 Tadeusz Kupis, "Dziennikarze na tle innych zawodów inteligenckich," in Kupis, *Dziennikarskie Sprawy* (Warsaw: Książka i Wiedza, 1975), p. 41.
81 T. Kupis, "Dziennikarki," in *Dziennikarskie Sprawy*, p. 43.
82 Kupis, "Na tle innych zawodów," p. 41.
83 Ibid.
84 Małgorzata Szejnert, "Dziennikarze," *Literatura* (20 January 1975), p. 8.
85 Dzięcielska, *"Sytuacja Społeczna," p. 65.*
86 *Skrzypek, "The Profession of Journalism in Poland: A Profile," Journalism Quarterly* (1974), XLIX, p. 124, quoted from *Prasa Polska* (July, 1969), p. 5.
87 Zbigniew Pis, "Skąd Brać Dziennikarzy?", *Biuletyn* (May, 1970), p. 54.
88 Tadeusz Kupis, "Zawód Dziennikarski-Zawód Otwarty," in Kupis, *Dziennikarskie*, p. 61.
89 T. K., "Dziennikarze w Polsce Ludowej," in *Encyklopedia Wiedzy o Prasie* (Wrocław: Ossolineum, 1976). p. 73.
90 See chapter 8 of this volume and Jane L. Curry, "Poland's Press – After the Crackdown," *Columbia Journalism Review* (September–October, 1984), pp. 36–40.
91 Stowarzyszenie Dziennikarzy PRL, *Komunikat*, no. 3 (May, 1983).
92 Zbigniew Krzystek, "Kim Jesteśmy?," *Prasa Polska* (August, 1977), p. 1.
93 Kupis, *Zawód Dziennikarza w PRL*, p. 106.
94 Krzystek, "Kim Jesteśmy?"
95 Kupis, *Zawód*, p. 105.
96 Werner, "Koniec i Początek," *Prasa Polska* (April, 1983), p. 47.
97 Kupis, *Zawód*, p. 105–6.
98 Dzięcielska, "Syhiego," p. 191.
99 *Ibid.*, p. 170–71.
100 Stenogram Walny Zjazd Nadzwyczajny, November, 1980.
101 Dzięcielska, *Sytuacja*, 167, and Kupis, *Zawód* as well as 1976 studies.
102 The 1976 survey results show that journalists in the non-Warsaw areas spend more time together (27.9 per cent ranked journalists as their prime social companions) than do journalists in Warsaw, who have more opportunities to meet other professionals in social gatherings (16.3 per cent listed journalists as their prime companions). With the exception of relationships with academics which are clearly more feasible in the capital,

journalists in and out of Warsaw distributed their social time in the same ways. Journalists in editorial positions ranked social contacts with other journalists slightly less frequently than did staff journalists (33.3 per cent of those who only edit, and 37.4 per cent of those who both write and edit, listed journalists in the first two levels of social contact while 43.4 per cent of those who only write listed journalists in the top two rankings). Editors tended also to spend less social time with political activists: 16.1 per cent of staff journalists listed them in the top two categories of their social contacts while 14.3 per cent of those who write and edit ranked political activists in these levels. (It must be noted here that the survey results do not include the political members of the staff, the editors-in-chief.) Three cohort groups tend to spend the most time with other journalists: those who recently entered the profession and are becoming established in it (30.6 per cent of those who entered the profession between 1971 and 1975), those who are at the midpoint of their career (25 per cent of those who entered between 1961 and 1965), and those who entered in the Stalinist period and had the most intense recruitment socialization and interaction (27.3 per cent of those who entered between 1951 and 1955). No discernible relationship exists between the amount of time spent in the profession and the level of social contact with political activists. Personal factors, such as the war and personal experiences were given as the reasons in the higher percentage of journalists between 31 and 50 who associate with political activists.

103 In 1976, Party members reported associating as often with other journalists as do those with no Party affiliation (22.7 per cent to 23.6 per cent). But even that association is quite small since 33.8 per cent stated that they had no social contact with Party activists. Work in professions other than journalism did affect the level of interaction with other journalists (21.3 per cent of those who had worked in other professions associated with their journalist colleagues) and 32.1 per cent of those who had not worked outside of journalism associated with fellow journalists.

104 Of working-class journalists, 26.1 per cent listed other journalists as their primary social contact (10.9 per cent as their second order contact). Educational level was not statistically significant in 1976 in relation to interprofessional social relations. Journalists from both the working and intelligentsia classes associated to an equal degree with academics. Clearly, in this case, professional affiliation was a justification for making contact with more educated people. University background was slightly more significant in predicting social contacts between journalists and literary writers as well.

Interaction by journalists with members of staffs other than their own, an argument for professional group behavior, is high. Not only are relations between journalists on a single staff close, but journalists relate socially and professionally with members of other staffs with high frequency.

105 Skilling, "Political Change," p. 225.

106 See descriptions of journalists' work in Paul Lendvai, *The Bureaucracy of Truth* (New York: Pegasus, 1970); Dzirkalis, Gustafson, and Johnson, "The Media and Intra-Elite Communication"; Owen Johnson, "The Media in Eastern Europe," unpublished manuscript; and Ellen Miczkiewicz and Thomas Remington's works.

107 Paul Zinne, *Revolution in Hungary* (New York: Columbia University Press, 1962), and *National Communism and Popular Revolt in Eastern Europe* (New York: Columbia University Press, 1956); Josef Maxa, *A Year is Eight Months* (Garden City, New York: Doubleday, 1970); Robin Remington, *Winter in Prague* (Cambridge: MIT Press, 1969); and H. Gordon Skilling, *Czechoslovakia's Interrupted Revolution* (Princeton: Princeton University Press, 1976).

108 See Remington and Johnson for studies of the rest of the East European and Soviet media profession.

2 Postwar roots of the profession

1 In interviews in 1976 and 1979, journalists constantly used 1956 and their role in it as the benchmark of professional life. For a more complete discussion of the earlier history of the Polish journalistic profession, see Jane Curry, "The Professionalization of Polish Journalists and their Role in Policy-making" (dissertation, Columbia University, 1979), chapter 2.

2 "Pragi Głos," *Prasa Polska*, I, no. 2–3 (July–August, 1947), p. 3.

3 Interview data, 1976 with prewar journalists involved in the reestablishment of the union after the war.

4 "Dopływ nowych sił do dziennikarstwa w latach 1945–1947," *Prasa Polska*, III, no. 1 (January, 1949), p. 16. See also *Stenogram Walny Zjazd 1956* on subject of discrimination against prewar journalists in the Stalinist era.

5 "Walne Zgromadzenie Członków Oddziału Warszawskiego," *Prasa Polska*, II, no. 11 (April, 1948), p. 15. The heads of the Warsaw branch reported that they intervened in six cases involving work conditions and three regarding pay scales on various journals. Nine requests were made for work by journalists: five were placed.

In addition, the heads of the Warsaw branch reported that they got fifty rooms or apartments for members, forty typewriters, and 2 radio sets. They also distributed 63 kilograms of lemons and 160 sets of shoelaces.

6 "Znów Trudności," *Prasa Polska*, II, no. 16 (September, 1948), p. 18.

7 Zbigniew Grotowski, "Zawód dziennikarski jest ciężki," *Słowo Polskie*, no. 117 (20 April, 1948), p. 1.

8 Ibid.

9 "Krytyka musi być publiczna," *Prasa Polska*, II, no. 16 (September, 1948), p. 7.

10 "Walne Zgromadzenie . . . Warszawskiego," *Prasa Polska*, II, no. 11 (April, 1948), p. 18.

11 E. J. Strzelecki, "Sprawozdania Sek. Gen.," *Prasa Polska*, II, no. 17–18 (October–November, 1948), p. 22.

12 "Walne Zgromadzenie . . . Warszawskiego," *Prasa Polska*, II, no. 11 (April 1948), p. 11.

13 "Sprawozdanie . . . Wrocławskich.", *Prasa Polska*, II, no. 17–18 (October–November, 1948), p. 25.
14 "Sprawozdania Strzeleckiego," *Prasa Polska*, II., no. 17–18 (October–November, 1948), p. 22.
15 Uchwały Plenum KCZZ," *Prasa Polska*, II, no. 17–18 (October–November 1948), p. 3.
16 "Pod znakiem szkolenia dziennikarzy," *Prasa Polska*, II, no. 12–13 (May–June 1948), p. 15.
17 Ibid.
18 Article from *Sztandar Młodych* (5 May, 1953) translated in "The Fettered Fourth Estate," *News From Behind the Iron Curtain*, I, no. 7 (June 1953), p. 35.
19 Jaromir Ochęduszko, "Pod Znakiem Odpowiedzialności," *Przęglad Kulturalny*, III, no. 21 (27 May–2 June 1954), p. 5.
20 Kupis, *Zawód*, p. 53.
21 Ibid., p. 50.
22 Ibid., p. 61.
23 Ibid., p. 50.
24 Mieczysław Kafel, *Ekonomiczne Oblicze Zawodu Dziennikarskiego w Polsce* (Cracow: PAN, 1945).
25 Mieczysław Kafel, *Prasoznawstwo*, (Warsaw: Państwowe Wydawnictwo Naukowe, 1966), pp. 70, 76–78.
26 Ibid., p. 76–77. According to Tadeusz Kupis in his article, "Wkład Uniwersytetu w Rozwój Kadrowy Zawodu Dziennikarskiego w Polsce Ludowej," *Biuletyn Prasoznawczy* (1965), no. 8, as reprinted in Kupis, *Dziennikarskie Sprawy* (Warsaw: Książka i Wiedza, 1975, p. 217, of the 700 people on the program in 1954, 20 per cent (140) were members of the PZPR and 90 per cent were members of the ZMP. (There was some overlapping membership between the Communist Party and the Communist Youth Organization.) He also reports that 70 per cent of the students in the program in the early fifties were from worker–peasant backgrounds.
27 In the first year class in 1950, 66 per cent of the students were of worker–peasant origin, thus "allowing for a class change in the journalism profession," ibid., p. 216 as reprinted in Kupis, *Dziennikarskie Sprawy* p. 216.
28 Mieczysław Kafel, "Zjazd Absolwentów Ṣtudiów Dziennikarskich," Życie Szkoty Wyższej, no. 4 (1955), p. 91.
29 Ikołowski, "Historia," p. 12; Stenogram, SDP Walny Zjazd (30 November – 1 December, 1956), p. 78.
30 Edward Puacz, "Kongres Związków Zawodowych," *Prasa Polska*, III, no. 3 (May–June 1949), p. 1.
31 *Prasa Polska*, V, nos. 1–2 (January–February 1950), p. 1.
32 "Ogniwa Związkowe w Redakcjach," *Prasa Polska*, IV, nos. 3–4 (May–June 1949), p. 29.
33 "Ulepszyć pracę ideową i wychowawczą," *Prasa Polska*, IV, no. 1 (January–February 1949), p. 2.
34 Rafał Praga, "Doświadczenia i Wnioski," *Prasa Polska*, IV, no. 3 (May–June 1949), p. 5.

35 "Ulepszyć Pracę Ideową," p. 2.
36 Kupis, *Zawód*, p. 55.
37 Ibid., p. 62.
38 Ibid., p. 55.
39 Mieczysław Krzepkowski, "Planowanie Pracy w Redakcji," *Prasa Polska*, IV, no. 4 (April, 1949), p. 5, and M. Żywicki, "Plan Oszczędnościowy w Pracy Redakcji," *Prasa Polska*, IV, no. 2 (March, 1949), p. 4.
40 Edward Puacz, "Błędy dziennikarzy przy współpracy z redakcjami gazetek ściennych," *Prasa Polska*, V, no. 5 (May, 1949), p. 15, and M. Krzepkowski, "Pokłosie dnia prasy w prasie codziennej," *Prasa Polska*, IV, no. 3 (March, 1949), p. 7.
41 Andrzej Ziemięcki, "Referaty Prasowe w Instytucjach i Przedsiębiorstwach," *Prasa Polska*, IV, no. 4 (April, 1949), p. 16.
42 "Nie wolno kneblować zdrowej krytyki," *Prasa Polska*, IV, no. 2 (February, 1949), p. 24.
43 Kafel, *Ekonomiczne*, 50; Aleksander Szpakowicz, "Lenin jako twórca prasy radzieckiej, *Prasa Polska*, V, no. 1 (January, 1950), pp. 5–6; Zofia Lewartowska, "Kontakt z czytelnikiem," *Prasa Współczesna i Dawna*, 1959, no. 2, pp. 19–27.
44 Lewandowska, "Kontakt," p. 25.
45 "Jeszcze o Płaceniu," *Korespondent*, no. 10 (October, 1954), p. 3 and Kafel, *Ekonomiczne*, pp. 45–52.
46 Lewandowska, "Kontakt," p. 50.
47 Szkoła Partyjna Przy KC PZPR, "Masowa Praca Redakcji Gazety" (Warsaw, 1950), p. 14, and Kafel, *Ekonomiczne*, p. 48.
48 Zbigniew Brzeziński, *The Soviet Bloc* (Cambridge: Harvard University Press, 1960), p. 237.
49 Ostrym Piórem, "Pierwsza Jaskółka," *Prasa Polska*, VIII, no. 12 (December, 1953), p. 36.
50 These were a sign of growing consciousness of the importance of the profession in the lives of those who performed professional functions.
51 Barbara Sobierajska, "Absolwent Wydziału Dziennikarskiego rozpoczyna pracę zawodową," *Prasa Polska*, VII, no. 12 (December, 1953), pp. 15–18.
52 Unpublished accounts in SDP Archives, Warsaw, Poland from contests run in 1964.
53 Henryk Korotyński, "O niektórych żywotnych zagadnieniach naszej prasy," *Prasa Polska*, VII, no. 11 (November, 1953), p. 7.
54 Kupis Zawód, p. 63.
55 Henryk Korotyński, "O niektórych," p. 6.
56 Ibid., p. 8.
57 Ibid., pp. 9–11.
58 Ibid., pp. 11–16.
59 Ibid., p. 270.
60 Ibid., p. 21. This statement can only be taken as an attack on chief editors and others who were political appointees with no journalistic skills.
61 Ibid., p. 22.

62 Jerzy Kowalewski, "Podsumowanie Dyskusji," *Prasa Polska*, VIII, no. 12 (November, 1953), p. 61.
63 Ibid., p. 62.
64 "Oddział Warszawski SDP rozpoczął pracę," *Prasa Polska*, VIII, no. 12 (November, 1953), p. 24.
65 Ibid., p. 25.
66 Tadeusz Lipski, "Po wyborach delegatów w redakcjach warszawskich," *Prasa Polska*, VIII, no. 3 (March, 1953), p. 27.
67 Ibid., p. 27.
68 Ibid., p. 28.
69 Adam Perłowski, "Jak" Życie Warszawy Oświetlało problemy IX Plenum, *Prasa Polska*, VIII, no. 3 (March, 1954), pp. 2–4, and Kamila Chylińska, "Szpilkom trzeba jeszcze więcej wielkiego gniewu," *Prasa Polska*, VIII, no. 3 (March, 1954), pp. 4–6.
70 Chyliński, "Szpilkom trzeba jeszcze więcej wielkiego gniewu," pp. 4–6.
71 Stenogram, 15–16 May, 1954, pp. 254–59.
72 Ibid., p. 240.
73 Ibid., p. 260.
74 Henryk Korotyński, "O najważniejszych ideowo-politycznych zadaniach prasy," *Prasa Polska*, VIII, no. 5 (May, 1954), p. 15.
75 Ibid., pp. 18, 19, 22, 25–27.
76 Ibid., p. 22.
77 Jerzy Morawski, *Stenogram*, May, 1954, p. 13.
78 Ibid., p. 17.
79 Ibid., p. 16.
80 Ibid., p. 17.
81 Zbigniew Mitzner, *Stenogram*, 1954, p. 172.
82 Stefan Bankowski, *Stenogram*, 1954, p. 131.
83 Lehrer, *Stenogram*, 1954, p. 176. He went on to say that interwar journalists were much more in touch with the broad population than postwar journalists and that "before World War II, journalists were seen as protectors and not just as writers."
84 Bańkowski, *Stenogram*, 1954, p. 133.
85 Jaszuński, *Stenogram*, 1954, p. 91.
86 Mienkiewicz, *Stenogram*, p. 44.
87 Krasiński, *Stenogram*, 1954, p. 53, said, "Let journalists know enough about foreign affairs to connect with national affairs."
88 Krasiński, *Stenogram*, 1954, p. 56.
89 Wolanowski, *Stenogram*, 1954, p. 187.
90 Wodzeńska, *Stenogram*, 1954, p. 113.
91 Bańkowski, *Stenogram*, 1954, p. 125. This he made as a direct criticism of IX PUWP Plenum pronouncements.
92 Korotyński, *Stenogram*, 1954, p. 240, and Adamski, *Stenogram*, 1954, p. 38.
93 Adamski, *Stenogram*, 1954, p. 32.
94 Tarłowski, *Stenogram*, 1954, p. 228.
95 Ibid., p. 220.

96 Kraak, *Stenogram*, 1954, p. 247.
97 "II Krajowy Zjazd Delegatów Stowarzyszenia Dziennikarzy Polskich," *Prasa Polska*, VIII, no. 5 (May, 1954), p. 2.
98 *Stenogram*, 1954, Electoral Committee list.
99 Ibid.
100 Ibid.
101 Kraak, *Stenogram*, 1954, p. 263.
102 Interview data, 1976, and "The Fading Flame, Part II," *East Europe* (October, 1958), pp. 11–13.
103 Stowarzyszenie Dziennikarzy Polskich, *Biuletyn Komitetu 300 – Lecia Prasy Polskiej* (Warsaw, 18 January, 1961), p. 104.
104 Interview data, 1976. This group was significant enough by late 1956 for the SDP to establish an auxiliary press agency to give work to these journalists and to discuss this as a critical problem in the follow-up meeting in 1957.
105 *Biuletyn Komitetu*, p. 105.
106 Ibid.
107 "Notes on the Polish Press," *East Europe*, no. 9 (September, 1961), pp. 22–26, and "The Fading Flame, Part III," *East Europe* (November, 1958), pp. 17–26.
108 Interview data, 1976. One prominent Communist Party journalist for instance, commented: "My skin crawled when I realized I had condemned my old professor who now became a hero wronged in actions that went against everything I thought the Party I joined had stood for. Never again have I believed anything I did not see with my own eyes.'
109 Interview data, 1976, and Stanisław Świerad, "Zawsze z Partią" (SDP Archives, 1974).
110 Paul Zinner, ed., *National Communism and Popular Revolt in Eastern Europe* (New York: Columbia University Press, 1956), p. 39.
111 Danuta Bieńkowska, "Dlaczego przetrwały," *Przegląd Kulturalny*, II, no. 46 (November 18–24, 1954), p. 3.
112 Kupis, *Zawód*, p. 71.
113 SDP, *Biuletyn Komitetu*, p. 96.
114 Ibid.
115 Kupis, *Zawód*, p. 233.
116 Ibid., pp. 64–65.
117 *Stenogram*, 1956, p. 187.
118 Mond, "Uwagi i refleksje o terenie," *Prasa Polska*, x, no. 4 (April 1956), p. 4.
119 *Stenogram*, 1956, p. 192.
120 Kupis, *Zawód*, p. 69.
121 Władysław Wanat, "Gdy celem staje się pieniądz," *Horyzonty*, no. 10 (December 15, 1955), p. 3.
122 Stanisław Brodzi, Stenogram, SDP Walny Zjazd (1956), p. 24.
123 "Po Plenarnych Obradach," *Prasa Polska*, x, no. 2 (February, 1956), pp. 1–2.
124 Kafel, "Studia Dziennikarskie i Rozwój Badań nad Prasą na U. W." *Biule-*

tyn Prasoznawczy Studium Dziennikarskie U. W. i Osrodek Dziennikarski przy SDP, no. 8, 1965 and *Prasoznawstwo*, p. 82.

125 Kafel, "Rozwój badań," p. 29, and *Kwartalnik Prasoznawczy* was published by the Center for Press Research and *Horyzonty Prasoznawcze* by former students and assistants at the School of Journalism.

126 "Po plenarnych obradach," *Prasa Polska*, x, no. 2 (February, 1956), pp. 1–2.

127 Michał Szulczewski, "Problemy etyki dziennikarskiej," *Biuletyn Naukowy*, no. 1/17 (March, 1958), p. 24.

128 *Stenogram*, 1956, p. 3–8.

129 Jerzy Mond, "Uwagi i refleksje o terenie," pp. 4–7, and *Stenogram*, 1956 (31 November–1 December 1956), pp. 16–46.

130 Maciej Wiktor, "Dyskusja jako metoda pogłębiania pracy dziennikarzy," *Prasa Polska*, x, no. 5 (May, 1956), pp. 28–30; G. "Z Sekcji twórczych SDP," *Prasa Polska*, x, no. 3 (March, 1956), pp. 38–39; Kazimierz Dziewanowski, "Sztuka chwytania rzeczywistości za rogi," *Prasa Polska*, no. 4 (April, 1956), pp. 7–9.

131 Mond, "Uwagi i refleksje o terenie," p. 4.

132 Ibid., p. 105.

133 Ibid., p. 3.

134 Ibid., p. 3.

135 *Stenogram*, 1956, pp. 17–46.

136 Mond, "Uwagi i refleksje," pp. 3–5.

137 Ibid., p. 2.

138 Ibid., p. 2.

139 Ibid., p. 5.

140 Ibid., p. 1.

141 Ibid., p. 3.

142 *Stenogram*, 1956, p. 308 and 320.

143 Ibid., p. 305.

144 Ibid., p. 227.

145 Ibid., p. 333.

146 Ibid., p. 332.

147 Ibid., p. 285.

148 Ibid., p. 305.

149 Ibid., p. 185.

150 Ibid., p. 515.

151 *Stenogram, Walny Zjazd SDP*, 2–3 March, 1957, pp. 54–55.

152 Ibid., p. 10.

153 Ibid., p. 38.

154 Ibid., p. 17.

155 Ibid., p. 49.

156 Ibid., p. 84.

157 Ibid., p. 17.

158 Ibid., p. 22.

159 Ibid., p. 108.

160 Ibid., p. 42.

161 Ibid., p. 37.
162 Ibid., p. 20.
163 Ibid., p. 52.
164 See *Stenogram*, 1957.
165 Jane L. Curry, *The Media and Intra-Elite Communication in Poland: Organization and Control of the Media* (Santa Monica, California: Rand Corporation, December 1980), appendix, and Jane L. Curry and Ross Johnson, *The Media and Intra-Elite Communication in Poland: A Summary Report* (Santa Monica, California: Rand Corporation, December 1980), pp. 28–31. See also, Michał Radgowski, *Polityka i jej czasy* (Warsaw: Iskry, 1981), pp. 7–50.
166 Interview data, 1976. See chapter 6 for statistical data for the number of 1956 governing board members who returned later to the governing board. In addition, the continuing presence of Ignacy Lassota, the editor of *Po Prostu*, in the profession and on the governing board as well as the presence of many of the *Po Prostu* staff members on journals such as *Polityka* and *Życie Warszawy* is striking evidence of this continuity in the profession.
167 "Na Zjeździe Związku Literatów," *Nowe Drogi*, October, 1964.
168 In effect, although journalists from the Stalinist press saw him as a real alternative, he had been either the target of their press verification in the late forties or had been out of their Party circles from the time they began to work in the media in the early fifties.
169 Interview data, 1976 as well as Gomułka's own statements. See, for example, Gomułka's repudiation of Stalinist era regulation of the media (Władysław Gomułka, "Przemówienie tow. Władysława Gomułki na XIV Zjeździe Związku Literatów Polskich w Lublinie," *Nowe Drogi*, October, 1964, pp. 3–12).
170 The factionalism of the Gomułka era has been extensively documented. Interviews with journalists from the period indicated that they were well aware of the Party divisions and of the fact that they could use them to protect their ability to publish.
171 W. Kruczek, "8th Plenum CC PUWP," *Trybuna Ludu* (18 May, 1967), p. 1.
172 Władysław Sokorski, 8th Plenum, CC PUWP, *Radio Free Europe Polish Press Survey*, no. 2073, p. 14.
173 Władysław Gomułka, "Sprawozdanie KC i wytyczne rozwoju PRL w 1966–1970," *Nowe Drogi* (July, 1964), p. 127.
174 Mieczysław Rakowski, "Successful Propaganda," *Polityka* (17 May, 1969), mimeograph, translation (interview with Party press chief Jan Szydlak).
175 "Przemówienia tow Gomułki," *Nowe Drogi* (April, 1968), p. 20.
176 Czesław Domagała, "8th Plenum KC PZPR," *Trybuna Ludu* (5 May, 1967).
177 W. Gomułka, "XIII Plenum CC PUWP, 4 July, 1963 (O aktualnych problemach ideologicznej Pracy Partii," *Nowe Drogi* (August, 1963), p. 30. In this instance, Gomułka specifically criticized "an attack by the revolt-

ing libeler Jerzy Urban, done in a most impermissible manner, on an old social activist and fanatic in the fight against alcohol."

178 Artur Starewicz, "Decyduje ideowa postawa dziennikarza," *Prasa Polska* (January, 1965), p. 20.

179 "Walne Zgromadzenie . . . Warszawskiego," *Prasa Polska*, II, no. 16 (September, 1948), p. 7.

180 E. J. Strzelecki, "Sprawozdania Sek. Gen., "*Prasa Polska*, II, no. 17–18 (October–November, 1948), p. 22.

181 "Uchwały Plenum KCZZ," *Prasa Polska*, II, no. 17–18 (October–November, 1948), p. 3.

182 Ibid.

183 "Sprawozdanie z Wrocławskich Obrad," *Prasa Polska*, II, no. 17–18 (October–November, 1948), p. 24.

184 "Pod znakiem szkolenia dziennikarzy," *Prasa Polska*, II, no. 12–13 (May–June, 1948), p. 15.

185 Ibid.

186 "Walne Zgromadzenie . . . Warszawskiego," *Prasa Polska*, II, no. 11 (April, 1948), p. 11.

187 "Sprawozdanie . . . Wrocławskich," *Prasa Polska*, II, no. 17–18 (October-November, 1948), p. 25.

188 Ibid.

189 In the 1948 editions of *Prasa Polska* discussions of capitalist press systems were much more common than discussions of the Soviet press.

190 "Sprawozdania. . . Strzeleckiego," *Prasa Polska*, II, no. 17–18 (October-November, 1948), p. 22.

191 Modest Dobrzyński, "Informacja w gazecie," *Prasa Polska*, II, no. 17–18 (October–November, 1948), p. 21.

192 Mieczyslaw Kafel, "W obronie socjologii prasy," *Prasa Polska*, II, no. 12–13 (May–June, 1948), p. 9.

193 Dobrzyński, "Informacja," p. 21.

194 Antoni Pokorski, "Rola prasy i związku dziennikarzy w ruchu zawodowym," *Prasa Polska*, III, no. 4 (June, 1949), p. 50.

195 Ibid., p. 61.

196 Ibid., p. 50.

197 *Prasa Polska*, IV, no. 1–2 (January–February, 1950), p. 1.

198 "Ogniwa związkowe w redakcjach," *Prasa Polska*, IV, no. 3–4 (May–June, 1949), p. 29.

199 Kupis, *Zawód*, pp. 50–51.

200 Ibid.

201 Ibid., p. 63.

202 Ibid.

203 "Ulepszyć pracę ideową i wychowawczą," *Prasa Polska*, IV, no. 1 (January–February, 1949), p. 2.

204 Rafał Praga, "Doświadczenia i wnioski" *Prasa Polska*, IV, no. 1 (January–February, 1949), p. 5.

205 "Ulepszyć pracę ideową," p. 2.

206 Kupis, *Zawód*, p. 55.
207 "Udany eksperyment," *Prasa Polska*, v, no. 1 (January, 1950), p. 7., was a report on an experiment done in a number of editorial offices to increase "basic production norms" to eliminate the payment of journalists by the lines they published.
208 Kupis, *Zawód*, p. 62.
209 Ibid., p. 55.
210 Mieczysław Krzepkowski, "Planowanie pracy w redakcji," *Prasa Polska*, iv, no. 4 (April, 1949), p. 5, and M. Żywicki, "Plan oszczędnościowy w pracy redakcji," *Prasa Polska*, iv, no. 2 (March, 1949), p. 4.
211 *Biuletyn 300-Lecia*, p. 46. Tadeusz Cieślak, *Prasa Pomorza Wschodniego w XIX i XX Wieku* (Warsaw: Państwowe Wydawnictwo Naukowe, 1966).
212 Witold Giełżyński, *Prasa Warszawska 1661–1914* (Warsaw: Państwowe Wydawnictwo Naukowe, 1962), pp. 390–91; Jerzy Łojek, *Moja droga do dziennikarstwa* (Warsaw: PAN, 1974); and Kazimierz Olszański, *Prasa galicyjska wobec Powstania Styczniowego* (Cracow: Komisja Nauk Historycznych, PAN, 1975), p. 21.

About the interwar role of the profession, see Zdzisław Dębnicki, "O podniesienie poziomu ideowego prasy," *Prasa*, ii, no. 1 (January, 1931), p. 1; Stefan Krzyszewski, "O autorytet moralny prasy," *Prasa*, viii, no. 10 (November, 1937), p. 1; "Rola prasy," *Prasa*, vii, no. 11 (November, 1936), p. 1; and "Przedstawiciele prasy w parlamencie," *Prasa*, ix, no. 12 (December, 1938), p. 5.
213 Interview data, 1976. This extended to the point where, aside from central Party publications (*Nowe Drogi, Trybuna Ludu*, and video copies of the nightly news) top Party leaders received only *Polityka* and *Życie Gospodarcze* to supplement the news summaries and secret bulletins they got regularly in the seventies.
214 *Encyklopedia Wiedzy o Prasie* (Warsaw: Ossolinium, 1976), pp. 38–60; *Polish Mass Media, Press Research, Journalism* (Cracow: *Zeszyty Prasoznawcze*, 1978), pp. 7–21 and Jerzy Mond, "La Presse, les intellectuals, et le pouvoir en Union Sovietique et dans des Pays Socialistes Europeans," La Documentation Français, Secrétariat General du Gouvernement (1970), for detailed statistics on the media system and its development.

3 Living and learning journalism

1 Bolesław Garlicki, "Organizacja pracy redakcji," Ośrodek Badań Prasoznawczych (Cracow, 1972), n., p. 8.
2 See survey data 1976 reported in chapter 1.
3 Interview data, 1976. Henryk Korotyński, "Nie beznamiętnie, nie bezszelestnie," *Zeszyty Prasoznawcze*, xxvi (no. 1), pp. 43–54; *Różnie bywało* (Warsaw: Książka i Wiedza, 1972); and Michał Radgowski, *Polityka i jej czasy* (Warsaw: Iskry, 1981).
4 Interview data, 1983. See also Dariusz Fikus, *Foksal 81* (London: Aneks, 1984), and *13 miesięcy i 13 dni Gazety Krakowskiej 1980–81* (London: Polonia, 1985).

5 M. Krz. "Czego chcemy od szkolenia?" *Prasa Polska* (June, 1965), p. 30; Mieczyslaw Kafel, "Po 14 latach pracy," *Prasa Polska* (August, 1964), p. 3; and Kafel, "Studia Dziennikarskie i Rozwój Badań nad Prasą na U.W.," *Biuletyn Prasoznawczy Studium Dziennikarskie U.W. i Osrodek Dziennikarski przy SDP*, no. 8, 1965, pp. 32–33.

6 Direct manipulation includes: allotment of paper allocations on a totally political basis, assigning journalists to specific journals, sending out directives on appropriate treatment of specific subjects, direct censorship regulations and calling journalists into meetings to criticize them or advise them on coverage. Indirect manipulation is best exemplified by the low pay scales in the Gomułka era. By all indications this reflected Gomułka's lack of interest in the press rather than any direct desire to pressure journalists. Its effect was, however, to limit the risk taking of journalists and their willingness to do creative, critical research. Journalists still considered these basic professional ideals but were unwilling to take the risks involved, given how limited was their earning power.

7 See Jane L. Curry, *The Black Book of Polish Censorship* (New York: Random House, 1984).

8 Interview data, 1979 and 1983. A surface comparison of the actual treatment of the Pope's visit in 1979 and the instructions for its coverage showed little observance of the orders in terms of the "play" or specific coverage of the trip.

9 Interview data 1979 and 1983. See M. Rakowski, *Przesilenie Grudniowe* (Warsaw: Państwowy Instytut Wydawniczy, 1981) in which he describes one such meeting on the 1976 price increases in which they were asked to help with plans for coverage and mobilization but given no specific information on the increases.

10 Interview data, 1976. In fact, this has become a standard signal of non support; journals with possibilities for coverage do not use their own reports but anonymous Polish Press Agency, or even more negative in the case of foreign affairs, Soviet agency reports. In this way, individual professionals and staffs do not have to be compromised by giving false reports. They may, however, elect to do "private" factual reports with the intention of these receiving only a limited circulation but insuring that the leadership knows the facts.

11 *13 dni* and interview data, 1983.

12 Anna Malinowska, "Zmiana zawartosci dzienników po zwiększeniu ich objętości," Ośrodek Prasoznawozych, version III (1974), pp. 20–23.

13 GUKPPIW, *Book of Directives and Recommendations*, para. 101.

14 Interview data. See Jane L. Curry, *The Media and Intra-Elite Debate in Poland; The System of Censorship* (Santa Monica: Rand, 1980) for a full discussion of censorship institutions.

15 Interview data, 1976 and "Dyskusja o modelu organizacyjnym redakcji dziennika," *Prasa Polska* (April, 1972), pp. 6–7).

16 Interview data and observations, 1976 and 1979.

17 "Informacja Cenzorska," no. 15, and "Plan pracy nad realizacja treści III Plenum KC" (14 April, 1976), p. 2.
18 Journalists interviewed both waited anxiously for these documents to be issued and, at the same time, made it clear to this interviewer that their coverage was not really affected by what the Party instructed. Reviews of instructions on the Pope's trip to Poland or on the coverage of the American Bicentennial backed this up; even specific instructions as to coverage were not observed.
19 *Trybuna Ludu* (18 May, 1967), p. 1.
20 Saturnin Sobol, "Prasa a podział administracyjny kraju," *Prasa Polska* (February, 1976), p. 19.
21 Interview data, 1979. By 1979, *Polityka*, in spite of Rakowski's Central Committee post, was one of the two most censored journals in Poland and it was not uncommon for the Central Committee bureaucrats to call and order Central Committee member–editors around.
22 Fikus, *Foksal*, pp. 37–38 and 44–49.
23 Ryszard Rosiński, *Prawo dziennikarza do informacji w polskim ustawodawstwie Prasowym* (Masters Thesis, University of Warsaw, 1983), and Kodeks Podstawowych Administracji, 1964.
24 1976 Survey (39.7 per cent of low to middle level journalists said they had trouble with access information sources and 36.8 per cent said they had trouble in gathering information).
25 Interview data, 1976 and 1976 Survey.
26 *13 dni* and interview data, 1983.
27 Malinowska, "Zmiana," p. 30.
28 Rosiński, *Prawo dziennikarza . . .*
29 Interview data, 1976. This happened explicitly in the strangling of *Świat*, Poland's model of *Life*, in the late sixties.
30 George Mond, "La Presse, les intellectuals, et le Pouvoir en Union Sovietique et dans des Payes Socialistes Europeans," La Documentation Francais, Secretariat General du Gouvernement (1970), p. 7.
31 Ibid.
32 Interview data, 1983. See Madeline K. Albright, *Poland: The Role of the Press in Political Change* (Washington, DC: Washington Papers no. 102, 1983), for a full discussion of what was published in the heyday of Solidarity.
33 Interview with a censor, 1979.
34 Curry, *System of Censorship*.
35 Ibid. and, for samples of the reports see Curry, *The Black Book*.
36 Interview data, 1976 and 1979. See Curry, *The Black Book*, chapter 2.
37 Curry, *System of Censorship*.
38 Interview data, 1979 *Tygodnik Powszechny* editors knew their censor well enough to ask about the health of his individual children and his vacation. Editors on other special publications also had stories about their "censors." One told of meeting his censor in the line for milk and talking about "girding for battle" with him that day.

39 This was done as a result of the censors' response to the liberalization of 1956. See Curry, *System of Censorship*.
40 Ibid.
41 Ibid.
42 Ibid.
43 See Curry, *The Black Book*.
44 Interview data, 1976. In the 1976 survey, 46.0 per cent said they had no trouble using the information they gathered and 56.3 per cent said they had no trouble getting articles published. This was borne out by the fact that only 13.2 per cent said they had not had all the articles they wrote the preceding month published.
45 Typically, in interviews, journalists reported on how often they were contacted openly and not anonymously by readers. Evaluations of dissatisfaction with media policy were made in terms of the increase in the number of anonymous letters that had been received. See Walery Pisarek, "Zaufanie do dziennikarzy i prasy," *Zeszyty Prasoznawcze*, no. 4 (1984), p. 34. Ośrodek Badań Prasoznawczych as well as individual journals and programs did regular studies of readership, individual feature and writers' popularity, and credibility throughout the seventies and eighties. These went largely unpublished except when they dealt with readership of specific journals or features. But, most were known to journalists and were seen as measures of the success or failure of media policy and the popularity of political leadership.
46 Interview data, 1983 and *13 miesięcy*.
47 Pisarek, "Zaufanie do dziennikarzy," *Zeszyty Prasoznawcze* (April, 1984), pp. 35–36 as well as unpublished research done at the Center for Press Research, 1976, on the presentations and perceptions of professional and occupational groups in the Polish press.
48 Stanisław Kwiatkowski, "Inteligent – kto to taki?" *Polityka* (March 30, 1985), p. 3.
49 Tadeusz Kupis, "Czy dziennikarze są sympatyczni?" *Prasa Polska* (May, 1983), p. 51, and Włodzimierz Wesołowski, *Teoria, Badania, Praktyka* (Warsaw: Książka i Wiedza, 1978), pp. 134–140.
50 Pisarek, "Zaufanie . . . ," pp. 35–36.
51 Ibid., p. 37.
52 Zbigniew Bajka, "Opinie o mediach w minionym dziesięcioleciu,' *Zeszyty Prasoznawcze*, XXVI, no. 1 (Winter, 1985), pp. 7–15.
53 Andrzej Duma, "Rola Polskiego Radia i Telewizji Jako Instytucji Skarg i Wniosków," Ośrodek Badań Opinii Publicznej i Studiów Programowych, Komitet do Spraw Radia i TV, no. 128 (1974), p. 33.
54 Walery Pisarek, "Co w dorobku 30 lat prasy polskiej uważam za najdonialejsze?" *Nasze Problemy* (1975), no. 3, p. 10.
55 Bajka, "Opinie o mediach," p. 8.
56 Komitet do Spraw Radia i Telewizji, Ośrodek Badania Opinii Publicznej i Studiów Programowych, "Zaufanie do Telewizji jako źródła informacji" (June, 1981) and see also Zbigniew Bajka, "Zmiany w Strukturze Czytel-

nictwa Prasy" (Ośrodek Badań Prasoznawczych, 1982) and "Opinie o mediach" for further discussions of this phenomenon in the post-Solidarity era.

57 "Czytelnicy o swoich pismach," *Prasa Polska* (May, 1965), p. 30.

58 Interview date, 1976 and 1979. See *13 dni*, pp. 19–21, and Fikus, *Foksal*, pp. 12–13.

59 Interview data, 1976. See J. Curry, *The Mass Media and Intra-Elite Debate: Organization of Media Work* (Santa Monica: Rand, 1980).

60 Mond, "La Press," p. 10.

61 Garlicki, "Organizacja," p. 118.

62 Ibid., p. 168.

63 Kupis, *Zawód dziennikarza w PRL* (Warsaw: Książka i Wiedza, 1972), p. 248.

64 "Organizacja pracy w dzienniku," *Teoria i praktyka w dziennikarstwie* (Warsaw: Państwowe Wydawnictwo Naukowe, 1964), p. 169.

65 Garlicki, "Organizacja," p. 8.

66 Ibid.

67 Radgowski, *Polityka*.

68 Interview data, 1979 and Fikus, *Foksal*.

69 Andrzej Osiecki, "Kwalifikowanie materiałów w *Życiu Warszawy*," *Biuletyn* (January, 1974), p. 60.

70 Ibid.

71 Garlicki, "Organizacja," pp. 122–23.

72 Ibid.

73 Interview data, 1983, and Albright, *The Role of the Press*.

74 Garlicki, "Organizacja." p. 3.

75 Władysław Masłowski, "Warunki Pracy Działów Łączności w Redakcjach Prasowych" (Cracow: Ośrodek Badań Prasoznawczych 1970), p. 19–21.

76 Interview data, 1983 and T. Pis, "Skąd brać dziennikarzy?" *Biuletyn* (May, 1970).

77 Interview data, 1983; Tadeusz Kupis, "Losy absolwentów dziennikarstwa," in Kupis, *Dziennikarskie Sprawy*, pp. 276–77.

78 Fikus, *Foksal*, pp. 1–19.

79 Ibid., pp. 16–19.

80 Garlicki, "Organizacja," p. 32.

81 Mieczysław Wasilewski, "Poszukiwanie metod ustalenia funduszów płac dla redakcji," *Biuletyn* (January, 1971), p. 20.

82 Garlicki, "Organizacja," p. 16.

83 Ibid.

84 Ibid.

85 Aleksander Matejko, *Postawy zawodowe dziennikarzy* pp. 63–67.

86 Garlicki, "Organizacja," p. 32.

87 Ibid.

88 See Jane L. Curry, *The Media and Intra-Elite Communication in Poland: The Role of Special Bulletins* (Santa Monica: Rand, 1980).

89 Interview data, 1983. Many of these, in fact, used the same acronyms as their government counterparts.

90 Garlicki, "Organizacja," and interview data, 1976.
91 Garlicki, "Organizacja," p. 32.
92 1976 Survey. Their own ideas were the prime source followed by readers and editors' suggestions. The least used were external authorities suggestions.
93 Interview data, 1976. Most journalists, beyond entry level, stay in the same department and work on the same problems for long periods. They make friendships and reputations in their own areas and reinforce them with their involvement in specialists' clubs at the SDP.
94 Interview data, 1976 (Radgowski, *Polityka na co dzień*).
95 Interview data and observations, 1976 and 1979.
96 Interview data, 1976. None of the journalists ranked as "authoritative" was known for his "scoops." Rather, all were known for their authoritative analyses of long-term events.

4 Professional associations and professional politics

1 Corine Gilb, *Hidden Hierarchies* (New York: Harper and Row, 1966) provides the model for both formal and informal professional interaction.
2 Interview data, 1983. For a memoir of Association life and work of this period, see Dariusz Fikus, *Foksal 81* (London: ANEKS, 1984).
3 Ibid., p. 29 and interview data, 1983.
4 Zdzisław Kazimierczuk was the one former secretary of the ZG SDP who stayed on in the administration of the new organization. Other lesser bureaucratic workers in the SDP also stayed on (Fikus, *Foksal*, p. 62).
5 In all 1983 interviews, SDP activists made clear distinctions between what their personal political concerns were and what they did as SDP officers. Stefan Bratkowski was, reportedly, criticized for dragging the SDP into his political involvement and, for that reason, his fellow officers were willing to have him step down in order to preserve the SDP after it was suspended under martial law.
6 See Gilb, *Hierarchies*, p. 65 for the importance of this right to a profession and professional organization.
7 See Gilb, *Hierarchies*, pp. 109, for the significance of external regulation to the professional group.
8 Five members of his staff – past and present – on *Polityka* were either interned initially or were on the original internment lists.
9 *Tymczasowy Aneks do Dziennikarskiego Kodeksu Obyczajowego Na Okres Stanu Wojennego*, 1982.
10 Interview data, 1981. Letters were sent seeking aid to Walter Cronkite and others as representatives of journalism organizations.
11 Interview data, 1983. See Fikus' report on his final conversations with Rakowski in *Foksal*, p. 155–56.
12 'Jak powstało Stowarzyszenie Dziennikarzy Polskiej Rzeczpospolitiej Ludowej," *Prasa Polska* (December, 1982), pp. 3–16.
13 Ibid. and Komunikat SDPRL (3 May, 1983).
14 Heinz Eulau and John D. Sprague, *Lawyers in Politics* (Indianapolis: Bobbs-

Merrill, 1964), pp. 11–30 and 54–86 provides ample evidence of this same phenomenon occurring among lawyers in the West.

15 No attempt is made here to say that the Associations do not and have not performed functions for the political leadership. They put out propaganda statements and provide for continued political education of professionals. These activities are, however, optional for the members.

16 Gilb, *Hierarchies*, p. 109.

17 Ibid., p. 65.

18 Ibid., p. 65.

19 Ibid.

20 Ibid., p. 165.

21 Ibid., p. 128.

22 Ibid., p. 65.

23 Ibid., p. 165.

24 Ibid., p. 165.

25 Ibid., p. 65.

26 Ibid.

27 Ibid.

28 Izabela Dobosz, "Prawo Prasowe PRL" (unpublished paper, University of Warsaw), p. 11.

29 John W. C. Johnstone, Edward J. Sławski, and William W. Bowman, *The News People* (Urbana: University of Illinois Press, 1976), p. 112.

30 *Ibid.*

31 Jan Brodzki, "O zmianach w statucie i aktach normatywnych," *Prasa Polska* (January, 1965), p. 19; Aleksander Matejko "Postawy zawodowe dziennikarzy na the systemu społecznego redakcji" (Warsaw, unpublished paper dated 1962–63 and written for the Krakowski Ośrodek Badań Prasoznawczych), p. 80.

32 Tadeusz Kupis, *Dziennikarskie sprawy* (Warsaw: Książkai Wiedza, 1975), p. 11–12.

33 Ibid., p. 11.

34 Stenogram, Extended Session III Walny Zjazd (1956) 2–3 March, 1957, p. 5.

35 Ibid.

36 Ibid.

37 Ibid.

38 Ibid.

39 Ibid.

40 Kupis, *Sprawy*, p. 9.

41 Ibid., p. 10.

42 Stenogram, V Walny Zjazd (24–25 April, 1961), p. 47.

43 Ibid., p. 250.

44 Stenogram, VII Walny Zjazd (14–15 March, 1968), p. 333.

45 "Z Prac Prezydium ZG SDP," *Prasa Polska* (January, 1972), p. 18.

46 Stanisław Wiechno, "Z mandatem delegata," *Prasa Polska* (April, 1983), pp. 3–5.

47 "Tymczasowy Statut Stowarzyszenia Dziennikarzy Polskiej Rzeczpospolitej Ludowej," *Prasa Polska* (December, 1982), p. 17.

48 Budget data in the *Sprawozdanie z działalności Zarządu Głównego SDP* (Governing Board Reports of the SDP) from 1968–71 (35) and 1971–74 (13) shows that money came from the following sources (in thousands of zloties):

	1968	1969	1970	1971	1972	1973
(1) own earnings (membership dues, profits on use of facilities, and the small industry of the SDP – the crossword puzzle magazine	6,381.9	6,716.6	6,807.2	7061.1	7,564.1	9,052.5
(2) Bureau of Publications Contributions	1,220.7	1,424.3	1,573.6	3,439.3	4,115.3	5,369.5
(3) Ministry of Culture and Art	2,200.0	2,200.0	2,039.6	2,097.0	2,001.0	2,223.8

In addition, reports from regional units show that some money was received on a project from the Trade Unions. This often went to support a local journalism Association building which doubled as an Intelligentsia Club.

49 See *Sprawozdanie* for reports of Association activities in these areas.

50 Meat has always been available in the Warsaw SDP restaurant even when it is not available in other public restaurants. The restaurant was reported to have been supplied by the Central Committee stores in the 1970s. In theory, only members of the SDP and their guests may eat there. In addition, for members, there is a special daily meal that is well below the cost of a meal in any other establishment.

51 Budget reports from the *Sprawozdanie* of 1968, 1971, and 1974 show the following total annual payments for awards to journalists (in zlotys):

1965	265,000	(1968, p. 40)
1966	356,000	
1967	382,000	
1968	409,000	(1971, p. 36)
1969	520,000	
1970	564,000	
1971	549,000	(1974, p. 14)
1972	558,700	
1973	567,700	

The sharp jump from 1965 to 1966 resulted from an attempt by the SDP leadership to compensate for inability to get increases in journalists' salaries.

52 Interview data with officials of the SDP, 1976 and 1983.

53 Ibid.

54 Interview data, 1983. In these interviews, it was claimed he was recruited and brought from outside Warsaw because he had created an exciting, critical and popular journal and it was felt he would do the same for Prasa Polska, thus making it – when things calmed down – more than just a professional vehicle.

55 Rank ordering[a] of use of professional organization by journalists surveyed, 1976 (absolute numbers)

	1	2	3	4	5	6	Yes[a]	No[a]	n.a.
Specialist clubs	61	12	9	7	5	1	23	36	20
Center for journalism education	14	21	18	13	12	4	15	57	20
Cultural and social activities	11	17	17	17	8	3	14	67	20
Material aid (stipends, etc.)	4	4	4	7	9	29	3	94	20
Journalists' building as a meeting place[b]	13	24	19	11	11	4	10	62	20
Publications of SDP[c]	17	15	15	9	16	13	16	53	20

[a]A large number of respondents did not rank order but responded "yes" or "no" by each alternative.

[b]The high regional representation shows this response as not all regional units have actual buildings.

[c]The dominant publication is clearly *Prasa Polska*: 68.4% claimed to read it regularly while 15.3% claimed to read *Nasze Problemy* (the closed circulation editors' journal) and 35.6% claimed to read *Zeszyły Prasoznawcze* (the academic journal).

Source: Survey data, 1976.

56 Helena Jabłońska, "Kluby twórcze z perspektywy", *Prasa Polska* (April, 1967), p. 14.

57 Sprawozdanie (1971–74), p. 215.

58 Mieczysław Kieta, "Protrzebna bliższa współpraca klubow terenowych," *Prasa Polska* (March, 1965), p. 30.

59 Ibid., p. 30–33.

60 *Sprawozdanie, 1971–74*, p. 8.

61 Ibid.

62 Jabłonska, "Kluby", p. 15.

63 *Sprawozdanie, 1971–74*, p. 8.

64 Mieczysław Rakowski, "Sprawy i Problemy SDP," *Zeszyty Prasoznawcze*, 1961, no. 1–2, p. 77.
65 *Sprawozdanie, 1964–1968*, pp. 47–48.
66 "Przed I Zjazdem Stowarzyszenia Dziennikarzy Polskiej Rzeczpospolitej Ludowej," *Prasa Polska* (February, 1983); "I Zjazd SD PRL zakończył obrady," *Rzeczpospolita* (6 June, 1983), p. 1.
67 Private archives, SDP leadership for 1980–81 with mimeographed reports on all SDP governing board meetings.
68 In the Polish case, the expectation that the SDP would represent journalists' interests was clear from their answers to the question: "How would you formulate the most important tasks for the SDP: in the legal affairs of the profession, in the livelihood of the profession, and in raising the qualifications of the members of the SDP?" Journalists listed multiple tasks for the SDP. The area of livelihood and living conditions was most often mentioned: 43.2 percent of the respondents thought the SDP should work to improve the earnings of the profession; 24.7 per cent housing conditions; 8.6 percent work conditions; 13 percent general questions of journalists' material privileges; and 13.6 percent, rewriting the "Work Code" for journalists. Secondly, journalists felt that the SDP should focus on legal and ethical regulation: 54 percent of the respondents thought the SDP should work to develop a national legal code and 26.5 percent felt the SDP should focus on developing and enforcing an ethical code for the profession. Specific activities to raise professional qualifications were considered much less crucial; 35.8 percent of the respondents did not see any aspect of this as an important goal.
69 Ibid.
70 Ibid.
71 In interviews, Association leaders fell always into discussions of the political leadership and what that leadership permitted them to do.
72 Tadeusz Kupis, "Dziennikarskie zdrowie," in Kupis, *Sprawy*, pp. 191–201.
73 Tadeusz Kupis, *Zawód dziennikarza w PRL* (Warsaw: Książka i Wiedza, 1966), pp. 164–66.
74 Ibid. p. 1.
75 *Sprawozdanie 1965–68*, pp. 113–17.
76 Kupis, *Zawód*, pp. 164–66.
77 Ibid., 177.
78 Ibid., 178.
79 Ibid.
80 Ibid., p. 1.
81 T.T., "Plenum i układ," *Prasa Polska* (May, 1964), p. 1.
82 Ibid., p. 2.
83 Ibid., p. 3.
84 Ibid., p. 13.
85 Tadeusz Rojek, "Co zostało zrobione?" *Prasa Polska* (August, 1964), p. 7.
86 Ibid.
87 Ibid.

88 T.R., "Plenum," p. 13.
89 Kupis, *Zawód*, p. 181.
90 Ibid.
91 Ibid., 207–8.
92 *Sprawozdanie 1965–68*, p. 108.
93 Ibid., p. 109.
94 According to research paid for by the SDP and done by doctors and sociologists, journalists had a much higher mortality rate than any other profession in Poland.
95 Kupis, "Zdrowie," pp. 193–99; "Problemy zdrowia i warunków pracy dziennikarzy," *Prasa Polska* (April, 1966), p. 1.
96 "Problemy zdrowia i warunków pracy dziennikarzy," *Prasa Polska* (April, 1966), p. 1.
97 Stanisław Mojkowski, "Nowy układ zbiorowy pracy," *Prasa Polska* (July, 1967), p. 12–14.
98 Ibid., 114.
99 Ibid.
100 The health difficulties of journalists were almost universally brought up in the course of interview discussions in 1976.
101 *Układ zbiorowy pracy*, 1972.
102 Interview data, 1983. See references to this in "Jak powstało" and in the rapidity with which the new SDPRL dealt with this issue.
103 *Układ zbiorowy pracy*, 1982.
104 Janine Wedel, *Private Poland* (Facts on File: 1986).
105 Interview data, 1976 and 1983, on what the executives of the SDP did.
106 "Journalistic Code of Ethics," *Kwartalnik Prasoznawczy* (foreign language edition), II (1958), pp. 82–84.
107 Dobosz, "Prawo," p. 26.
108 Interview data, 1976. A survey of *Prasa Polska* showed that, in addition to private action, the professional journal often raised this issue.
109 Interview data, 1976. See Jane L. Curry and Ross Johnson, "The Media and Intra-Elite Debate: Case Studies of Press Controversies" (Rand Corporation, 1981).
110 Zbigniew Kwiatkowski, "Uchwała rzecz ważna," *Życie Literackie* (19 March, 1978), p. 12.
111 Gilb, *Hierarchies* p. 128. "Leadership" here is equated with the Governing Board (*Zarząd Główny*). This level was selected because it was the only level which represented purely professional activity and, yet, required a heavy time commitment and had a national base. The delegates to the National Conventions were: (1) too large a group; (2) elected as delegates from local units to fill the seats allocated to that unit on the basis of the size of the professional population; and (3) did not represent any significant time commitment of the professional. The top elite in the SDP was not used because it tends to be a full-time, bureaucratic post and not to be something that journalists compete for. However, the Governing Board is: (1) a medium-sized group; (2) elected on a national basis at the National

Convention on the basis of factors other than a set regional distribution of seats; and (3) requires a time commitment while at the same time not taking the place of full-time professional work. It, thus, can be used most effectively to measure the factors which are significant in the politics of the organization.

112 Ibid., p. 129.

113 Warsaw *versus* provincial regions in percentage membership in SDP.

Year of convention	Warsaw %	Provincial regions %
1954	63	37
1956	55	45
1958	59	41
1961	62	38
1964	61	39
1968	61	39
1971	63	37
1974	61	39

Source: Archive SDP

Warsaw *versus* provincial representation on the governing board of the SDP (percentage)

Year of convention	Warsaw %	Provincial Regions %
1954	75.5%	24.5%
1956 (a)	n.a.	n.a.
1958	n.a.	n.a.
1961	55.5	44.5
1964	55.8	44.2
1968	72.5	27.5
1971	55.0	44.5

[a]Identification by journal was not given in the reports of either convention as it was felt that journalists on the governing board should represent the profession as a whole. However, the news commentary on the convention stated that the governing board was "war based" but representative of the entire country.

Source: Stenograms, Walny Zjazd (1954, 56, 58, 61, 64, 68 and 71).

114 Most of the Warsaw journalists on the governing board claimed to be friends in the sixties and seventies. This same problem was cited by

journalists writing about the Solidarity period – because they were in Warsaw, the most active officers were from Warsaw even though there had been a clear attempt to make sure the other regions were represented. Fikus, *Foksal*, p. 1.

115 For instance, in 1964–68, all of the members on the Qualifications Committee, the Legal Regulations Committee, the Planning and Finance Committee, and the Education Committee were members of Warsaw media staffs. In 1968–71, when there was a major shift toward regional representation, all the members of the Qualifications Committee, the Legal Regulation Committee, and the Planning and Finance Committee were from Warsaw. Only on the Education Committee did regional journalists make up half of the committee. And those "regional" delegates were all from around Warsaw or from the Ośrodek Badań Prasoznawczych in Cracow (the Center for Press Research).

116 Review of Club notes, 1960–76 and 1980–81.

117 *13 Miesięcy i 13 dni* (London: ANEKS, 1985).

118 The formal slate had far fewer nominees than there were positions. Most of those elected were nominated from the floor. The balloting was by closed ballot. Stenogram, III Walny Zjazd (30 November to 1 December, 1956), pp. 59–74.

119 Stenogram, III Walny Zjazd (30 November to 1 December, 1956), p. 460.

120 Seven of the Governing Board elected in 1961 were chief editors, most of whom had been journalists earlier in their careers.

121 In 1964, six of the thirteen members on the planning group for the 1968 convention were either prominent editors or journalists.

122 Of the governing board from 1964, only half returned as delegates in 1968.

123 Stenogram, IV Walny Zjazd (14–15 March, 1968), p. 31.

124 Stenogram, VIII Walny Zjazd (1974), p. 225.

125 Fikus, *Foksal*, p. 35–38.

126 Stenogram, Nadzwyczajnego Zjazdu Delegatów Stowarzyszenia Dziennikarzy Polskich (internal manuscript) (29–31 October, 1980), pp. 65–164.

127 Fikus, *Foksal*, p. 35.

128 Interview data. A review of their past histories shows connections through their specializations and through work on journals such as *Polityka*, *Kultura*, and *Życie Warszawy*.

129 Interview data, 1983 and "Jak powstało . . ."

131 Małgorzata Szejnert, "Dziennikarze," *Literatura* (30 January, 1975), p. 8.

132 Szejnert, "Dziennikarze," p. 8.

133 Jerzy Urban has been blacklisted for his political activities four times in his career. Wiesław Górnicki was removed from *Życie Warszawy* in 1975. Before that, he was blacklisted for sending an open cable, which was reported in the Western press, opposing Poland's support of the Arabs in the 1967 Arab–Israeli War.

134 Interview data, 1983 and Andrzej Kępiński and Zbigniew Kilar, *Kto jest kim w Polsce Inaczej* (Warsaw: Czytelnik, 1985), pp. 335–50 and 389–408.

135 Interview data, 1983. In 1987, this was played out in the curious drama of

the Thirtieth Anniversary celebration of *Polityka* initial publication. The young, post 1980–81 entrants and those who had remained on the journal after martial law wanted former staff members who had left or resigned in protest to be included in the celebration. This they felt would not only truly represent the paper's proud history, but also, by association with these former stars, lend more authority and legitimacy to their work on the post martial law paper. Officials, including former editor Rakowski and government press spokesman Jerzy Urban felt this would be inappropriate and those who had left also made it clear they were unwilling to lend their presence to an official, public celebration. So, the staff decided to hold *two* anniversary celebrations, an official ceremony for those currently on the staff and Party government officials and an unofficial ceremony – paid for by donations from current staff members – to include all former and present members of the staff with the exception of Urban and Rakowski whose presence was too objectionable for many former staff members. But, just prior to the informal party, in response to complaints by the excluded Rakowski and Urban, the informal party was cancelled by *Polityka's* chief editor. As a result of this and the lack of prestige in the official ceremony, many present staff members ostentatiously avoided the formal anniversary ceremony as well.

136 The group was formed in 1973 and Association leaders made a conscious effort to court it.

137 Interview data, 1983. See *Rubikon, 1981* (Warsaw: Niezależna Oficyna Wydawnicża, 1986), a series of interviews with those who elected to leave prominent positions or the profession as a whole rather than associate with the profession after martial law. In the period between 1981 and 1983, the snubs of the establishment and its "selling out" were prime concerns of journalists.

138 Stenogram, Meeting of *Komisja Ogólna SDP* (General Commission), 9 March, 1964, p. 3.

139 Ibid., p. 9.

140 Ibid.

141 In 1956, for example, the entire discussion of the National Convention was reprinted. Subsequent conventions until 1980 have been reported only in part, omitting the critical comments on censorship and broader regime policies.

142 Ross Johnson, "The Moczarist Debate," in Curry and Johnson, *Case Studies*.

143 Reports of this began in mid-1964 (April) and continued monthly: lists of who was dropped from the Association in what region and for what reason throughout the period. They were published monthly in *Prasa Polska*. The reasons given were almost exclusively: "nonpayment of dues," "left the area" or "moved to another profession."

144 Interview data, 1976. When queried, journalists involved in the Moczar movement stressed, in retrospect at least, that it was individuals' lack of training rather than their "Jewishness" that fueled their attacks. Whether or not this was merely justification of their actions, it is paralleled in published discussions.

145 This was a constant topic in such journals as *Prawo i Życie* from 1963, when the journal was heavily involved in discussions of the Administrative Code. In many of the articles which heavily criticized the administration of specific institutions, criticism was also made of their failure to respond to the press.

146 See Ross Johnson's discussion of the press articles from 1968 in Curry and Johnson, *Case Studies*.

147 Most of their journalists had worked elsewhere, were well established in the profession, and earned the highest salaries. *Polityka* was persecuted in 1968 for its refusal to join the campaign. It was moved out of its office space and, for a period, did not have an office in Warsaw. Its phones were cut off and its building surrounded by police. In addition, pressure was placed on Gomułka to appoint Rakowski to the ambassadorship to West Germany or to the post of Assistant Minister of Culture. Kąkol was to take his position. Rakowski refused all of these positions and threatened "if his journal was taken away from him" to retire and live on his wife's income. All of these actions were taken by supporters of Moczar in the Ministries and the Party. They were considered "shocking" by Warsaw journalists. One Moczarist (the only *Polityka* staff member to attend the National Convention in 1968 as a delegate) was assigned to the journal. The staff refused to hold meetings when he attended. Offers of other positions to the journalists were not accepted and Rakowski ignored complaints against his staff. Most informants felt that Rakowski finally appealed to Gomułka personally to stop the persecution of his journal. By this point, Gomułka felt that *Polityka* was an ally and should be saved.

148 *Trybuna Ludu* journalists interviewed claimed that they were approached by Moczarists but, since they knew all the details of factionalism in the Party, they rebuffed these approaches. According to them, few journalists left *Trybuna Ludu* and those who did, left of their own volition. In fact, *Trybuna Ludu* was criticized at the 1968 Convention for being pro-Israeli (Stenogram), V Walny Zjazd (March 14–15, 1968), p. 272.

149 *Stenogram*, 1968.

150 *Stenogram*, 1968. It should be noted that many of the critical remarks made at the National Convention were not reported in *Prasa Polska* after the meeting. In addition, three Party speakers were claimed to have attended and participated in that meeting (Zenon Kliszko, Artur Starewicz, and Stefan Olszowski) but only remarks by Kliszko were given and no acknowledgement of the others was given in the journal's report, "Pragniemy ze wszystkich swych sił służyć narodowi, klasie robotniczej, parti," *Prasa Polska* (April, 1968), pp. 1–35.

151 Stenogram, 1968, p. 7.

152 Ibid., p. 9.

153 Ibid., p. 31.

154 Ibid., p. 16.

155 Ibid., pp. 22–23.

156 Ibid., p. 91.

157 ibid., p. 65.
158 Ibid., p. 85.
159 Ibid., p. 69–74.
160 Ibid., p. 76–78.
161 Ibid., p. 81.
162 Ibid., p. 168.
163 Ibid., p. 154.
164 Ibid., p. 114.
165 Ibid., pp. 335–340.
166 Stenogram, 1974, pp. 1–3.

5 Journalists as professional actors

1 Heinz Eulau, "The Skill Revolution and Consultative Commonwealth," *American Political Science Review*, LXVII, no. 1 (March, 1973); Terence Johnson, *Professions and Power* (London; Macmillan, 1972), pp. 43–61; Talcott Parsons, "Professions," on *International Encyclopedia of Social Sciences*, XII (New York: Macmillan and Free Press, 1968), p. 539; and H. Wilensky, "The Professionalization of Everyone?," *American Journal of Sociology*, LX (September, 1964), p. 143.

2 Survey, 1976, responses on "Reasons for Selecting Journalism as a Profession": "interesting," 83.3 percent of multiple responses; "role of press," 17.8 percent; "accident," 18.4 percent; "status," 9.2 percent; "financial," 2.9 percent; "family tradition," 6.9 percent. Also interview data, 1983 (with 20 younger generation journalists from various areas of the political spectrum). See Kupis, "Czy Dziennikarze SA?" pp. 51–53.

3 Based on interviews with journalists after they had done the survey questionnaire, 1976.

4 Karol Małcużynski in "Odpowiedzialność," p. 6.

5 Barbara Kalamacka and Larek Burczyk, "Kilka uwag o prasie jako informatorze i wyrazicielu opinii publicznej," *Biuletyn ZG RSW Prasa*, no. 147, p. 8.

6 Interview data, 1976. The extent of tolerance was clear both from interviewees' references to their editors' political positions as evidence of their papers' power and from the fact that the most respected journalists, by the 1976 survey, included a number who had held Party and state positions. Local leaders made clear to this researcher that journalists lent a veneer of credibility to their various organizations.

7 T. K., "Dziennikarze w Polsce Ludowej," in *Encyklopedia Wiedzy o Prasie*, Julian Maślanka, ed. Wrocław: Ossolineum, 1976), p. 73.

8 See, for example, Jerry Hough's discussion of the meanings of Party membership in the Soviet Union as in his book, *How the Soviet Union is Governed* (Boston: Harvard University Press, 1979), ch. 6.

9 In 1983, it was this power of their reputations that many cited for their reluctance to work visibly in the press after martial law as well.

10 "Zawodowa sieczka", *Prasa Polska* (February, 1963), p. 21; "Problemy prasy, telewizji, radia na forum Komisji Sejmowych," *Prasa Polska* (January, 1964), p. 13; "Dziennikarze-posłowie", *Prasa Polska* (July, 1965), p. 1;

"Zawodowa sieczka," *Prasa Polska* (January, 1968, p. 32 and "Zawodowa sieczka", *Prasa Polska* (November, 1968), p. 34.

11 *Prasa Polska* has yearly summary reports of what the Sejm delegates did. In addition, interviews with these delegates gave a clear indication of what their interests and involvements had been.

12 Interview data, 1983, and mimeographed bulletins prepared for the SDP Executive Committee on the work done on the press and censorship laws in 1980–81.

13 Mimeographs of his speeches from the SDP private archives.

14 Interview data, 1983 and *Diariusz Sejmowy*, 20 June, 1981.

15 Interview data, 1983, with Party and state activists.

16 Interview data, 1976 and 1983, dealing with the appearance of "mystery" authors in various journals.

17 Interview data, 1976, with editors of minor party and union or association journals.

18 Lucien Blit, *The Eastern Pretender – Boleslaw Piasecki* (London: Hutchinson, 1965); Andrzej Micewski, *Współrządzić czy nie kłamać?* (Paris: Libella, 1978)

19 Micewski, *Współrządzić czy nie kłamać?*, pp. 94–160 and interview data, 1983.

20 Interview data, 1983. Even though some of the leadership of the organization was included in the declaration of martial law, the journal had gone so far afield that its entire staff had to be reconstituted.

21 Micewski, *Wspołrządzić czy nie kłamać?* part 2.

22 Interview data, 1976 and Micewski, *Wspołrządzić czy nie kłamoć?*

23 J. Curry, "The Psychiatric Law Debate," in Jane Curry and Ross Johnson, *The Media and Intra-Elite Debate: Case Studies of Controversy in the Polish Press* (Santa Monica: Rand Corporation, 1981).

24 Interview data, 1983 and Fikus, *Foksal*, p. 97.

25 Fikus, *Foksal*, p. 98.

26 Ibid.

27 Interview data, 1976, and observation, 1976.

28 Interview data, 1976 and 1983, and observations, 1976, 1979, and 1983.

29 See Curry and Johnson, *Case Studies*, section 3.

30 Interview data, 1976. A review of the censorship documents smuggled out of Poland and presented in J. Curry, *The Black Book of Polish Censorship* gives evidence that, while these discussions were unpublishable, they were going on and their publication was attempted.

31 Interview data, 1976, with participants in this group.

32 Jan Józef Lipski, *KOR* (Berkeley: University of California Press, 1985).

33 Interview data, 1979 and 1983, as well as *Poland Today* (Armonk: M. E. Sharpe, 1981).

34 Interview data, 1976. Almost all journalists interviewed in 1976 stated that the psychiatric law, the social parasite law, and the labor and family code revisions – all of which were based on press criticism – were the major achievements of the profession. In addition, journalists in the survey done

in 1976 all focused on professional work that involved the criticism and analysis of broader policies as their most important form of professional work. In addition, in that survey, the journalists who were selected as professional leaders were all journalists renowned for their press criticism. And, in the Solidarity era and in the reconstruction of the establishment and underground media after martial law was declared, it was press criticism that journalists most wanted reconstructed. This is clear both from the focus on press criticism by journals like *Veto, Zdanie*, and *Przegląd Tygodniowy*, begun after martial law and from the use of that mode in the underground press as well.

35 Władysław Masłowski, *Akcje Prasowe* (Cracow): Ośrodek Badań Prasoznawczych, 1973), pp. 41–56.

36 Madeline Albright, *Poland's Press in Crisis*, Washington Papers, 1982, contains a complete discussion of the various issues and lines of press criticism that were raised.

37 This debate began in *Życie Warszawy*, involved awards for those who had been noted by citizens as particularly civil, and was paralelled by similar campaigns in other journals in 1973 and 1974.

38 Interview data, 1976. This campaign was spread for the period of 1972–74 throughout the Polish press.

39 See Curry and Johnson, *Case Studies*.

40 Ibid.

41 *Rubikon*, 1986.

42 Curry and Johnson, *Case Studies*.

43 Radio Free Europe, "Polish Communist History and Factional Struggle," Background Report no. 20 (2 July, 1968); "Polish Interwar History Reexamined," Background Report no. 32 (11 November, 1968); and "Notes on an Historical Discussion," Background Report no. 5 (20 March, 1969).

44 Michał Szulczewski, *Publicystyka* (Warsaw: Państwowe Wydawnictwo Naukowe, 1976); "Czego chcą redaktorzy naczelni?" *Kultura* (14 October, 1973), p. 1.

45 Interview data, 1979.

46 J. Curry, *The Black Book of Polish Censorship* (New York: Random House, 1976), p. 278.

47 In the seventies, all the editors were in high Party bodies. Since the position of *Tygodnik Powszechny* is anomolous as the staff is committed to criticism even though it does not have the resources to take such risks, it will not be discussed here.

48 All of the leading journalists, as ranked by fellow journalists, are on the staffs of, or regular contributors to, one of these journals.

49 It was to these central journals that journalists turned to see what was of interest and what should be covered. They were the journals most commonly reported to be read by all professionals; *Polityka, Kultura*, and *Życie Warszawy*.

50 The press criticism which preceded the 1968 upheaval was a unique phenomenon. Although it began on veiled historiographical topics in central

socio-political weeklies and was broadened to general social criticism in these journals, it was much more widespread than other instances of press criticism have been. In addition, it reflected more disparate views than normally occur in the Polish press. This was a product, in part, of inter-elite conflicts which were occurring within the Party. The focus of the articles was on the social and economic policy failures of the Gomułka regime. In fact, the underlying impetus for most of the articles, according to journalists involved, was the frustration felt by local journalists because their career mobility was blocked by untrained professionals who had entered the profession after the war. The attempt was, in part, to attack the patrons of top level journalists in order to weaken their tenure positions and open up those positions to younger journalists. What appeared as a striking case of national social criticism in the press was actually, according to the journalists who participated in the campaign, a reflection of the frustration of individual professionals and not societal criticism in the traditional sense.

51 See *Politika* series, "Studenci," from all of 1976; Radio Free Europe, "Polish Interwar History" 11 March, 1968) and the article by Stefan Bratkowski, "Where Are We?", from *Życie i Nowoczesność* (21 September, 1972) for some samples of the kind of issues that were discussed.

52 The number of letters requesting aid dropped dramatically and the number of anonymous letters (taken by journalists as indications that they were not trusted as holders of confidential information but were seen as handmaidens of the elite) increased.

53 Andrzej Duma, "Rola Polskiego Radia i Telewizji jako instytucji skarg i wniosków," *Ośrodek Badania Opinii Publicznej i Studió Programowch. Komitet do Spraw Radia i TV* no. 128 (1974), p. 42.

54 "O listach do redakcji i interwencjach prasowych," *Prasa Polska* (March, 1963), p. 1–11.

55 Andrzej Wróblewski, "Wrongs for Sale," *Polityka* (8 November, 1969), translated in Polish Press Survey, Radio Free Europe, no. 225, p. 2. Research by journalism institutes (the University of Warsaw, Institute of Journalism; Research Center of Polish Radio and Television; the Center for Press Research in Cracow) and individual journals evaluate the departments of connections in journals on the basis of the number of letters that they draw and the number of letters which are signed. This encourages journals to exaggerate the numbers of letters which they receive. In addition, letters are regularly categorized on the basis of the issues and requests made of the journal itself. It is continually repeated in these studies that the press competes easily with state and Party institutions for managing complaints and suggestions.

56 Hieronim Kubiak, *et al.*, "Oczekiwania i dążenia mieszkańców regionu krakowskiego w świetle listów do Gazety Krakowskiej" (Cracow: Institute of Sociology, Jagiellonian University, 1974), p. 78. Press responses to letters in Gazeta Krakowska are as follows (%):

Type of response	1969	1971	1973	Average
Publication of the letter	23.1	45.1	70.5	44.6
Letter with commentary	27.5	25.9	18.9	24.5
Discussion article	5.5	10.3	3.3	6.5
Short feature	4.0	3.1	1.4	3.0
Essay	2.1	1.4	0.7	1.5
Other	37.8	14.2	5.2	19.9

Source: Hieromin Kubiak, *et al.*, "Oczekiwania i dążenia mieszkańców regionu krakowskiego w świetle listow de Gazety Krakowskiej" (Cracow: Institute of Sociology, Jagiellonian University, 1974), p. 73.

57 Ibid., p. 72.

58 For a survey of the typical array of problems that are raised in letters from readers: institutions cited in complaints in letters to *Gazeta Krakowska* (%):

Institutions	1969	1971	1972	Average (1969–72)
State administration	4.2%	6.1	7.3	5.9
Socio-political organizations	0.2	0.5	0.3	0.4
Workplace	4.6	5.2	4.3	4.8
Trade institutions	7.1	8.0	11.6	8.9
Public services	10.8	9.8	10.2	10.3
Individuals	3.6	6.0	6.0	5.3
Not specified	69.5	64.4	60.3	64.4

Source: Hieronim Kubiak, *et al.*, "Oczekiwania i dążenia mieszkańców regionu krakowskiego w świetle listów do Gazety Krakowskiej" (Cracow: Institute of Sociology, Jagiellonian University, 1974), p. 48.

59 Journalists universally reported that they were encouraged or expected to forward compilations of letters and reports of the frequency of interventions on specific issues to the elite and that this was considered a key sign of popular opinion.

60 Masłowski, *Akcje prasowe*, pp. 7–26 and interview data, 1976.

61 Ibid., p. 10–11.

62 Interview data, 1976 and Masłowski, p. 10.

63 Author's observation, 1976.

64 Masłowski, *Akcje prasowe*, p. 124.

65 Ibid., p. 110.

66 In interviews done in 1979, journalists universally claimed that the country was poorly managed but that the Gierek elite was such a strong wall that changes could not be made.

67 Albright, *Polish Press*.

68 In general, journalists played down or belittled the importance of the inputs from bureaucrats, artists, and political groups committed to ideology.

69 *Polityka, Plan Roku 1969*.

70 See, for example, Mieczysław Rakowski, *et al. Polskie Przyśpieszenie, 1971–1975* (Warsaw: Interpress, 1975).

71 Benedykt Lewandowski, "Likwidujemy nieżyciowe przepisy, kampania z szerokim Odzewem," *Biuletyn* no. 149 (1972), pp. 58–60.

72 *Głos Pracy* ran a series of articles to educate its readers on the Labor Code revisions in 1975. All of these are leanings that characterize professionals' policy preferences in the West as well.

6 Solidarity and beyond: the critical test of professionals and professionalism

1 Observers found that reports on Poland's debt problems were treated, by the public, as unbelievable – an excuse to make the public resign itself to the situation. For this and other public opinion data as well as the use of the media in this period, see Stowarzyszenie Dziennikarzy Polskich, "Kryzys Polski 1980–1983: społeczeństwo-świadomość-informacja (Materiały raportu o stanie komunikaci spolecznej w Polsce)", Warsaw (manuscript: 1984), pp. 100–9.

2 Stefania Dzięcielska *Sytuacja społeczna dziennikarzy polskich* (Wrocław: Ossolineum, 1962), p. 188.

3 Ibid., p. 176.

4 Survey data, 1976.

5 Eulau, "The Skill Revolution and Consultative Commonwealth," *American Political Science Review*, LXVII, no. 1 (March, 1973).

6 Survey data, 1976.

7 Unpublished doctoral research, University of Warsaw, 1975, (the researcher requested anonymity).

8 1976 Survey data.

9 Dzięcielska, *Sytuacja*, 178.

10 "Leading journalists" assessment is based on professionals' assessments in surveys and interviews as well as published identification of leading journalists, Małgorzata Szejnert, "Dziennikarze," *Literatura* (30 January, 1975), p. 1.

11 Ibid.

12 Ibid., p. 178.

13 These were journalists on prominent national socio-political weeklies or known commentators on central dailies or television. Their views were part of a letter sent to the Gdańsk strikers by sixty-four intellectuals urging both sides "to take the path of compromise" ("Further Signs of Unrest in Polish Intellectual Circles" in *August, 1980*, p. 145).

23 Interview data, 1983.

24 The Gdańsk Agreement (31 August, 1980), August, 1980, p. 425.
25 Dariusz Fikus, *Foksal 1980* (London: ANEKS, 1981), p. 20.
26 "Listy otwarte – rezolucje – postulaty", *Prasa Polska* (October, 1980), pp. 2–16.
27 Ibid.
28 Fikus, *Foksal*, p. 29.
29 "Referat Prezydium Zarzadu Głównego SDP wygłoszony przez przewodniczacego ZG kol. Józefa Bareckiego," *Prasa Polska* (October, 1980), p. 20.
30 Editors, *Prasa Polska*, "Podziękowanie," *Prasa Polska* (October, 1980), p. 55.
31 Interview data, 1983 and Fikus, *Foksal*, pp. 29–30.
32 Interview data, 1983.
33 Interview data, 1983, and "Ostatnie plenum Zarządu Głównego SDP ubłegłej Kadencji," *Prasa Polska* (November, 1980), p. 16.
34 Interview data, 1983.
35 *Stenogram Nadzwyczajnego Zjazdu Delegatów Stowarzyszenia Dziennikarzy Polskich, 29–31 Października, 1980* (internal transcript printed by the SDP), p. 47.
36 "Referat – Bareckiego," *Prasa Polska*, (November, 1980), p. 24.
37 *Stenogram*, pp. 24–44.
38 "Uchwala w sprawie absolutorium dla ustępującego Zarządu Głównego SDP," *Prasa Polska* (November, 1980), p. 6.
39 Stenogram (such criticisms were voiced by many throughout the three-day conference).
40 Ibid., pp. 41–42 and "Nadzwyczajny Zjazd Delegatów SDP", *Prasa Polska* (December, 1980), p. 6.
41 Interview data, 1986.
42 "Wnioski Nadzwyczajnego Zjazdu Delegatów SDP", *Stenogram*, 1980 (Addendum, pp. 51–2).
43 *Prasa Polska*, December, 1980, p. 5.
44 Interview data, 1983.
45 Stenogram, 1980, p. 5.
46 Ibid.
47 Ibid.
48 Ibid., p. 6.
49 Ibid., p. 6.
50 *Stenogram*, 1980.
51 "Nadzwyczajny," p. 9.
52 Fikus, *Foksal*, pp. 76–78.
53 Interview data, 1983. For instance, Fikus has written extensively about his continued work with *Polityka* while he was on the staff of the SDP. Others who were prominent as professional representatives followed the same pattern of carrying on both professional leadership and professional work as writers.
54 He was a former film critic and friend of Krakow's more liberal local Party leadership.

55 See *13 miesięcy i 13 dni Gazety Krakowskiej 1980–1981* (London: Polonia Book Fund, 1985) for a description of this.
56 Interview data, 1983.
57 Interview data, 1983.
58 Interview data, 1983 and Fikus, *Foksal*, pp. 55–58.
59 Interview data, 1983.
60 Interview data, 1983. See Fikus, *Foksal*; *13 Dni*, and *Społeczeństwo-świadomość-informacja* for various specific instances of journalists' mediation.
61 *Społeczenstwo*, part I.
62 Fikus, *Foksal* p. 72. See also Radio Free Europe, "Developments in the Polish Media" (8 May, 1981) and *Społeczeństwo*, parts 3 and 4. For two of the many surveys done of the liberalization of the Polish press, see Anthony Barbieri, "Polish Press Drops Passive Role to Speak in Its Own Voice," *Baltimore Sun* (16 May, 1981) and Madeline Albright, *Poland: The Role of the Press in Political Change*, Washington Papers, 1983.
63 Interview data and SDP archives, 1983. (See, for example, "Dokumentacja do oświadczenia SDP z dn 10.08.1981," in Fikus, *Foksal*, and *Społeczeństwo*, parts 3 and 4 for reprints of the most significant of these reports.
64 Mieczysław Rakowski, *Polityka* 17 January, 1981), p. 1.
65 Interview data, 1983.
66 Interview data, 1983. This practice of using elipses, however, was limited by editors to the non-party press, especially the Catholic press.
67 "Oświadczenie ZG SDP" (13 February, 1981).
68 Fikus, *Foksal*, p. 81.
69 Interview data, 1983. Participants on both sides reported this sense of betrayal as a pervasive one.
70 *Prasa Polska* (January, 1981–October, 1981) ran regular reports on journalists' court hearings.
71 Interview data, 1983.
72 Interview data, 1983. Reports of numbers of such incidents are recorded in *Społeczeństwo*, Fikus, *Foksal*; and *13 miesięcy*.
73 *Uchwała Rady SDP*, (2 September, 1981).
74 "O znaczeniu środków komunikacji społecznej w Polsce i roli SDP w ich rozwoju, ocena wstępna wniosków z dyskusji," (unpublished documents) and Stanisław Brodzki and Jerzy Surdykowski, "Stan komunikacji w Polsce u progu lat 80-tych" (unpublished manuscript).
75 Fikus, *Foksal*, pp. 95–98.
76 Fikus, *Foksal*, 98–101. "Projekt modyfikacji funkcjonowania RSW Prasa-Książka-Ruch w związku z reformą gospodarczą" (unpublished document, 14 October, 1981).
77 Interview data, 1983.
78 Interview data, 1983.
79 "Oświadczenie Zarządu Głównego SDP (8 October, 1981) reprinted in Fikus, *Foksal*, p. 168.
80 Interview data, 1983.
81 Fikus, *Foksal*, pp. 122–25.

82 Ibid.
83 Maciej Iłowiecki, "VI Sesja Rady SDP" (typescript).
84 Interview data, 1983.
85 Interview data, 1983.
86 Interview data, 1983; "Oświadczenie ZG SDP (20.08.1981)" (typescript).
87 Józef Gosławski, *Ustawa o kontroli publikacji i jej realizacja* (Masters Thesis, Warsaw, 1983), pp. 18–71; and "Censorship: Issues and Documents," Radio Free Europe Situation Report, no. 23 (20 December, 1986), pp. 42–48.
88 Interview data, 1983.
89 Interview data, 1983.
90 "Wystąpienie Macieja Iłowieckiego w Sejmowej Komisji Kultury" (typescript with marginal notes on other speakers) and "Speech by Karol Małcużyński at 12 June Sejm Session," FBIS (June 15, 1981), p. 17–19.
91 *Diariusz Sejmowy* (July 31, 1981).
92 Fikus, *Foksal*, pp. 136–7.
93 Ibid.
94 Stefan Bratkowski, "List do członków komitetu Centralnego PZPR" and "Pełny tekst listu otwartego Macieja Szumowskiego do wszystkich członków Partii, który ukazał się w Gazecie Krakowskiej" (19 October, 1981) and mimeographed letters from various regional journalists' organizations in the archives). For a discussion of journalists' attitudes on the subject, see *13 Miesięcy*, p. 68.
95 Interview data, 1983. One source reported that the delegates were so concerned that they might be arrested or detained that they went in two groups and left their personal valuables behind in Poland.
96 Fikus, *Foksal*, pp. 136–40.
97 Ibid.
98 Interview data, 1983.
99 Interview data, 1983, and Fikus, *Foksal*, pp. 53–55 and 136–38.
100 Interview data, 1983.
101 Interview data, 1983. For a discussion of the variety of stories and issues that appeared in the early Solidarity era establishment press, see Madeline Albright, *Poland*.
102 See reprint of major documents, Fikus, *Foksal*, pp. 169–76.
103 Interview data, 1983.
104 Interview data, 1983.
105 Interview data, 1983, and SDP Council meeting notes, 1980–81.
106 Interview data, 1983.
107 Interview data, 1983.
108 Interview data, 1983.
109 Interview data, 1983.
110 Interview data, 1983.
111 Interview data, 1983.
112 Interview data, 1983.

113 Interview data, 1983.
114 Interview data, 1983.
115 Interview data, 1983. Tadeusz Dziewanowski and Artur Hajnicz as well as Wanda Falkowska and Ernest Skalski all had left their management positions and taken background roles by the late summer, 1981.
116 Układ Zbiorowy SDP, November, 1981 (internal document).
117 This statement is based on internal Solidarity accounting reported to this researcher in 1983.
118 "Polish Council of Ministers Communique Proscribing Unions" (13 December, 1981).
119 Interview data, 1983.
120 "Tymczasowy Aneks do Dziennikarskiego Kodeksu Obyczajowego na Okres Stanu Wojennego, 1982" (carbon copy).
121 For a full discussion of their decisions and motivations, see the series of interviews with those who left the profession or elected to work at less visible jobs in *Rubikon* (Warsaw: NOWA, 1986). See also such summary reports as "Bratkowski's Letter to Members of the Polish Union of Journalists" (20 February, 1982) in *Uncensored Polish News Bulletin* (London: 16 April, 1982), pp. 23–25 and "Journalist and the Press," in *Uncensored Polish News Bulletin* (14 May, 1982), pp. 12–14.
122 Claims vary from one source to another in large part because the definitions of "dropping out" and of "professional journalism" have varied dramatically. In the period prior to 1983, there was a general agreement that, counting retirements and moves to marginal journalism as well as refusals to be varifies, blacklisting and emigration, the general estimate was in the 2,000 range. This was held both by former SDP officials and, less publicly, from SDPRL officials. As time has passed, the number out of the profession has dropped. See, for instance, Andrzej Małachowski, who claims the number of officials departures was only 705. ("Dziennikarze", *Przegląd Tygodniowy* iv, no. 20 (19 May, 1985), p. 4.
123 Jane L. Curry, "Poland's Journalists After Martial Law", *Columbia Journalism Review* (Summer, 1984).

Select bibliography

Albright, Madeline. *Poland: The Role of the Press in Political Change* (Washington, D.C.: Washington Papers, 1983).

Andrews, Nicholas, *Poland, 1980–81* (Washington, D.C. National Defense University Press, 1985).

Bachrach, Peter and Morton S. Baratz. *Power and Poverty* (New York: Oxford University Press, 1970).

Ben-David, Joseph. "Professions in the Class System of Present-Day Society," *Current Sociology*, XII (1963/64), pp. 247–330.

Biuletyn Komitetu 300–lecia Prasy Polskiej (Warsaw: Stowarzyszenie Dziennikarzy Polskich, 1961).

Brumberg, Abe. *Solidarity* (New York: Random House, 1984).

Brzeziński, Zbigniew. *The Soviet Bloc* (Cambridge: Harvard University Press, 1960).

Cieślak, Tadeusz. *Prasa Pomorza Wschodniego w XIX i XX Wieku* (Warsaw: Państwowe Wydawnictwo Naukowe, 1966).

Crozier, Michael. *The Bureaucratic Phenomenon* (Chicago: University of Chicago Press, 1964).

Curry, Jane L. *The Black Book of Polish Censorship* (New York: Random House, 1984).

The Media and Intra-Elite Communication in Poland: Case Studies of Press Controversy (Santa Monica, California: Rand Corporation, December, 1980).

The Media and Intra-Elite Communication in Poland: Organization and Control of the Media (Santa Monica, California: The Rand Corporation, December, 1980).

The Media and Intra-Elite Communication in Poland: The Role of Special Bulletins (Santa Monica, California: The Rand Corporation, December, 1980).

The Media and Intra-Elite Communication in Poland: A Summary Report, (Santa Monica, California: The Rand Corporation, December, 1980).

The Media and Intra-Elite Communication in Poland: The System of Censorship (Santa Monica, California: The Rand Corporation, December, 1980).

"Poland's Press – After the Crackdown," *Columbia Journalism Review* (Summer, 1984).

Dzięcielska, Stefania. *Sytuacja społeczna dziennikarzy Polskich* (Wrocław: Ossolineum, 1962).

Dzirkalis, Lillith, Thane Gustafson, and A. Ross Johnson, *The Media and Intra-Elite Communication in the Soviet Union* (Santa Monica, California: The Rand Corporation, 1984).

Eulau, Heinz, "The Skill Revolution and Consultative Commonwealth," *American Political Science Review*, LXVII, no. 1 (March, 1973).

Eulau, Heinz and John Sprague, *Lawyers in Politics* (Indianapolis: Bobbs-Merrill, 1964).

Fikus, Dariusz. *Foksal 1980* (London: Aneks, 1984).

Friedson, Elliot. *Professional Dominance: The Social Structure of Medical Care* (New York: Atherton Press, 1970).

Giełżyński, Witold. *Prasa Warszawska, 1661–1914* (Warsaw: Państwowe Wydawnictwo Naukowe, 1962).

Garton-Ash, Timothy. *The Polish Revolution* (New York: Charles Scribners, 1983).

Gilb, Corine. *Hidden Hierarchies* (New York: Harper and Row, 1966).

Glaser, William. "Doctors and Politics," *American Journal of Sociology*, LXVI, no. 3 (November, 1960).

Goode, William. "Community within a Community," *American Sociological Review*, XXII, no. 2 (April, 1957).

Hopkins, Mark. *Mass Media in the Soviet Union* (New York: Pegasus, 1970).

Johnson, Chalmers, ed. *Change in Communist Systems* (Stanford: Stanford University Press, 1970).

Johnson, Terrance. *Professions and Power* (London: Macmillan, 1972).

Johnstone, John W. C., Edward J. Sławski, and William W. Bowman. *The News People* (Urbana: University of Illinois Press, 1976).

Jowitt, Kenneth, "Inclusion and Mobilization in European Leninist Regimes," *World Politics*, XXVIII, no. 1 (October, 1975).

Kafel, Mieczysław. *Ekonomiczne Oblicze Zawodu Dziennikarskiego w Polsce* (Cracow: PAN, 1945).

Prasoznawstwo (Warsaw: Państwowe Wydawnictwo Naukowe, 1966).

Korotyński, Henryk. *Różnie Bywało* (Warsaw: Książka i Wiedza, 1972).

Kępiński, Andrzej and Zbigniew Kilar. *Kto jest kim w Polsce Inaczej* (Warsaw: Czytelnik, 1985).

Krzystek, Zbigniew. "Kim Jesteśmy?," *Prasa Polska* (August, 1977).

Kupis, Tadeusz. *Zawód Dziennikarza w Polsce Ludowej* (Warsaw: Książka i Wiedza, 1960).

Dziennikarskie Sprawy (Warsaw: Książka i Wiedza, 1975).

Lane, David. *The End of Inequality* (London: Penguin, 1971).

Lane, David and George Kolankiewicz. *Social Group in Polish Society* (New York: Columbia University Press, 1973).

Lendvai, Paul. *The Bureaucracy of Truth* (New York: Pegasus, 1970).

Lenin, V. I. *Collected Works*, Vol. 1 (Moscow: Progress Press, 1967).

Lipski, Jan Józef. *KOR* (Berkeley: University of California Press, 1985).

Lodge, Milton C. *Soviet Elite Attitudes Since Stalin* (Columbus, Ohio: Charles E. Merrill, 1969).

Łojek, Jerzy. *Moja droga do dziennikarstwa* (Warsaw: Polska Akademia Nauk, 1974).

Maślanka, Julian, ed. *Encyklopedia Wiedzy o Prasie (Wrocław: Ossolineum, 1976).*

Masłowski, Władysław. *Akcje Prasowe* (Cracow: Ośrodek Badań Prasoznawczych, 1973).

Matejko, Aleksander. *Postawy zawodowe dziennikarzy na tle systemu społecznego redakcji* (Kraków: Ośrodek Badań Prasoznawczych, 1962–63).

Maxa, Josef. *A Year Is Eight Months* (Garden City: Doubleday, 1970).

Micewski, Andrzej. *Współrządzić czy kłamać?* (Paris: Libella, 1978).

Miller, Marek. "Kto Opuścił dziennikarstwo?" (Łódź: Pracownia Reporterska, 1982).

Mond, Jerzy. "La Presse, les intellectuals, et le pouvoir en Union Sovietique et dans des payes Socialistes Europeans" (La Documentation Français, Secretariate General du Gouvernement, 1970).

National Communism and Popular Revolt in Eastern Europe (New York: Columbia University Press, 1956).Olson, Mancur. *The Logic of Collective Action* (New York: Schocken Books, 1968).

Olszański, Kazimierz. *Prasa galicyjska wobec Powstania Styczniowego* (Cracow: Komitet Nauk Historysznych PAN, 1975).

Parsons, Talcott. "Professions," in *International Encyclopedia of Social Sciences*, XII (New York: Macmillan and Free Press, 1968), pp. 536–45.

Pis, Zbigniew. "Skąd Brać Dziennikarzy?" *Biuletyn* (May, 1970).

Poland Today (Armonk, New York: M. E. Sharpe, 1981).

Polish Mass Media, Press Research, Journalism (Cracow: *Zeszyty Prasoznawcze*, special edition, 1978).

Radgowski, Michał. *Polityka i jej czasy* (Warsaw: Iskry, 1981).

Radio Free Europe. *August, 1980: The Strikes in Poland*, (Munich: October, 1980).

Rakowski, Mieczysław. *Polskie Przyśpieszenie, 1971–75* (Warsaw: Interpress, 1975).

Przesilenie Grudniowe (Warsaw: Państwowy Instytut Wydawniczy, 1981).

Ramundo, Bernard A. "The Answer to *Pravda*," *The University of Illinois Law Forum* (Spring, 1964).

Remington, Robin. *Winter in Prague* (Cambridge: MIT Press, 1969).

Reminton, Thomas. "Politics and Professionalism in Soviet Journalism," *Slavic Review*.

Remnek, Richard B. *Social Scientists and Policy Making in the USSR* (New York: Praeger, 1977).

Rubikon, 1981 (Warsaw: Niezależna Oficyna Wydawnicza, 1986).

Schwartz, Joel J. and William R. Keech, "Group Influence and the Policy Process in the Soviet Union," *American Political Science review*, LXIII, no. 3 (September, 1968).

Siebert, Fred, *et al. Four Theories of the Press* (Urbana, Illinois: University of Illinois Press, 1956).

Skilling, H. Gordon. *Czechoslovakia's Uninterrupted Revolution* (Princeton: Princeton University Press, 1976).

Skilling, H, Gordon and Franklyn Griffiths. *Interest Groups in Soviet Politics* (Princeton: Princeton University Press, 1971).
Skrzypek, "The Profession of Journalism in Poland: A Profile," *Journalism Quarterly*.
Stewart, Phillip D. "Soviet Interest Groups and the Policy Process: The Repeal of Production Education," *World Politics*, XXII, no. 3 (October, 1969).
Surdykowski, Jerzy. *Notatki Gdańskie* (London: ANEKS, 1982).
Szejnert, Małgorzata. "Dziennikarze," *Literatura* (20 January, 1975).
Szulczewski, Michał. *Publicystyka* (Warsaw: Państwowe Wydawnictwo Naukowe, 1976).
Teoria i praktyka w dziennikarstwie (Warsaw: Państwowe Wydawnictwo Naukowe, 1964).
13 miesięcy i 13 dni Gazety Krakowskiej (London: Polonia, 1985).
University of Warsaw Institute of Journalism, *Polish Mass Media and National Culture* (Warsaw University, 1978).
Weaver, David H. and G. Cleveland Wilhot. *The American Journalist* (Bloomington, Indiana: Indiana University Press, 1986).
Weber, Max. *The Theory of Social and Economic Organization* (New York: Free Press, 1964).
Wedel, Janine. *Private Poland* (Facts on File, 1986).
Wesołowski, Włodzimierz. *Teoria, Badania, Praktyka* (Warsaw: Książka i Wiedza, 1978).
Wesołowski, Włodzimierz and Kazimierz Słomczyński. *Investigations on Class Structure and Social Stratification in Poland* (Warsaw: Polish Academy of Sciences, 1977).
Wilensky, H. "The Professionalization of Everyone?" *American Journal of Sociology*, LXX (September, 1964).
Zinnes, Paul. *Revolution in Hungary* (New York: Columbia University Press, 1962).

Journals

Prasa Polska; Prasa (pre-World War II); *Biuletyn RSW Prasa; Zeszyt Prasoznawczy; Ośrodek Badań Opinii Publicznej i Studiów Programowych; Przegląd Opini i Prasa Współczesna i Dawna*; Korespondent (1947–55); *Nowe Drogi: Przegląd Kulturalny* and *Kultura; Polityka; Przegląd Tygodniowy*; and *Diariusz Sejmowy*.
Radio Free Europe Situation Reports, Background Reports, and Polish Press Summaries as well as the *Uncensored News from Poland* and other underground sources.

Unpublished Sources:

Journalists' own archives of speeches, circulars, and other documents as well as censored articles.
SDP archives from past National Congresses, executive board meetings, and memoir files done by journalists.

SDP Stenograms and Yearly Reports from all National Congresses since the reestablishment of the SDP after World War II.

Other documents:

Garlicki, Bolesław. "Organizacja pracy redakcji," Cracow: Ośrodek Badań Prasoznawczych, 1972).

Malinowska, Anna. "Zmiana zawartości dzienników po zwiększeniu ich objętości" (version III) (Ośrodek Prasoznawczy, 1974).

SDP, "Kryzys Polski 1980–1983: Społeczeństwo-świadomość-informacja (Materiały raportu o stanie komunikacji społecznej w Polsce)" (Warsaw: manuscript, 1984).

Szkoła Partyjna Przy KC PZRR, "Masowa Praca Redakcji Gazety" (Warsaw, 1950).

Gosławski, "Ustawa o kontroli publikacji i jej realizacja" (Masters' thesis, University of Warsaw, 1983).

Rosiński, Ryszard. "Prawo dziennikarza do informacji w polskim ustawodawstwie prasowym" (Masters thesis, University of Warsaw, 1983).

Index

Soviet and East European Studies

53 ANITA PRAŻMOWSKA
Britain, Poland and the Eastern Front, 1939

52 ELLEN JONES AND FRED GRUPP
Modernization, value change and fertility in the Soviet Union

51 CATHERINE ANDREYEV
Vlasov and the Russian liberation movement
Soviet reality and émigré theories

50 STEPHEN WHITE
The origins of détente
The Genoa Conference and Soviet-Western relations 1921–1922

49 JAMES MCADAMS
East Germany and détente
Building authority after the Wall

48 S. G. WHEATCROFT AND R. W. DAVIES (EDS.)
Materials for a balance of the Soviet national economy 1928–1930

47 SYLVANA MALLE
The economic organization of war communism, 1918–1921

46 DAVID S. MASON
Public opinion and political change in Poland, 1980–1982

45 MARK HARRISON
Soviet planning in peace and war 1938–1945

44 NIGEL SWAIN
Collective farms which work?

43 J. ARCH GETTY
Origins of the great purges
The Soviet Communist Party reconsidered, 1933–1938

42 TADEUSZ SWIETOCHOWSKI
Russian Azerbaijan 1905–1920
The shaping of national identity in a muslim community

41 RAY TARAS
Ideology in a socialist state
Poland 1956–1983

40 SAUL ESTRIN
Self-management: economic theory and Yugoslav practice

39 S. A. SMITH
Red Petrograd
Revolution in the factories 1917–1918

38 DAVID A. DYKER
The process of investment in the Soviet Union

36 JEAN WOODALL
The socialist corporation and technocratic power
The Polish United Workers Party, industrial organisation and workforce control 1958–1980

35 WILLIAM J. CONYNGHAM
The modernization of Soviet industrial management

34 ANGELA STENT
From embargo to Ostpolitik
The political economy of West German–Soviet relations 1955–1980

32 BLAIR A. RUBLE
Soviet trade unions
Their development in the 1970s

31 R. F. LESLIE (ED.)
The history of Poland since 1863

30 JOZEF M. VAN BRABANT
Socialist economic integration
Aspects of contemporary economic problems in Eastern Europe

28 STELLA ALEXANDER
Church and state in Yugoslavia since 1945

27 SHEILA FITZPATRICK
Education and social mobility in the Soviet Union 1921–1934

23 PAUL VYSNÝ
Neo-Slavism and the Czechs 1898–1914

22 JAMES RIORDAN
Sport in Soviet society
Development of sport and physical education in Russia and the USSR

14 RUDOLF BIĆANIĆ
Economic policy in socialist Yugoslavia

The following series titles are now out of print:

1 ANDREA BOLTHO
Foreign trade criteria in socialist economies

2 SHEILA FITZPATRICK
The commissariat of enlightenment
Soviet organization of education and the arts under Lunacharsky, October 1917–1921

3 DONALD J. MALE
Russian peasant organisation before collectivisation
A study of commune and gathering 1925–1930

4 P. WILES (ED.)
The prediction of communist economic performance

5 VLADIMIR V. KUSIN
The intellectual origins of the Prague Spring
The development of reformist ideas in Czechoslovakia 1956–1967

6 GALIA GOLAN
The Czechoslovak reform movement

7 NAUN JASNY
Soviet economists of the twenties
Names to be remembered

8 ASHA L. DATAR
India's economic relations with the USSR and Eastern Europe, 1953–1969

9 T. M. PODOLSKI
Socialist banking and monetary control
The experience of Poland

10 SHMUEL GALAI
The liberation movement in Russia 1900–1905

11 GALIA GOLAN
Reform rule in Czechoslovakia
The Dubcek era 1968–1969

12 GEOFFREY A. HOSKING
The Russian constitutional experiment
Government and Duma 1907–1914

13 RICHARD B. DAY
Leon Trotsky and the politics of economic isolation

15 JAN M. CIECHANOWSKI
The Warsaw rising of 1944

16 EDWARD A. HEWITT
Foreign trade prices in the Council for Mutual Economic Assistance

17 ALICE TEICHOVA
An economic background to Munich
International business and Czechoslovakia 1918–1938

18 DANIEL F. CALHOUN
The united front: the TUC and the Russians 1923–1928

19 GALIA GOLAN
Yom Kippur and after
The Soviet Union and the Middle East crisis

20 MAUREEN PERRIE
The agrarian policy of the Russian Socialist-Revolutionary Party
From its origins through the revolution of 1905–1907

21 GABRIEL GORODETSKY
The precarious truce: Anglo-Soviet relations 1924–1927

24 GREGORY WALKER
Soviet book publishing policy

25 FELICITY ANN O'DELL
Socialisation through children's literature
The Soviet example

26 T. H. RIGBY
Lenin's government: Sovnarkom 1917–1922

29 MARTIN CAVE
Computers and economic planning
The Soviet experience

33 MARTIN MYANT
Socialism and democracy in Czechoslovakia 1944–1948

37 ISRAEL GETZLER
Kronstadt 1917–1921
The fate of a Soviet democracy